The World Was Never the Same: Events That Changed History

J. Rufus Fears, Ph.D.

THE
GREAT
COURSES

PUBLISHED BY:

THE GREAT COURSES
Corporate Headquarters
4840 Westfields Boulevard, Suite 500
Chantilly, Virginia 20151-2299
Phone: 1-800-832-2412
Fax: 703-378-3819
www.thegreatcourses.com

J. Rufus Fears, Ph.D.

David Ross Boyd Professor of Classics
University of Oklahoma

Professor J. Rufus Fears is the David Ross Boyd Professor of Classics at the University of Oklahoma, where he holds the G. T. and Libby Blankenship Chair in the History of Liberty. He also serves as David and Ann Brown Distinguished Senior Fellow of the Oklahoma Council of Public Affairs. Professor Fears was formerly Professor of History at Indiana University, where he was chosen as the first Distinguished Faculty Research Lecturer. From 1986 to 1990, he was Professor of Classics and chairman of the Department of Classical Studies at Boston University. Professor Fears received his Ph.D. from Harvard University.

Professor Fears is an internationally distinguished scholar and author of numerous studies in Greek and Roman history, the history of freedom, and the lessons of history for our own day. His books and monographs include *Princeps a diis electus: The Divine Election of the Emperor as a Political Concept at Rome*; *The Cult of Jupiter and Roman Imperial Ideology*; *The Theology of Victory at Rome*; and *The Cult of Virtues and Roman Imperial Ideology*. He has published a three-volume edition of the *Selected Writings of Lord Acton*, the great British historian of freedom.

Professor Fears has been a Danforth Fellow, a Woodrow Wilson Fellow, and a Harvard Prize Fellow. He has also been a fellow of the American Academy in Rome and the Guggenheim Foundation, and twice a fellow of the Alexander von Humboldt Foundation in Germany. Professor Fears's research has been supported by grants from the American Philosophical Foundation, the American Council of Learned Societies, the National Endowment for the Humanities, the Zarrow Foundation, and the Kerr Foundation. He has been a distinguished visiting professor and scholar-in-residence at numerous institutions, including Washington and Lee University, Miami University, and the Franz Doelger-Institut at the

University of Bonn. He is listed in *Who's Who in America* and *Who's Who in the World.*

Professor Fears's teaching has been the subject of numerous feature articles, and he has been recognized for teaching excellence on more than 25 occasions. In 1996, 1999, and again in 2000, students chose him as the University of Oklahoma Professor of the Year. In 2003, he received the University Continuing Education Association (UCEA) Great Plains Region Award for Excellence in Teaching. UCEA is the national association for colleges and universities with continuing education programs. In 2005, Professor Fears received the National Award for Teaching Excellence from UCEA, which cited "his outstanding teaching, imaginative scholarship and contribution to continuing education." Also in 2005, Professor Fears received the Excellence in Teaching Award from the Classical Association of the Middle West and South and was named Most Inspiring Professor by University of Oklahoma students. In 2006, the state-wide Oklahoma Foundation for Excellence awarded him its Medal for Excellence in College and University Teaching.

Professor Fears is very active in speaking to broader audiences about the lessons of history for our own day. He has appeared regularly on national talk radio, and interviews with him have been carried in newspapers and television across the country. He leads annual study trips to historical sites in Europe and America.

The World Was Never the Same is the eighth course Professor Fears has produced with The Great Courses. His other courses are *A History of Freedom*; *Famous Greeks*; *Famous Romans*; *Churchill*; *Books That Have Made History: Books That Can Change Your Life*; *The Wisdom of History*; and *Life Lessons from the Great Books.* ■

Table of Contents

Table of Contents

SUPPLEMENTAL MATERIAL

The World Was Never the Same:
Events That Changed History

Scope:

This course is a set of 36 lectures exploring world history through the study of great events that have shaped history. The course rests on the conviction that history is not the story of anonymous social and economic movements. History is made by great individuals, great ideas, and great events.

In this course, we will study great individuals who have shaped events from ancient Mesopotamia to our own day. We will study the great ideas that propelled these events, from the idea of equality under the law to the vision of bringing freedom to the world. We will study events that were great in themselves and those that no human planned, such as the Black Death of the Middle Ages and the stock market crash of 1929.

Three criteria were used in choosing these great events: (1) The event was important in itself; (2) the world was never the same after the event, and (3) the event had consequences that still reverberate with us today.

This course builds on seven other courses I have taught for The Great Courses. Thus, a fourth criterion was that this lecture series should discuss different events from those covered in the earlier courses. In a few cases, I was unable to avoid repeating events, but in those instances, the events are discussed from a different perspective in this course. The history of the world is multifaceted. My understanding of history grows each day, and the world itself changes each day. We will never run out of great events to discuss.

The arrangement of the lectures is chronological. If we are to understand how an event changes history, we must see it in its correct chronological order.

This course gives equal attention to politics, culture, religion, economics, and society. But it is also a lesson of this course that there can be no separation of political history from intellectual or social, religious or economic history. History is a multicolored but seamless garment.

Ideas make political history, as we see from the Battle of Marathon to the Bolshevik and Chinese Revolutions. Political history shapes art and literature. Michelangelo's Sistine Chapel is an enduring work of art, but it is also the product of the political aspirations of Pope Julius II. Dante's *Divine Comedy* is a masterpiece of philosophy and literature, but it is also the product of the politics of Florence that drove Dante into exile.

Great individuals shape history, but the political and intellectual climate must be right. We see in this course that Martin Luther was only one of many who sought to reform the Church, but the times were right for Luther. Untimely reformers, as Machiavelli pointed out, tend to be burned at the stake.

Technology goes hand in hand with intellectual currents in shaping political events. The invention of printing enabled Luther to get his ideas out to millions, and the university system gave the impetus to both the Reformation and the Catholic Counter-Reformation. Science is never "pure" science. It is the product of the political and intellectual currents of its time. In our course, we explore science from the Oath of Hippocrates in 5th-century B.C. Athens to Darwin's *On the Origin of Species* and from the development of the atomic bomb to the scientific discoveries of our day, such as cloning.

Lectures 1 through 12 explore our heritage from the classical civilizations of the Middle East, China, India, Greece, and Rome. The beginning of civilization in the Middle East (3000 B.C.) and later in China and India (around 1700 B.C.) was characterized by four features: writing, metallurgy, monumental architecture, and complex governmental forms. The law code of King Hammurabi of Babylonia offers the springboard for us in Lecture 1 to discuss the question of what government is supposed to do. How should government be organized, and what are the proper limits for government? The Middle East has, throughout its history, chosen absolute monarchy. Hammurabi is the model of the benevolent ruler. The law code he issued begins the legacy of the Ten Commandments, the Roman civil law, and the U.S. Constitution. Greece and Rome rose to greatness under democratic forms of government. Lectures on Solon, the Battle of Marathon, Hippocrates, and

Julius Caesar give us the opportunity to consider the lessons of Greece and Rome for modern democracy (Lectures 5 through 8).

The most enduring and immediate legacy of the ancient world, however, is spiritual. Three of the world's great religions arose in the Middle East: Judaism, Christianity, and Islam. Ancient India gave rise to both Hinduism and Buddhism, which still shape the everyday lives and beliefs of hundreds of millions of people. China in the 6th century B.C. was the scene of the teaching mission of Confucius. His ideas have shaped and continue to shape 2,500 years of Chinese tradition. We reflect on the seminal events in this religious legacy of the ancient world in Lectures 2–4 and 9–11.

In Lecture 12, we look at the founding of the University of Bologna in 1088. Greece and Rome, Judaism, Islam, China, Buddhism, and Hinduism all established means of discovering, systematizing, and transmitting knowledge to new generations. But the University of Bologna is the alma mater of contemporary higher education, the most powerful intellectual force in the world today.

Lectures 13 through 36 discuss decisive events in the shaping of the modern world. Dante (Lecture 13) serves as our transition. This visionary poet is a Janus-like figure who looks back to Greece, Rome, and medieval Christendom to look forward into the Renaissance, a bold new age of discovery and transformation.

The Renaissance world was shaped by the events of the Black Death (Lecture 14), the discovery of the New World (Lecture 15), the art of Michelangelo (Lecture 16), the invention of printing (Lecture 17), and the political consequences of Martin Luther and the Reformation (Lecture 18). The defeat of the Spanish Armada (Lecture 19) was as decisive for American as it was for British history. The defeat of the Turks at Vienna in 1688 began the decline of the Ottoman Empire, an event that still reverberates in the Middle East today (Lecture 20).

The Battle of Lexington began the American Revolution (Lecture 21). It is a central theme of this course that the founding of the United States is the decisive event in the modern world. Lectures 22, 29, 31, 32, 34, 35, and 36 deal with other seminal events in American and world history: the Battle of Gettysburg, the crash of 1929, the inauguration of Franklin Roosevelt, the dropping of the atomic bomb, the assassinations of John Kennedy and Martin Luther King Jr., and the terrorist attack of September 11, 2001.

It is another major tenet of this course that America has followed a unique path. That path's uniqueness is best illustrated by decisive events in the other great nations of the modern world: the assassination of Archduke Franz Ferdinand (Lecture 27), the Bolshevik Revolution (Lecture 28), the rise of Adolf Hitler and the Third Reich (Lecture 30), and the communization of China by Mao Zedong (Lecture 33).

The destructive curse of revolution in Russia, Germany, and China was shaped by the economic ideas of Karl Marx, while the economic course of America since its own revolution followed Adam Smith. Lecture 23 gives us the opportunity to compare Smith and Marx as decisive minds in economic thought and political reality.

Science and technology have added a new dimension of infinite proportion to the modern world that separates it from all that has gone before. Science and technology gave to the 20th and 21st centuries the opportunity to bring peace and prosperity to the entire world. That same science and technology have also given us the opportunity to destroy the world. Lectures 24–26 and 32 discuss decisive events in the world of science and technology: Darwin's early work in the modern science of life, Pasteur and the development of modern medicine, the Wright Brothers and the modern conquest of space and time, and the science and politics of the atomic bomb.

There are those who believe that science and technology have negated the importance of history, that through science and technology, humans have moved to a new dimension where the lessons of history have no meaning. This course shows how false that view is. Human nature does not change. Men and women still have the same intellect and the same passions they did in the Babylonia of Hammurabi and the Florence of Dante. As long as human nature remains the same, history will be our best guide to life. The aim of this course is to make us think historically: to use the lessons of the past to make decisions in the present and to plan for the future.

History was the guide of the founders of the United States as they shaped a new world of freedom out of political and economic crisis. This course is aimed at allowing us to better follow their example. ∎

The Defeat of the Spanish Armada (1588)
Lecture 19

> From all over this vast [Spanish] empire came the resources, until ultimately, a fleet of 130 ships was available, of which a considerable number were the most modern kind of warship, the galleon. That was the Trident missile of its day, the Nautilus submarine of its day. It was the cutting edge of naval warfare.

The defeat of the Spanish Armada in the summer of 1588 meant the failure of the attempt by King Philip II of Spain to conquer England and to reconquer the Netherlands. It also marked the decline of Spain as a great empire and launched the ascent of England to superpower status.

In August of 1588, Queen Elizabeth spoke to her troops in the town of Tilbury, casting "foul scorn" on Philip of Spain, who dared to invade the realm of England, and promising her own blood in his defeat. For his part, Philip believed that God had given him a mission to crush Protestantism in England and the Netherlands.

By 1540, in response to the Protestant Reformation, the church had launched the Counter-Reformation. Stringent rules were put in place, corruption was curtailed, and a better-educated class of priests was created. Philip II was part of this attempt to restore the power of the church. In 1588, he became convinced that he must use his military might to bring England and the Netherlands back to Catholicism.

For the expedition against England, Philip assembled a fleet of 130 ships. Spanish tactics for naval battles rested on blasting the enemy with one round of cannon fire, then closing and boarding the enemy's ship with the ferocious Spanish infantry. After defeating England, Philip planned for his Armada to sail to the Netherlands to join the Spanish forces there, which were led by the duke of Parma. The duke advised against this plan, citing the strength of the Dutch and English navies and the lack of a suitable port for embarkation of his army, but Philip prevailed.

The British fleet outnumbered the Spanish fleet and had a larger number of galleons, as well as a new strategy. The British galleons were more maneuverable than the Spanish ships and had a wider range of armament, with both large and small cannons. The British strategy was to sail as close to the Spaniards as possible, then blast them with the smaller cannons. Furthermore, the British planned to wear the Spaniards down with minor skirmishes, hoping that the enemy might make a mistake or that a storm would destroy their ships.

When the battle was over, the Spanish fleet was in disarray.

As the Spanish fleet approached Plymouth, the British ships took advantage of a favorable wind to sail northward, forcing the Spaniards to chase them. The Spaniards were compelled to make harbor at Calais, where the British launched fireships against them, breaking up the close formation of the Spanish ships. The next day, August 8, 1588, the two forces clashed at Gravelines, off the coast of Flanders, and England was victorious. When the battle was over, the Spanish fleet was in disarray and was forced to sail around the British Isles before heading southward to Spain. The Dutch fleet had blockaded the duke of Parma, who remained in the Netherlands with his troops.

In the fall, the Spanish fleet crept back to its ports, having lost as many as 20,000 men and half of its ships. Within two decades of this defeat, by the year 1607, Englishmen would make their way across the Atlantic Ocean and establish a colony at Jamestown; later, these colonists would bring the traditions of free government to their land. The reign of Elizabeth would launch the golden age of English expansion and place the queen in a position to maintain the balance of power on the continent. ∎

Suggested Reading

Mattingly, *The Defeat of the Spanish Armada.*

McDermott, *England and the Spanish Armada.*

Questions to Consider

1. What other despots have destroyed their power by preemptive wars? Do we think of Xerxes, of Napoleon, of Hitler?

2. What role did Protestantism and Catholicism play in the different courses of freedom taken in England and Spain?

The Defeat of the Spanish Armada (1588)
Lecture 19—Transcript

The theme for this lecture is the defeat of the Spanish Armada, the summer of the year 1588. The defeat of the Spanish Armada immediately changed history. It meant that the attempt by the king of Spain to conquer England failed, and in the immediate aftermath it became clear that the Spanish king was also going to fail ultimately in his attempt to re-conquer the Netherlands.

Out of the defeat of the Spanish Armada would come the independent Dutch Republic. It also meant that the Spanish king, Philip II, would fail in his efforts to re-conquer all of Europe for the Catholic faith. It also meant that Spain would begin to decline as a great empire. In the summer of 1588, when the Armada sailed, Spain was one of the two superpowers of the world, Spain and the Ottoman Empire. It also meant that England would begin its climb to becoming the superpower, and the empire of England would spread across the Atlantic. Ultimately, it still reverberates with us today. We speak English and we are free to worship as we choose. It also meant that the instruments of freedom—parliament, the idea of individual freedom, of freedom of conscience—would spread to the New World and become our greatest heritage from England.

To understand this event that changed history, I want you to go back with me to a day in August of the year 1588. We are right off the coast of England with Queen Elizabeth, on land, standing amidst our loyal troops who have been gathered to fight the Spaniards if the Spaniards should carry out their plan of landing an amphibious force on the sacred soil of England. We are at Tilbury, and that is where Queen Elizabeth has come with her general and with her closest advisors. There we are, these fierce warriors of England, many of us clad in breastplates, iron helmets, and many of us holding the pike that is such a deadly weapon, almost 18 feet long. We have come to fight and to see our queen because she has come to be with us.

Her speech is another way in which history was changed by the Spanish Armada because it also shows us that history is made not just by great men, but also by great women. Queen Elizabeth is one of the greatest of all figures in history. She is the greatest ruler in English history. She is the greatest monarch of England, greater than William the Conqueror, greater than Richard the Lionheart. She is a woman of late middle age now, around 55 years of age. She has never married because her heart is devoted to her country. She is extremely well-educated. She has learned Greek and Latin. She likes to debate theological questions. But, she is a convinced Protestant and head of the Church of England, the position that her father, Henry VIII, had created for himself.

She loves music and is a good dancer, and she knows politics. She is a devoted disciple of the teachings of Machiavelli, about how to get power and how to keep it. She studies and learns from history, the way Machiavelli taught. She is also a very, very fine speaker. She uses all those talents today as she addresses her troops. Let me paraphrase. "I have," she says, "but the body of a weak and frail woman, but I have the heart of a king and indeed the heart of a king of England. My advisors have told me that it might be dangerous for me to come here amidst my troops. Little do they know, nowhere am I safer than among my beloved subjects. I have lived my life and I have governed in such a way that you, my loyal Englishmen, you are the bastion of my safety, and I have come here to fight and, if need be, to die alongside you. I will give my blood in the pursuit of our victory. I cast foul scorn upon Philip of Spain and his minion, the general, the Duke of Parma, or to any prince who would dare to invade our realm, this realm of England. And so we shall fight, and so we shall win. I know how brave you've already been, and I will be your general. I will be your judge, and I will be the one to reward you for your gallantry on the field of battle."

Her troops gave rousing cheers, and then she rode amongst them, their general, to guide them in this critical struggle. Off the coast, there was the Armada of Spain. What had brought Elizabeth there to Tilbury? What had brought this Armada all the way from Spain? It was the desire of the king of Spain, King Philip II, to restore the Catholic Church. That was his mission. God had given him that mission. He was a man also of middle age in 1588, a rather small man, somewhat handsome, a dapper though conservative dresser, and an absolutely pious Catholic. Among his titles was the title king of England. He had in fact been married to Mary, the half sister of Queen Elizabeth. He had held the title of king of England, and he was reasserting that right as well as the determination of that most Catholic king, as well as the invocation of the pope, to crush Protestantism in England and in the Netherlands.

The revolt against Spanish authority had begun in the Netherlands as part of the broader rise of the Protestant reformation. Martin Luther had begun that reformation in 1517, and by 1540, the Catholic Church was responding in the most vigorous of all fashions. Not only had troops been sent by the emperor of the Holy Roman Empire, by the emperor Charles V, but also the church had begun to reform itself internally, what is called the Counter Reformation. Far more stringent, rules were put in place. Corruption was put an end to. A better educated class of priests was created. Above all, figures like Ignatius Loyola had created the Society of Jesus, the Jesuits, to restore the power and glory of the Catholic faith. Philip II was part of this great attempt to restore the power of the church.

In 1588, after a number of negotiations with Elizabeth, he had become convinced that he must crush England by military force and that he must use his military power not only to crush England, but also the Netherlands. Working in his magnificent palace, though rather grimly situated, the El Escorial, far away from the distractions of Madrid, he planned his strategy by which this most Catholic Armada would restore the Catholic faith.

El Escorial, it was the creation of Philip II. He planned every aspect of it. He was devoted to St. Lawrence. You'll recall in one of our lectures we had described how St. Lawrence was roasted alive on a grill. El Escorial, which we can still visit today, is shaped in the form of a grill. There, Philip, from a rather small, sparsely clad room, ruled over one-half of the world. He was king of Spain and Portugal. He held the land of Naples and Sicily. He ruled over the Netherlands. Of course, he ruled over that vast empire of Spain in the New World. The gold and silver from the New World had filled the coffers of the Spanish Empire. He was the absolute ruler of the superpower of his day.

But, he had spent and spent in a very extravagant fashion to restore the Catholic faith. He planned his strategy for this mighty naval force. The captain he chose was an experienced admiral, but died shortly before the expedition was reaching fruition. Philip turned to an extremely Catholic and very high-born Spanish Grandee, the Duke of Medina Sidonia, the oldest dukedom in all of the kingdom of Spain. Philip told him, "You are going to be admiral of this great Armada." The admiral said, "One, I'm really not an admiral. I know almost nothing about the navy. Two, I have no real concept of how to fight a naval battle. Three, I get terribly seasick. Please choose someone else." But, no, Philip's mind was made up. From all over this vast empire came the recourses, until ultimately a fleet of 130 ships were available, of which a considerable number were the most modern kind of warship, the galleon. That was the trident missile of its day, the nautilus submarine of its day. It was the cutting edge of naval warfare. It was huge, able to carry many, many hundreds of tons of goods, but also heavily armored and great oaken planks, and able to carry something like 42 cannons, and cannons that were capable of hurling 32-pound shots one-third of a mile across the ocean. They were very, very powerful war ships that were entirely done by sail, three and four great masts.

He also had though older-type ships—the galley. The galley was rode by generally convicts, galley slaves, and it was suited for warfare in the Mediterranean, much less suited for the wilder waters of the Atlantic. But, the Spanish navy was first rate. In fact, in the year 1571, it had achieved a startling and decisive victory over the fleet of the Ottoman Empire at the Battle of Lepanto. But, that was fought in the Mediterranean. The Mediterranean lacking tides, far more calm than the Atlantic, is a very different place of battle for a fleet. But, there was some of these older fashioned galleys, and Spanish tactics rested upon blasting the enemy with one round of cannon fire and then closing and boarding the enemy's ship. The Armada also sailed with large numbers of the ferocious Spanish infantry on with their pikes and heavy slashing swords. The idea would be to blast them with the cannons, then close and defeat the English on shipboard.

That was only part of the overall strategy of Philip II. The other part of that strategy was that this great, most Catholic Armada, the Invincible Armada, as it was called, sailing under a Papal banner, that it would join up with the army of Spain in the Netherlands. There the Spanish army, some 30,000 men strong, capable of going up to 55,000 men strong, was under the generalship of one of the finest commanders of the age, the Duke of Parma. It had won a series of victories in the Netherlands. He was a ruthless commander, capable of winning battles that were pitched, as well as battles that were carried out by siege. However, from the very beginning of this plan of Philip, the Duke of Parma said, "This really raises some serious issues. One, there's not a port suited for us to carry out this kind of embarkation of my army onto ships. Two, we do not have control of the sea. The British have a strong fleet, but so do these Dutch rebels, and it is going to be very hard for us to carry out any kind of combined operation with such a powerful set of opponents as the Dutch navy, as well as the English navy. Moreover, I think we should concentrate right now on conquering the Netherlands. England is a very, very difficult project." But, no, Philip was an absolute ruler. There was no bounds whatsoever on his power, and thus the Duke of Parma must give in to this strategy.

The great fleet sailed, and by July, it had cleared the Bay of Biscay and was making its way towards the English coast. England knew it was coming. England was prepared. As soon as the great Armada was sighted off of the English coast, beacon lights from Cornwall all the way across England and up towards Scotland carried the flash that the armada was coming. Riders rode at top speed to Plymouth, where the English fleet was situated. It was said that Sir Francis Drake, who would be one of the great admirals of the British fleet in this battle, was there playing a game of bowls, bowling. The rider came up and said, "The Armada is off the coast." Drake said with unflappable calm, "Let's finish our game, and then we will take care of the Spaniards."

The British fleet outnumbered the Spanish fleet. The British fleet had a larger number of these galleons, these best kinds of ships in the world. The British fleet had a new kind of strategy. One, the galleons that were part of the British fleet were more suited to naval warfare than the Spanish ships. The Spanish galleons were best at transporting large amounts of goods. That is how they had really been developed, to carry large amount of trade goods back and forth between Spain and its empire. But, they were adapted to warfare, and even as merchant ships they were heavily armed. But, they sat higher in the water, and they were not as maneuverable as the way the British had adapted their galleons. The British galleons had a wider range of armament. They had some of these big cannons that could hurl a 32-pound ball a third of a mile, but they also had large numbers of smaller cannons. These cannons hurled only a 4-pound ball. They could hurl it a third of a mile as well, but they used less powder, and moreover, they were very effective at close range of about 100 yards. The British had the strategy of getting as close to the Spaniards as possible, without allowing themselves to be boarded, and then blasting the Spaniards with these 4-pound balls, which, at that distance of 100 yards, even 200 yards, could smash through the heavy oak planks of the Spanish ships.

The British had a very keen awareness of how fine the Spanish navy was, and they wanted to avoid at any cost having to fight the Spaniards on board their ships. The British had developed, or the English had developed, a strategy. The English navy also, because of Queen Elizabeth's ability to pick the right people, had a superb overall commander, Earl Howard, who was an experienced sailor and who developed the overall strategy, which was to avoid as long as possible fighting a major battle with the Spanish fleet. There are two kinds of strategy in warfare. One is to come to grips with the enemy force as soon as possible and fight a big battle and decide it right then and there. The other is to kind of go around the enemy, poke at the enemy a little bit, but avoid a big battle. Wear down the enemy and maybe wait for the enemy to make a mistake. That is what Earl Howard insisted that the English fleet do, that they stay close to the Spanish Armada, but avoid a big battle, see if storms did not come up that would dash the Spanish Armada to pieces, get the Spanish Armada in a convenient place, and perhaps launch fireships at the Spanish Armada.

But, do not believe the way we sometimes are told that the British fleet was a kind of briefly put together, quickly put together, ad hoc fleet made up of little small boats. No, it was probably the best navy in the world already, with a very capable admiral in charge, and then superb commanders there with the fleet itself. Sir Francis Drake, the most gallant, daring seaman of his day, had already the year before sailed into the port city of Cadiz and singed the beard of the Spanish king by wreaking havoc among the ships there. He had carried out bold buccaneering expeditions to the New World. In one of these he brought back enough gold for the queen that it was more than all the rest of the income she received that entire year. He was one of her favorites and a man of absolutely steel nerves. With him was Sir John Hawkins, another bold buccaneer, and with them, seamen who had sailed all over the world and were devoted, one, to their queen, two, to their country, and three, to their Protestant faith. That was the greatest terror of all, that the Spaniards would not only conquer, but impose this religion of Catholicism back upon the English nation. These were the bold spirits that guided the English destiny.

As soon as the Spanish fleet began to pull in towards Plymouth, the question was raised: Do we want to do battle with them? Earl Howard, along with the agreement of Drake and Hawkins, said, "No, let's avoid it." The Spanish fleet was now keeping very closely together in a crescent-shaped formation. But, making use of the superior maneuverability of their galleons, the English caught the wind. For the rest of this period of battling with the Spanish fleet, the English had the advantage of the wind. That is to say, they had seized the initiative. With that advantage of the wind, they avoided the Spanish fleet and began to sail further northward. The Spaniards had to come after them. But, since the English would not give them battle and the Spaniards had no port there in England where they could rest their ships, they had to sail then across the channel to Calais. There they went into the Harbor at Calais, still in their crescent-shaped formation, a very sturdy, difficult-to-break formation, and waited for the English. But, the English held back, and then suddenly the Spaniards saw bearing down upon them on the 7th of August eight fireships. To do this the English had sacrificed eight of their galleons, filling them with all matter of combustible material, pitch, and towing them until they hit the Spanish fleet. Some Spanish ships were burned, but most of them were scattered. That is what the English had waited for, scattering the Spanish fleet, so that they could not keep this stern, close-ordered formation.

The next day at Gravelines, off the coast of Flanders, right on the border of Flanders and France, the great battle was fought, August the 8th, 1588. The

English were absolutely victorious. The Spaniards could not get close enough to board the English ships. Also, from one of the captured Spanish ships, Drake had learned that the way the Spanish ships were rigged out, their guns did not run back and forth. In other words, they did not run out in fire and then were pulled back in through the porthole, but instead, they were really meant to fire one time. Then the gunners would join the boarding party. This meant that the English had very important information, intelligence about the Spanish fleet, but also that they could fire many shots to the few that the Spaniards could fire. When the battle was over, the Spanish fleet was in disarray. It had no choice but to sail back home. But, the English fleet blocked their return the way they had come, blocked the southward return to Spain, and so poor, seasick Admiral Medina Sidonia did the only thing he could do. He had to sail all the way around the British Isles. The Duke of Parma, he had never shown up. He said quite rightly, he did not have the right kind of ships to take him across the channel. The Dutch fleet was blockading him. Many of his men were sick from dysentery. He really couldn't do a thing, so there he stayed in the Netherlands, and that whole half of the strategy of King Philip failed.

Thus, the Spanish fleet began its horrible, disastrous trip around Scotland. Gales blew, bitter cold, and the stores began to give out. The water turned putrid. The salt pork had so many maggots in it that the sailors had to eat it at night, so they wouldn't see the little creatures crawling around when they bit down into the salt pork. The sailors got sick from dysentery sweeping through this fleet. Ships crashed upon the shores in Scotland and then as they tried to make their way around Ireland. There the English were waiting for them, particularly in Ireland, and every one of them captured in Ireland was put to death, if the English could get their hands upon them. The English fleet was safe. The wind and the rain and, as they saw it, God, did their work for them.

In the fall, the Spanish fleet crept back to its Spanish ports. The king of Spain sent as much aid as he could to the sailors once they were back in port, but even with all the aid and doctors he could send them, men continued to die until probably as many as 20,000 of the Spaniards died as a result of this defeat of the Spanish Armada. One-half of its ships, 65 ships, were lost. The

English losses were utterly without consequence, negligible. The mighty Catholic invincible armada had failed.

"God has given us this victory," Elizabeth said, "and it is the proclamation of God, of the truth of our Protestant religion." King Philip sought again guidance from God, how indeed he could plan another expedition, but it would never be. The Spanish Armada had been defeated. Within 19 years of this defeat, by the year 1607, Englishmen would make their way across the Atlantic Ocean, and there, at Jamestown, set up the first colony that endured, naming it, quite rightly, Virginia, after the virgin queen, Elizabeth. There, in the year 1619, 12 years after having founded Jamestown, these colonists created the first legislative body here in what would become the United States—the House of Burgesses—and the traditions of free government would come from England of Elizabeth to here, to this land.

Elizabeth was a strong ruler, but she was not a despot. She had a parliament, and to get any money from parliament, she had to present good cause, and no taxes could be raised without the consent of parliament. It was the free parliament of England that paid for this fight against the Spanish Armada. Then the Protestant religion, following their Puritan faith in 1620, brave men and women would sail across the Atlantic again and establish a colony in Massachusetts so they could be free to worship the way that they chose. Elizabeth, her England would be the England of Shakespeare, who would celebrate this realm, this sceptred isle that was England. Her rule would go down as the golden age, the beginning of English expansion. England would take her position as a great power, and England would also take her position as the guarantor of a balance of power on the continent. That is why the English under Queen Elizabeth had aided the Dutch in their rebellion against the Spaniards. Yes, for the Protestant religion, but even more so, so that no one power could dominate the continent and ever threaten England again with subjugation, so the balance of power and the rule of the sea. Britannia rules the waves—rule Britannia. Britons will never be slaves. From that moment down until World War II, the British navy was not only the strongest navy in the world, it was the guarantor of the freedom of England.

Spain, its decline would go in ever faster form. The money that Philip had spent on this huge expedition would plunge it ever further into debt. Not all the riches of the New World could balance the treasury of the Spanish Empire. With weaker and weaker rulers, it would gradually subside into a pitiful relic. The empire of Spain would finally reach its ultimate humiliation with the Spanish American War and the utter end of that empire that Philip believed had been called by God to rule the world.

The Battle of the Spanish Armada is one of the most decisive naval battles in all of history. It takes its place right alongside the Battle of Salamis in 480, when the freedom of Greece triumphed over the despotism of the king of Persia. It takes its place alongside the Battle of Trafalgar, where the English fleet destroyed once and for all the hope of Napoleon to rule the sea. As Winston Churchill would say, both at the time of the Spanish Armada and at the time of Trafalgar, "That line of storm-tossed ships alone stood between England and the continental tyrant with his goal of world dominion."

Do you know what Winston Churchill's favorite movie was? It was *Fire over England*, that magnificent portrayal produced in 1937 with Lawrence Olivier of the great days of danger when Spain threatened all of England with conquest. He would watch it time and time again in that grim year of 1940, knowing that as in 1588, so to in 1940, freedom would triumph.

The Battle of Vienna (1683)
Lecture 20

It was but one more event in the long struggle between the values of the Middle East and the values of Europe, the struggles described by Herodotus in his history of the Persian Wars, and one more illustration of our maxim: that the Middle East is the crucible of conflict and the graveyard of empires.

The Battle of Vienna was the culmination of a summer-long siege of the city by the forces of Sultan Mohammed IV of the Ottoman Empire. Arrayed against the Turks were the troops of the Holy Roman Empire, under King John Sobieski of Poland. After this battle, the Turks would cease to be a superpower of Europe. The later fall of the Ottoman Empire, at the end of World War I, left behind problems in the Middle East that still challenge us today.

The Ottoman Empire arose in the 14th century A.D. from the decaying corpse of the Byzantine Empire. By 1453, the Turks had spread into the Balkans and occupied large parts of Greece, along with modern-day Bulgaria and Serbia. In that year, they took the city of Constantinople and made it the capital of their vast empire. Two hundred years later, that empire stretched from Iran across the Holy Land to Egypt and Morocco; it encompassed Greece, Bulgaria, Romania, Croatia, Serbia, and Hungary. The next goal was the capture of Vienna, a trading center and bastion of the Catholic faith.

The army of the Ottoman Turks was one of the most powerful military forces ever to move across the Middle East. It consisted of a superb cavalry and the fearsome infantry troops known as the Janissaries. The grand vizier of the sultan, Kara Mustafa Koprulu, convinced Mohammed to use these forces in a campaign to launch a renewed Islamic struggle against Christianity, represented by the city of Vienna. In the spring, the army marched out, and large numbers of refugees fled from their path.

The Holy Roman Emperor, Leopold, had time to prepare for the onslaught of the Turks; he assembled an army of about 60,000 and made a treaty with the king of Poland, John Sobieski, to bring aid with about 20,000 more. By July 14, 1683, the Turks were at the walls of Vienna, and the citizens of the city had dug in to endure a siege.

The strategy of the Turks was to dig trenches as close to the walls of a city as possible. From there, they would dig under the walls, place mines to bring down the city's defenses, and storm their enemies with the ferocious Janissaries. But the troops inside Vienna, holy warriors on the side of the pope and Christianity, were able to drive back repeated Turkish assaults.

The army of the Ottoman Turks was one of the most powerful military forces ever to move across the Middle East.

By early September, rations in Vienna were growing slim, and the general left behind by Leopold waited eagerly for the arrival of assistance. On September 12, when Kara Mustafa saw the Christian relief forces approaching, he realized that he had to take Vienna immediately. Mines were laid, and one large portion of the wall was blown apart, but the Viennese discovered another large mine and diffused it. Kara Mustafa was forced to turn and face an assault from Sobieski's army.

Sobieski unleashed the German infantry to attack the Ottoman flank, and a ferocious battle raged throughout the day. Late in the afternoon, he launched his cavalry at top speed into the Turkish army, routing the feared Janissaries. Caught between the infantry and the cavalry, the Turkish troops fled. In the coming months, Kara Mustafa was executed and Mohammed IV was deposed. The Austrian Empire would rise to great power status, while the Ottoman Empire declined, leaving a legacy of instability and violence that is still with us today in the Middle East. ∎

Suggested Reading

Inalcik, *Social and Economic History of the Ottoman Empire.*

Stoye, *The Siege of Vienna.*

1. Do you believe that there is a fundamental difference between the values of the Middle East and the values of Europe and America?

2. Do you see any similarity between the decline of Spain and the decline of the Ottoman Empire?

The Battle of Vienna (1683)
Lecture 20—Transcript

Our theme in this lecture is the Battle of Vienna, fought on the 12th of September in the year 1683, the culmination of the summer-long siege of the city of Vienna by the army of the Ottoman Turks, the army of Sultan Mohammed IV, ruler over the vast domains of the Turkish Empire and sultan and head of the faith in terms of the warrior faith of Islam. The army of the Holy Roman Empire gathered under the forces of King John Sobieski, the last great king of that noble nation of Poland.

We are with Sobieski on this great day that will change history forever. For the siege of Vienna and the victory of the army of the Holy Roman Empire and the army of Poland would immediately mark the high water of Ottoman expansion in Europe. The Turkish army, as a result of this defeat, would fall back into the Balkin Peninsula and step-by-step would cease to be the superpower of Europe and become, in the words of the 19th century, the sick man of Europe. Europe was saved on this day, and the longer-term result still reverberates with us right now, for the fall of the Ottoman Empire at the end of World War I has left behind problems in the Middle East that confront us, our American foreign policy, every day of our lives now.

What brought these men to Vienna to fight and to die, and the one army for the faith of Islam and the other army for the faith of Christianity? It was but one more event in the long struggle between the values of the Middle East and the values of Europe, the struggles described by Herodotus in his history of the Persian wars, and one more illustration of our maxim, that the Middle East is the crucible of conflict and the graveyard of empires.

The Ottoman Empire began in the 14th century A.D., of course, there in Asia Minor of what we now call Turkey. It arose upon the decaying corpse of the Byzantine Empire. Already in 1075 A.D. the empire of Constantinople had suffered a crushing defeat at the hand of Turkish forces at the battle of Manzikert. From that time onward, more and more of Asia Minor, which had been Greek, had Greek as its language and the Orthodox faith as its religion, was taken over by small Turkish principalities. It was on its way to being transformed into what we call it today, Turkey, the land of the Turks. The Turks speak a distinctive language. It is not related to Greek or Latin or to Chinese, for that matter. It is a beautiful musical language. The Turks themselves had come out of central Asia. There are close connections linguistically and in terms of ethnicity and culture between the Mongols of Genghis Khan and the Turks who would overrun the Byzantine Empire.

The Ottoman Turks were one such small principality, and one of their first great rulers was Othman—thus the name the Turks of Othman are the Ottoman Turks by which they are known to history. In 1453 they achieved their great triumph. They had already spread into the Balkans, occupied large parts of Greece, destroyed the army of the king of Serbia and occupied what we call Bulgaria and Serbia today. But one bastion of Christianity, the city of Constantine, had held out against them all these years. But, in 1453, Mohammad the Conqueror, or Muhammad Faqih, the Law-giver, as the Ottomans knew him, but Mohammed, that great ruler, breached the walls of Constantinople, making use of heavy cannon, and the last of the emperors of Rome, Constantine XI, fell fighting near the Romanos gate, sword in hand, worthy to be the last emperor of Rome. The city of Constantinople now became the capital of this vast empire.

It would by our year 1683 consist of a territory reaching all the way from the border with Iran, for the Ottomans were never able to conquer Iran. There was a long series of wars between the Shiite Iranian Empire and the Sunni Empire of the Ottoman Turks. But, the empire stretched all the way from Iran, including, of course, Iraq as part of the Ottoman Empire, across the Holy Land. Egypt was part of the empire of the Ottoman Turks. The influence of the Ottoman Turks spread all the way out to Morocco, and the fleets of the Ottoman Turkish sultan sailed all over the Mediterranean, raiding deeply into Italy, and then, of course, Turkey itself, and then on up to the Balkans. Greece, Bulgaria, Romania, Croatia was on the borders of the Ottoman Empire, but Serbia very much in the grip of the Ottoman Empire. All of these still today bear a strong imprint of their days under Turkish rule. More than that, all the way up through Hungary, and in 1526 the chivalry of Hungary had been destroyed at the Battle of Mohawks. Budapest itself was an Ottoman city. The next great goal was the capture Vienna, not just because it was a trade center, but far more than that it was a bastion of the Catholic faith. In 1529, the great Sultan Suleiman the Magnificent had begun a siege of Vienna after his victory over the Hungarians, but had given it up.

The Ottoman Empire began as a Ghazi empire. Ghazi is one of the highest accolades you can have in the Islamic religion. It means a warrior who is willing to fight and to die, if need be, to spread the faith of Islam and to rid the world of the infidel filth. The early sultans of the Ottoman Empire took enormous pride in having won the title of Ghazi. This desire to spread Islam was always fundamental to the foreign policy of the Ottoman Turks.

The army of the Ottoman Turks was one of the most powerful military forces ever to move across the Middle East. It consisted of a superb cavalry, elite troops trained for specialized duty, devastating with their use of the bow, as well as with their swords. But, at the core of the empire's army were the infantry troops, the Janissaries. The name means literally the new troops, and they were a newly created troop among the Ottoman army about the 15th century. But, they were not born Turks, nor were they born Muslims. The Janissaries were taken from the subject nations of the empire, above all from the Balkans, from lands that we would call Albania, Serbia, Bulgaria, and Greece. Every year, the devşirme it was called—the roundup, quite literally—was carried out, in which children of about four or five were taken away from their parents, never to come home again, to be trained as Muslims, to develop an absolutely fanatical devotion to the sultan, knowing nothing else than their devotion to the sultan and the face of Islam. They were educated to be absolutely fanatical as followers of the teachings of the prophet.

They were armed very early on with firearms. They were superb at the use of these heavy muskets of the day. Above all, they were terrifying for their use of the pike. Nothing in Europe could stand up to the attack of the Janissaries carrying their 16-foot long pikes, with a great ax at the end of it. Their hats carried in them a wooden spoon—great floppy hats and a wooden spoon was pinned into it—as a sign of their submission to the sultan, but also as a sign of the sultan's duty to feed them soup every day. When they got mad and were ready to revolt, the Janissaries would turn over their soup pots with this heavy stew in it, a kind of minestrone with lots of pasta. They carried this spoon in their hats. They were feared throughout all of Europe and the Middle East. The Ottomans were also superb at cannon. Very early on they became masters in the use of artillery, frequently making use of Germans who had become renegades and come to the Ottoman Empire to show them the use of artillery.

By 1683, some of these organizations had begun to decline. The Janissaries were no longer drawn entirely from these Christian young boys. Instead, many times sons and even grandsons of Janissaries were allowed into this core. The core had become somewhat more concerned with its own privileges than with its ferocity on the field of battle. The sultan, Mohammed IV, was a pale reflection of the mighty warriors like Mohammed the Conqueror, as well as Suleiman the Magnificent. In fact, Mohammed IV was called "The Hunter," and that was what he was most devoted to was hunting. But, to take the place as an immediate giver of policy, the sultans had their Grand Vizier. This was the second in command of the empire. The Ottoman sultan was an absolute despot. Everybody in his empire, from the lowliest peasant to the high Grand Vizier, was just his slave. Many times these Grand Viziers has originally been slaves who had risen up through the ranks, and at any moment the highest and most powerful official in the empire could be laid low by the sultan and all of his worldly goods confiscated.

But, Mohammed IV had a very strong Grand Vizier, an enormously capable man, whose family had for several generations held the post of Grand Vizier: Kara Mustafa. Swarthy Mustafa, he was called. He was a stern, very capable man, with a reputation for harshness, a reputation as a good general, and a reputation for being extremely avaricious—greedy. He convinced Mohammed IV to take a little bit of time from his hunting and to give thought to a conquest of Vienna. It is an enormously wealthy city, but above all, he said, it will give a new impetus to our Ottoman Empire. It will once again make us the center of the Islamic struggle against the Christians. "I can take Vienna if I can march out with an army of 275,000 men." Mohammed IV gave his permission.

In the spring of that year, Mohammed IV accompanied his ferocious army all the way to the city of Edirne, what was once called Adrianople, right there still today on the border of Turkey and Bulgaria. There at Edirne the sultan, Mohammed IV, had an elaborate hunting lodge, and he waved farewell to his army. The roads had been repaired all the way as far as the Hungarian border. Bridges had been repaired, and troops had been levied from throughout the empire. Riding alongside the Turkish Calvary were Tartars, Mongols from the land of the Crimea. They were riding out in front of them, the most ferocious of all the Ottoman troops who killed and plundered every village they came across if it offered any resistance, spreading terror. Large numbers of refugees began to flow towards Vienna out of the fury of the Ottomans. The church bells all along the way began to ring out—the Turkin bells, they were called, the Turkish bells, *Turkin Glocken* in German—ringing out that the Turks were on the march one more time. The great kettledrums of the Turkish forces boomed out. The camels brought their caravans along with all the necessities, including 300 cannons, to batter the walls of Vienna into submission.

Turkey had already, before the spring, declared war upon the Holy Roman Empire. The Holy Roman Emperor, Leopold, had plenty of time to prepare for this great onslaught by the Turks. Leopold was neither a particularly capable nor very war-like emperor, and he had enough sense to entrust this great struggle against the Turks to capable generals and to make a treaty with the king of Poland, John Sobieski, to give aid to the Holy Roman Empire.

The Holy Roman Empire, we met it in our lecture about Luther. It was the descendent, so the Holy Roman Emperor said, of the empire of Julius Caesar and Augustus. It had begun again in the year 800 A.D. when Charlemagne was crowned in Rome as the new Roman Emperor. It had been renewed under Otto in the 11th century in Germany. It was a political entity of some 365 units—as I mentioned earlier, some no more than a knight with his castle, others large kingdoms, like Bavaria. The Holy Roman Emperor was elected by electors, and it was one of the reasons why the founders of our country thought of the electoral system. There was an imperial parliament called a diet, which could meet at various cities of the empire, and which acted as a check upon the Holy Roman Emperor. He was in no sense an absolute despot. He was elected. He had to have the permission of the diet of his parliament to do anything that he wanted to do. To get to be Holy Roman Emperor you generally had to spend large sums of money to buy the electors.

By the time of Leopold, the emperorship had almost become hereditary in the House of Habsburg. It began as a small noble family with a castle in what we call the Tirol today of Austria. The saying was, "Others have to make war; you, fortunate Austria, you marry." Through marriage alliances the power of the dynasty of the Habsburgs had spread over a good portion of the world. Charles V, who took it upon himself to break Martin Luther, was Holy Roman Emperor, ruled over the Netherlands, ruled over Spain, and ruled over the vast empire of Spain. But, the Protestant Reformation as well as all the duties of this empire wore him out, and he had retired to a monastery.

Leopold was now emperor of the Holy Roman Empire. As soon as the word came that the Turks were on the march, he asked for the help of the duke of the Lorraine, Charles the duke of Lorraine, one of the most capable military minds of his day and one of the subjects of the Holy Roman Empire. He set Charles of Lorraine to raising an army. Leopold sent out to the various political entities that made up his empire until ultimately he had close to 60,000 troops, and to these would then be added 20,000 troops from John Sobieski of Poland. These preparations were made all through the late spring and early summer as the Turkish army came ever closer, until by July the 14th, the Turks were at the walls of Vienna, that beautiful city on the Danube, a Roman city where the emperor Marcus Aurelius had died. It was one of the earliest places where Christianity began to make a foothold in Germany. It was a German-speaking city then as it is now, solid walls around it and beautiful steeples, like the church of St. Steven's rising up in to the sky.

Leopold didn't really have it in him to stay and endure siege. He had fled. He had gone further westward, as had about 80,000 of the citizens of Vienna. But, others stayed, and the Count Rudiger Von Stahrenberg took over command of troops of about 11,000 men there and the city of Vienna, also pressing into service a number of citizens. Heavy cannons manned the walls of Vienna, and they prepared to endure a siege and an onslaught by the Turks.

Siege warfare was very highly adapted in the 17th century. These great cannons that could hurl stones as big as 32 pounds for almost a mile at times, smashing into walls made it very difficult for any wall, no matter how thick, to withstand a long prolonged cannon aid. However, it was the practice of those who were being besieged, the Viennese, in this case, to use their heavy artillery to keep the enemy at a distance. The enemy was forced to dig trenches to get as close to the wall as possible. In fact, the favored technique—and it was very successful to the Turks—for capturing a walled city was to dig trenches. It was not surround the whole city, but to dig trenches from one central place—in this case where Kara Mustafa had his tent, his headquarters situated—as close to the walls of the enemy city as possible, so there would be about a mile of parallel trenches. Then, you get to the city wall, dig under the city wall, and place enormous gunpowder-filled mines, blow a hole in the wall, and then storm through the city with the ferocious Janissaries. It's what the Janissaries liked as well, because if the city simply surrendered, gave up without the Janissaries storming it, they didn't get to plunder the city. But, if the captured it by force, they could rape and plunder and take away as much as they wanted to from the city.

The siege began. There were plenty of supplies in Vienna, though at the end rations would grow short. The troops inside the city were most of them German, but there were gallants who would come from all over Europe to take part in this crusade. That in fact is what the pope had declared it. It was a crusade against the Turks. It would be in fact the last of the crusades. In the same way, the sultan had declared this to be a holy war, a jihad, against the Christians. The troops inside the city fought with enormous bravery, driving back Turkish assault after Turkish assault. Time and time again, the Turks sought to blow up the wall and storm through it.

By early September, rations were growing fewer and fewer, and the count, the general, Rudiger Von Stahrenberg, looked up day after day hoping to see an army coming to relieve the city of Vienna. Leopold waited in his distant retreat for the army that would come to relieve his capital city of Vienna.

It finally arrived by September the 12th, making its way along the Danube, stopping to meet with Leopold, with the two armies. One was drawn from the German portions of the empire, like Bavaria, Franconia, Swabia, the dukedoms and kingdoms of this Holy Roman Empire, under the lead of Charles, Duke of Lorraine, a handsome man, though his face was rather pockmarked, and at one time a candidate to be the king of Poland, a position now held by John Sobieski.

Sobieski was a great large man, well over six foot and reaching close to 250 pounds, an enormous swooping mustache, who had been a soldier his whole life long. He had fought against the brave Cossacks. He had fought Turks before. He had fought against Swedes. He had won the right to be king of Poland because of his sheer bravery on the field of battle and his ability as an organizer of the army. He had reorganized a Polish army, both its infantry, giving them large numbers of firearms, its artillery service, as well as its cavalry. It was a most formidable army. He is the organizer of the army of Poland and the best general on the entire field.

The disposition of the Turkish troops was in the hands of Kara Mustafa, and he had no particularly outstanding general, and he had almost no military training. He also, as I told you, was avaricious. One reason why the siege had endured so long, why the attempts to blow up the walls had been somewhat halfhearted, was that if the Janissaries stormed the city, they got the money, but if it surrendered, then Kara Mustafa got the money from the city of Vienna. He had held off, and now he'd held off almost too late because when he saw the army of the Christian forces appearing on the hills above Vienna, he realized that he must take the city right now. A huge set of mines were laid. Large portions of one part of the wall were blown down. All it needed was one more enormous mine being exploded, and the city could probably be stormed by the Janissaries. But, the Viennese inside the city knew what the Turks were up to, and brave Viennese would dig down like moles. That's what they were called. They discovered the biggest of the mines and diffused it.

Kara Mustafa had to turn and face an assault from this relieving army. They're not inside the city. They are up on the hills, the Christian army. There are

11,000 troops inside the city, but this battle will be fought between the armies of the Holy Roman Emperor and the Polish army, attacking down the hill into the Turkish forces. Kara Mustafa had left his flanks and his rear undefended. He had counted upon his Tartar troops, his Mongol troops, to defend his rear, but he had been very arrogant towards the Khan of the Mongols, and they just didn't fight. There were also Tartars, Mongols, fighting under Sobieski, who knew how to make use of their ferocious attacks with arrows, shooting from horseback. They wore straws in their helmets to distinguish them from the Mongols who were supposed to be fighting for the sultan.

Early in the morning, Sobieski unleashed the duke of Lorraine, Charles, with his infantry to attack the Ottoman flank. All day long the most ferocious battle raged between the two armies, back and forth. At five o'clock, the sun still high on this summer day, late summer, but sun's still high, Sobieski launched his cavalry. All 20,000—knights from Germany, the Polish Calvary, all in heavy breastplates, carrying lances—rode at top speed into the Turkish army, routing their Calvary and then routing the feared Janissaries themselves. Caught between the German infantry with their pikes and firearms and the Polish and German Calvary, the Turkish troops began to flee. They fled the whole battlefield, leaving behind all of their cannons, but taking time in a most brutal fashion to cut the throats of all the women that they had taking captive and made concubines out of during the siege, slitting their throats and leaving them there in their own blood before the Turks fled back down towards Hungary and Budapest. In fact the Turkish army would not really slow down until it reached Belgrade.

Kara Mustafa had tried to cover himself by putting blame upon his generals and having several of these generals executed. But, there at Belgrade on December the 25th, 1683, the sentence arrived. Six men bearing a silken rope came to Kara Mustafa and said, "You know what must happen to you, *Efendi*, my lord." "Yes," said Kara Mustafa, "just tie the knot properly, please, so I won't suffer too long." In the fashion of the Ottoman Empire, a high official like Kara Mustafa had a silken rope tied around his neck, and strangled him.

Not even Mohammed IV would survive all of this. He would be deposed, a new sultan put in place, because the Turkish Empire had received a mortal blow. The Austrian Empire had begun its rise to great power status. It would be the Austrian Empire aligned with the English under General Marlborough, the ancestor of Winston Churchill, who would defeat the attempt by Louis XIV to conquer Europe. It'd be the Austrian Empire again allied with the British who would defeat the attempt by Napoleon to establish a rule over all of Europe. The Austrian Empire would be one of the great powers of Europe, right down until the First World War.

But, the Ottoman Empire, step by step, would decline, leaving behind out of its ruins issues like Kosovo, for those in Kosovo today who are so proud to be Muslim but speak the language of the Serbians are part of the legacy of the Ottoman Empire. They are people who converted to get the advantages of being Muslims under the Ottoman Empire. Iraq, a totally artificial country created after World War I, again was left on the ruins of the Ottoman Empire to try to give some stability in that vital part of the world. In fact, the Ottoman Empire and all of its issues of ruling over a multicultural diverse empire of people hating each other would be inherited first by the British and the French after World War I and the collapse of the Ottoman Empire, and now, we have inherited the problems of the Middle East. That goes back to that day when the forces of Christendom crushed the Ottoman army there at Vienna.

The Battle of Lexington (1775)
Lecture 21

There have been so many armed revolts throughout history—armed revolts against the Ottoman Empire, armed revolts against the Austrian Empire, and armed revolts in England itself, a whole civil war in England. What is remarkable to me is that this revolution in these 13 colonies became not one more bloody, brutal revolt for insignificant questions but instead led to the Declaration of Independence.

No event in the ensuing centuries has changed history to the extent of "the shot heard round the world," fired on April 19, 1775. The battles of Lexington and Concord, fought that day, resulted in the declaration of independence of Britain's 13 colonies from their mother country. And the later victory of those 13 colonies led to the creation of the United States as a nation founded on law and moral principles.

On the morning of the first battle of the Revolution, 77 American militiamen gathered on the green in Lexington to face 700 British troops; these troops had been sent by the governor of Massachusetts to confiscate cannons being held in either Concord or Worcester. The Americans were armed with rifles, which could shoot farther than the British muskets, but the British were well trained in using bayonets. When the British troops arrived, the rebels were commanded to disperse. The Americans had been ordered to stand their ground but not to fire unless fired upon. Someone—it is not known whether the soldier was British or American—fired a shot, and the British charged the militia. Seven Americans were killed, the militia dispersed, and the British moved on to Concord.

The town of Concord was searched, but no cannons were found. A group of about 80 men was dispatched to the Concord River, but again, all seemed quiet. A few pickets were posted, and the rest of the men lay down to rest. About 11:00 in the morning, the British troops on the river were awakened by the approach of at least 1,000 militiamen. Both the British and the Americans took up positions, but the British retreated to Concord when the Americans began to fire. From there, the British were commanded back to Boston; all along the route, they fell victim to American snipers. By the time they reached Boston, the British had suffered heavy casualties and a disheartening defeat. Many of the American militiamen stayed on in Boston, ultimately forming an army of almost 16,000 men, and put the city under siege.

The American Revolution offers a fruitful and instructive study about what happens when a government decides that it knows what is best for its constituents. In the wake of the French and Indian War, King George III believed that he could follow the path of the benevolent despots of Europe. He wanted to guide a centralized, well-organized empire in which each of the subject nations paid its own way. To help pay the debt left over from the war against France, the British imposed taxes on the American colonists, not realizing how strongly the Americans would resist. The Americans declared that they would remain loyal subjects of the king but would not allow themselves to be governed by a body in which they had no representation.

In the spring of 1776, King George III and Parliament unleashed against the colonists the largest armada ever mustered by the British Empire. The Americans, in the aftermath of Lexington and Concord, were faced with the question of whether or not they should declare independence. The move for independence gained strength, and on July 4, 1776, the Declaration of Independence was released. This document

A small skirmish at Lexington, Massachusetts erupted into the American Revolution.

ensured that the battle against British troops at Lexington and Concord did not go down in history as just one more failed revolt but launched a nation that guides the world to this day. ■

Suggested Reading

Birnbaum, *Red Dawn*.

Higginbotham, *War of American Independence*.

Questions to Consider

1. The militia laws of the 13 colonies were essentially a military draft. Do you think the United States should have a draft today?

2. Were the colonists right in their assertion that British taxation of the colonies was unfair given that they were not represented in Parliament?

The Battle of Lexington (1775)
Lecture 21—Transcript

Our theme in this lecture is the battle of Lexington and Concord. It is April 19, 1775. The shot heard around the world. The battles there at Lexington and at Concord meant that the 13 colonies found themselves in armed conflict with the superpower of the day, the British Empire, their own country. In the aftermath, the Americans found themselves in a situation, given the determination of the king in parliament utterly to crush this rebellion, either of declaring their independence or surrendering. So would come, a little more than a year after the battle of Lexington and Concord would come, The Declaration of Independence. The United States would be the first nation in history founded upon moral principles. Victory would lead then to the constitution. The aftermath was the creation of the United States as a nation under law and moral principles. That united nation, the United States of America, would purge itself of slavery, go on to turn the tide in two great world wars, and become the bastion of freedom today. No event in the 18th, 19th, 20th, or so far in the 21st century has so changed history as April 19, 1775.

Go back with me to that date. You are you. You could be a boy of 16; you could be a man as old as me. You are there at the Green in Lexington, where 77 of you come together, part of the regularly organized and legal militia of Lexington. Go to Lexington with me today; it is still at the center very reminiscent of the town that you have come to on that morning. Some of you had a stop at Buckman's Tavern where you have had a pint or two. It is a gray, gray day just beginning to get light. You have been taken away from your fields that you have planned to plow and plant on this day. Some of you have had wives who have said, "Do you know what you are doing? You are going out to resist the troops of the king. You are going to become a trader. Do you know what they do to traders? They draw and quarter you. That is to say, they hang you by the neck until you are almost dead. They then pull you on a rack until your bones begin to pop out. They then disembowel you while you are still alive and burn your entrails before your expiring eyes. Who is going to take care of me and the children?" But, you have gone out.

You are not an inexperienced soldier. Every one of the thirteen colonies has a militia law in which men from the age of sixteen on up are required to be in the militia. If they cannot supply a weapon, they will have one supplied for them by their township. They train on a regular basis. Officers who command you there in Lexington, like some of your comrades, have served in the French and Indian War from 1756–1763, in which Britain has won its great empire in Canada. You know the British Army, you know how it operates, and you are not afraid of it. But, you are also willing to take this very grave decision.

Who are the British troops coming down the road to meet you there in the Green at Lexington? They are your fellow countrymen. They are on a legitimate mission, 700 of them sent out by the governor of Massachusetts in his authority both as military and civilian governor of Massachusetts, Governor Gage. They are the best, elite troops in the British Army and they approve of themselves on the field of battle in Europe and in North America as the best soldiers in the world, defeating the French. You call them Redcoats or Lobsterbacks. They wear a bright red jacket, white vest, white pants, and hobnail type boots. These are all elite troops, so they were either wearing a bearskin headdress or they are wearing a hat shaped a bit like a baseball cap. These are grenadiers and other crack troops—rangers, who carry in their belt a tomahawk they have learned to use in the French and Indian War. These are the best troops the king has, more than 2,000 of them stationed in Boston, and these 700 have been sent out, starting the night before, to confiscate weapons of mass destruction. This is because the governor has learned that there are cannons being held either in Concord or perhaps at the other town of Worcester. These cannons have no purpose other than, of course, to kill the king's troops. You have no legitimate right to these cannons. The English Declaration of Rights says quite specifically, "An Englishman may bear arms suited to his station." It's not an unlimited right to bear arms; an Englishman may bear arms suited to his station and it is not suited to your station without the permission of the governor to have these cannons. That is what they are there on mission to do.

But, all along the way, once they crossed by boat Boston Harbor, one if by land and two if by sea, to take the route to Concord. If they went by land, they were going to go to get cannons in Worcester, so they crossed their only way to Concord, as well as to Lexington. Lexington lies along the way about eight miles closer to Boston from Concord. All along the way they have seen lights in the windows. You farmers are supposed to be asleep this time of night. But, all along that route, riders have made their way, pointing out, shouting, knocking on doors: The British are coming! The Redcoats are coming! These were brave men like Paul Revere, a silversmith, a man of considerable wealth. If anybody ever tells you the revolution was made by wealthy men who just wanted to get more rich, that is nonsense. Paul Revere could have left the colony of Massachusetts, gone to London, opened up a shop as a silversmith, and made an even larger fortune. These are patriots and, as Lord Acton, the British historian of liberty said, "The Americans in 1775 were the most lightly taxed, freely governed people in the world." A pound of tea cost less in Boston than it did in London, but they were willing to rise up in the name of one word alone: Liberty.

The British troops are coming along on a perfectly legitimate mission, coming to confiscate these weapons, but knowing something was not quite right. They get there to Lexington. Seven hundred troops under their rather middle-aged and portly commander, Francis Smith, with John Pitcairn, a Major marine, second in command. There are these 77 militiamen, and they are not scraggily looking. They have first-rate muskets and also many of them are armed with rifles. A rifle can shoot considerably further than a musket. The musket in the hand of the English troops, the brown vest, is accurate at not much more than 75 yards. That is not a whole lot more firing power than a Roman javelin had. A rifle can hit accurately at about 200 yards, but there is a big difference. A rifle cannot carry a bayonet; the musket does. The British soldier through harsh discipline is the absolute master of using that bayonet. You, an American, fear that weapon. They will fire at you from their three ranks and then close with that bayonet. If you are using a rifle, you have no protection except to try to reload before he gets to you or use your rifle as a club.

The British arrive and Francis Smith looks out upon these armed men, almost all of them wearing a common uniform because the militia used uniforms and were proud of their uniforms, and Smith says: "Lay down your weapons and disperse, you damned rebels." But, Commander Parker, the commander of the militia says: "Boys, do not fire unless fired upon, but if they mean too have a war, then let it start right here." Nobody would ever know who, but someone fired—British or American, we do not know. The British fired first, the Americans got off one round, and then the British charged with those bayonets and the militia units began to break up. Eight Americans were killed, one man bayonetted before his front door, in front of his wife and children. Then, having dispersed this band of militia, the British moved on towards Concord.

But, by this time, the commander and the second in command, Major Pitcairn and his superior Francis Smith, began to get a little worried. They had shot down the king's subjects and they better find those weapons of mass destruction, so they went on to Concord. There did not seem to be many men in the town of Concord, but that really was not the main concern of the officers. They gave the strict demand, "Find those cannons!" The British soldiers began to go through every house and every barn, but they could not find any cannons. Then, just to make sure that something amiss did not happen, a group of about 80 troops was dispatched further on to the Concord River where the North Bridge flowed over the Concord River. There, nothing seemed to be happening. They had been up all night, marched all this 20 miles, and fought this battle at Lexington, so they were tired. Their officers said go ahead, just leave a few pickets out, and take a nap.

About 11:00 in the morning, drowsy, the British soldiers there at the North Bridge in Concord began to hear a kind of buzzing. It was almost like a bunch of honeybees. They got up and looked and coming over the hilltop were at least 1,000 more militiamen. From neighboring towns like Acton, they had come. Hearing the cry in the night, that the British are coming, and then learning that the British had fired upon militiamen and killed British subjects there at Lexington, they came down the hill. The British crossed the bridge to face them. The British took up their stand and formation while putting down a riot, four men behind one another. The Americans went into three lines just like well-trained British troops. Then, they unleashed a volley, then a second volley, and then a third. The officers calling out, "Front rank, fire! Second rank, fire! Third rank, fire!" The British troops broke and ran back across the bridge, while the American pursued them. While the British were sprawled out there, an American took a tomahawk and whacked him in the head. The British shouted out, "They are scalping us boys, they are scalping us!" Then, they raced back to Concord.

Now what are we going to do? We have not only killed the king's subjects, we have a battle going here. How many of them are there? I don't know. There are at least 1,000 and more are coming in every hour. Perhaps as many as 2,000 militiamen would show up there between Concord and Boston. All that is left for the British troops to do is for their officers to give the command, "Start on back boys, start on back."

But, all along the way, as they marched from Concord, the eight miles to Lexington, Americans fired upon them. They were firing from behind stone walls, firing from trees, firing out of house windows, and the British were under this constant bombardment and unable to do anything about it. The Americans would not stand and fight, so the British officers gave the command, "Go get 'em boys; go on, find them; burn that house down!" Some Americans were bayonetted as the British pursued them into their homes and pursued them into the woods. But, the Americans kept coming back firing again and again and not in formation, but individually. The British had already learned in the French and Indian War, these Americans were crack shots. The British troops, hungry, exhausted from having been up well over 24 hours, having marched 20 miles and now having to march back, through all the stress of battle, were just about to collapse. As they got to the town of Lexington, they began to hear that comforting sound of drums and fifes. There were 700 more British troops. The governor, General Gage, had become concerned that he had not sent enough troops. Several hours after the first group had left, he sent another group. There they were with cannons and mustering behind these fresh troops, the British retreating from Concord were saved.

The Americans still were not finished. When the British turned to begin to march, all 1,400 of them now, back towards Boston, the Americans continued to fire all along the way. Until, late that night the British Army straggled into Boston having suffered extremely heavy casualties—not only in dead, but also in wounded. You must remember that in 1775 if you got wounded in the hand, there was no one around to put antiseptic on it. It got gangrene and one out of every two battlefield wounds ended either in death or amputation. Amputation was almost, in many cases, like a death sentence. The British had suffered very heavy casualties and a very discouraging, disheartening defeat.

Now what was the governor to do? He had to write London and tell them that following their orders, he had started an armed revolt in the colony of Massachusetts. He knew what London wanted. London was determined to put down any resistance in these American colonies. He had been urged, General Gage, to show more force towards the Americans. He had done so and this was the result.

To me, the most extraordinary aspect of this is not the Americans firing upon the British, but the fact that they then stuck together and fought this war of the revolution. I fear today that if for some reason, hope it never happens, but if Americans were forced to fire upon the American Army, every one of those militiamen would be down at the courthouse the next day with an attorney trying to get a plea bargain in place—not these Americans. Instead, making use of their colonial legislatures, making use of the illegal, from the British point of view, Congress that was meeting in Philadelphia, they responded by raising an army. In fact, rather than going home, many of these farmers who had fired upon the British at Lexington and Concord, now stayed on there at Boston where they formed a large American Army almost 16,000 men strong. They were drawn from the New England colonies of Massachusetts, Connecticut, Rhode Island, and New Hampshire of course, to besiege the British there in Boston itself. They built siege works around the city of Boston and the British were cut off from any supplies except by sea. There the siege of Boston, under trained officers who had served under British command during the French and Indian War, like Israel Putnam, carried on into the month of June 1775.

By this time, more generals had arrived by sea to give aid to General Gage. More troops had arrived, but even so the American siege of Boston continued. There was one key to breaking that siege and that was to put heavy cannon up on Bunker Hill. From that position on Bunker Hill, there on the harbor of Boston, the American siege lines could be battered into non-existence by heavy British cannon. These American officers were very capable men. Israel Putnam saw this problem and sent a large number of troops, in the night of June 16th to June 17th, over to Bunker Hill. The next day when General Gage awakened and looked out, the Americans had built fortifications there at Bunker Hill to hold that position so the British could not seize it. That same day, in the afternoon, a large number of crack British troops time and time again suffering terrible losses carried out a frontal assault against Bunker Hill. Finally running out of ammunition, the Americans made an orderly retreat. Bunker Hill was seized, but the American siege of Boston continued.

In July of 1775, under the great elm tree in Cambridge, George Washington of Virginia took command of what was becoming the Continental Army. These 13 colonies found themselves in an absolute life and death struggle. There have been so many armed revolts throughout history—armed revolts against the Ottoman Empire, armed revolts against the Austrian Empire, and armed revolts in England itself, a whole civil war in England. What is remarkable to me is that this revolution in these 13 colonies became not one more bloody, brutal revolt for insignificant questions, but instead lead to The Declaration of Independence.

King George was not going to let this go. In fact, what had transformed these militiamen into armed rebels and traders because just a few years before in 1763 when the war with France had been brought to a glorious end, all over the colonies from New Hampshire all the way down to Georgia celebrations occurred and speeches were made. The American colonists declared themselves to be proud subjects of the great empire of Britain and proud subjects of King George III.

The American Revolution is a most fruitful and instructive study about what happens when a government decides that they know what is best for their constituents. That is exactly what the British decided after the French and Indian War was concluded. King George III believed that he could follow in the path of the emperor of Austria, follow in the path of various local rulers in Germany, the king of France, and be a benevolent despot, and that he could bring order into all of these anachronistic institutions that were holdovers from the Middle Ages. King George III wanted to guide a centralized, well-organized empire in which each part of the empire paid its own way. He had a huge debt left over from the war against France and he charged the ministers in his cabinet to find a way to pay that debt.

One of these ministers in 1767 was Charles Townsend. He was a very close friend, patron and supporter of Adam Smith, the economist. Adam Smith gave Townsend the bright idea of a stamp tax; he had already told Townsend this in 1764. Tax sugar; put a tax on the sugar that is used to make molasses. Put other taxes on articles like lead and tea. Adam Smith, as we shall see, was a great economist, but he was dead wrong about how Americans would respond to these taxes.

King George III was also a capable politician and he had packed parliament with his "cronies." They followed his policy. In fact, the more the Americans resisted the taxes that were put upon them, starting in 1763 and 1764, the more parliament was insistent upon its demands that the Americans recognize that parliament alone governed for the entire British Empire. Once again, in an event that changed history, the Americans said no. No government in which we do not have geographical representation can govern us. We will remain loyal subjects of the king, but we insist on our political freedom. That is to say, our political matters except for foreign policy will be handled by the individuals we elect, who represent us in our colonial legislatures, like Virginia or Connecticut. We insist upon our individual freedom, freedom to live as we choose as long as we harm no one else. We will not allow either of these freedoms to be infringed upon by the king or by parliament. In fact, we declare parliament's rule over us to be illegal.

You could say that, but in the spring of 1776, King George III and parliament unleashed the largest armada, naval and land forces, ever mustered by the British Empire up until that point. Their goal was the absolute conquest of the colonies. Boston had been abandoned by the British. Leave New England alone for a while; the British were determined to completely crush the rebellion in the middle colonies like New York and New Jersey. This large armada including 73 warships made its way across the sea until ultimately

King George III would have roughly 40,000 troops that spring to crush this rebellion.

The Americans, in the aftermath of Lexington and Concord, were faced with this great decision. Do we declare ourselves independent? When the Congress meeting in Philadelphia, representing the 13 colonies, adjourned in the fall of 1775, there was a great deal of ambiguity. In fact, a strong poll showed that most of the delegates representing the viewpoint in their colonies thought that this still could be worked out with the British. A declaration of independence would be an irrevocable decision.

In the course of that winter, Thomas Paine's *Common Sense* was published. It was a runaway bestseller and one of the most influential books ever written. It simply made the statement that independence is common sense. England is our mother country; are you going to live with your mom the rest of your life? England has taken care of us. England would take care of the Ottoman Turks, if there were profit in it. No, we are now grown up and we need to declare our independence based on freedom, not on the outworn idea of a divine king. In fact, what God in the world would put King George upon the throne? The idea of a divine right of kings is totally fraudulent. When they came back in the spring of 1776, the move was strong for independence. George Washington was strongly pushing it, so that the Americans would cease to be rebels and become men fighting for a real country. They could get recognition from France and perhaps from Spain.

On the 4th of July, that was the day that declaration of independence was set forth to the world. In the words of Thomas Jefferson and that whole Congress, "We hold these truths to be self-evident, that all men are created equal, and they are endowed by that creator with certain unalienable rights among which are life, liberty, and the pursuit of happiness. Governments are instituted among men to secure those rights. When a government no longer secures those rights, it is not only our right, it is our duty to overthrow it and replace it with a government based upon these natural rights."

America is the only nation in history founded on moral principles. In 1776, you were British because you were born there. A German will still tell you that you are a German because you speak the German language as a mother tongue. We alone say come here from anywhere in the world, speak any language. You become an American if you accept these fundamental principles, that all men are equal, that all men are endowed with the right of liberty, of life, and the pursuit of happiness, the right to live their lives in such a way that they leave the world a better place.

We are founded upon moral values and, this is just history, we are founded upon a belief that those moral values come from God. The Declaration of Independence ensured that firing upon some British troops in Lexington and Concord did not go down as one more failed revolt, but became a beacon that guides the world, and above all us, still today.

General Pickett Leads a Charge (1863)
Lecture 22

Lee, Davis, and the Confederate soldiers who fought from 1861 to 1865 were fighting because of the American Revolution. ... They had done nothing differently than their forefathers. They had declared their independence from a country that had become tyrannical, wanting to interfere with their—as they saw it—fundamental right to property.

Gettysburg represents the most decisive battle in American history and one of the most decisive battles in human history. The surrender of the Confederacy on July 4 in Vicksburg, after the Battle of Gettysburg, meant that the government of the South would never receive recognition by Britain or France, without which it had no hope of winning the Civil War. It's often said that war never solves anything, but the defeat of the Confederacy forever ended the question of secession and the terrible institution of slavery.

From almost the time of the Declaration of Independence, slave states and free states had pursued two different ideas of freedom. Many of the founders of the United States owned slaves and would have justified slavery as an aspect of human law, while acknowledging that it was not the will of God. Others asked whether America could exist as a free republic based on moral principles while allowing slavery.

Through the late 18th century, many believed that slavery would prove itself to be economically unfeasible and that the institution would fade away, but by 1860, slavery was expanding. Slaves were part of the industrial transformation of the South, and more than that, the southern states had found their self-identity in slavery. They saw no incompatibility between slavery and democracy. For many southerners, the question of slavery was not a matter of morality but individual choice.

Abraham Lincoln refused to believe this justification. He was convinced that the slaveholding states wanted more than tolerance for this immoral institution—they wouldn't stop until the Union was a slaveholding empire.

In 1860, Lincoln won an electoral majority against a hopelessly splintered Democratic Party and became president.

Lincoln approached the issue of slavery cautiously, hoping that it could be solved through a constitutional convention, but the war came and was longer and bloodier than anyone had imagined it would be. As the war raged on, Lincoln came to believe that it was impossible to save the Union and allow slavery to continue.

In late June of 1863, **Robert E. Lee** embarked on a strategy to capture the capital of Pennsylvania, Harrisburg, then engage the Army of the Potomac and sweep down toward Washington. On July 1, the Confederate forces discovered that Union troops were already entrenched in the high ground above the town of Gettysburg. The next day, Lee sought repeatedly to break the left flank of the Union, but it held. On July 3, he decided to try a direct frontal assault to break the Union center. The Confederate troops marched forward at 3:06 in the afternoon, at first inspiring awe in their enemies. Then the Union cannons began to fire, and the Confederates were forced to turn back at the crest of the hill.

Abraham Lincoln (1809–1865).

Library of Congress, Prints and Photographs Division, LC-DIG-ppmsca-19305.

The cause of the Confederacy was dead. Britain and France would never recognize it, and only the military genius of Robert E. Lee and the devotion of his soldiers to him kept the cause alive until 1865. Lee thought that slavery was a great moral wrong, but he believed that to allow the federal government to usurp the rights of the states would be to allow tyranny. He wanted slavery ended but by each state individually; unfortunately, it would take a war to make America "the bastion of freedom." ∎

Name to Know

Lee, Robert Edward (1807–1870): U.S. and Confederate soldier. As general of the Army of Northern Virginia, Lee's victories from 1862 to 1863 led him to be compared in the North and Europe to the greatest generals in history.

Suggested Reading

Foote, *The Civil War*.

Shaara, *The Killer Angels*.

Questions to Consider

1. Were slaveholding signers of the Declaration of Independence, such as Thomas Jefferson, hypocrites?

2. Do you still believe with Lincoln that the United States is the last best hope of the human race?

General Pickett Leads a Charge (1863)
Lecture 22—Transcript

The theme for this lecture is the Battle of Gettysburg, the most decisive battle in American history, one of the most decisive battles in all of human history. The battle of Lexington was of course very important battle and so was Yorktown, but we were still part of the British Empire until we actually won those battles. The Battle Of Gettysburg changed our history forever.

Starting with the 4th of July and the retreat of the confederate army and the surrender on that same day in the great port city of Vicksburg, it meant that the confederacy lost any hope of recognition by France and Britain. That was crucial in the same way that George Washington and Jefferson Davis, whose fathers had fought in the Revolution, knew that only ultimately recognition and help from France enabled us to win the American Revolution, so recognition and financial support from Britain and France was all that would enable the confederacy to win. In the aftermath of Gettysburg, that was no longer possible and the confederacy began its slow decline. With the defeat of the confederacy, the 13th, 14th, and 15th amendments, slavery was forever ended, and it became clear that you were first and foremost a citizen of the United States.

Someone challenged me the other day when I said, "No war ever solves anything, it is what we say but it is dead wrong." That person challenged me and said, "Who said war never solves anything?" I did something I never do almost. I went to the Internet and I checked and there were all these people ranting and raving about war solving or not solving anything, but I still do not know who said that. I think we all say it, but wars do solve things and there is no better proof of this than the Civil War. It was fought over the question of can a state secede, leave the union, and can you be a democracy and have slavery as well? The answer to both was no. The Civil War forever ended the question of secession and it forever ended that terrible institution of slavery. In the long term, America became the bastion of freedom, purged itself of slavery and World War I, World War II, all through the long cold war, had the moral authority to lead the world towards ever greater freedom.

To understand this decisive moment in our history, go back with me to July 3rd, 1863. We are in the small crossroads town of Gettysburg, Pennsylvania. It is exactly 3:06 in the afternoon and the most tremendous artillery barrage ever heard before or since in the western hemisphere has just come to an end—two hours which the Confederate army's artillery has pounded the Union posts. The Confederates are stretched out along a long slope by a little Lutheran Seminary. On the other side, three-quarters of a mile away, the Union forces are dug in along ridges with ominous names like Cemetery Hill and Little Round Top. For three days the struggle has gone on and it is about to reach its climax at 3:06 in the afternoon of July 3rd.

Let us be with the Confederate Army and the very center of the Confederate line. As we stand there, not one of us has a uniform the same as the other one. We begin to raise our hats before the man who represents for us, the cause for which we are fighting—Robert E. Lee, 56 years of age, handsome and once called the most handsome man in the United States Army. The ladies of the Confederate Army call him the most handsome man in all of Christendom. He has silver hair, silver beard, and is dressed in his finest uniform. Whenever Lee sees an officer, he of course salutes. But, whenever he sees an enlisted man, like those of us standing in front of him, he takes off his hat as a sign of the greatest tribute. Officers have told us not to cheer him, lest we give away how many of us there are in these woods, but some of us think it is almost like a halo around his head. He would give anything not to be here in Gettysburg, about to send us into a desperate fight with our fellow Americans. Lee has said, "I want no other flag than the stars and stripes. I want no other anthem than Hail Columbia. I want no other country than the United States of America. There is nothing I would not give up to save the Union except Honor and Liberty." This is indeed a struggle over conflicting ideals of liberty that go right back to the beginning of our country. That is what has brought us in gray and in blue to the field at Gettysburg, both of us Americans, Confederate and Union alike, but from The Declaration of Independence onward, we on two different courses about freedom.

The Declaration of Independence had declared that all men are created equal, but many of the delegates there including Thomas Jefferson owned slaves. Jefferson and other delegates were well educated and could have explained to you, unconvincingly to us today, but convincingly to themselves, that slavery was indeed the part of human law. God wanted all men to be free, but from the beginning of history some men had been enslaved. And so it was that Roman law itself said that slavery was contrary to the will of God, but it was a human institution.

Then, came the Constitution. The Constitution would never have been drafted, never would have been ratified, had it prohibited slavery. All the way from Georgia up through Delaware were slave states and they would not have a constitution that prohibited slavery. The Constitution, unlike The Declaration of Independence, did not mention God and the Constitution wrote slavery into it. If a slave ran away to a free state, the federal marshals were required by the Constitution to bring that slave back. The federal government even collected ten dollars in the early days of the republic on each slave that was imported. From the beginning this question had been there: "Can you be a free republic based upon moral principles and also a slave holding state?"

All through the late 18th century, there had been many who hoped that the issue of slavery would die a natural death. The Constitution had provided that after twenty years Congress could prohibit the importation of slaves and that happened without very much controversy at the appointed time. Many thought that slavery would prove itself to be economically unfeasible. But, in fact, not just the invention of the cotton gin changed all of that, but other industrial developments as well. By 1860, slavery was advancing; the number of slaves had increased. The price of slaves had gone very, very high. Slavery was becoming part of the industrial transformation of the South. From Maryland all the way out to Missouri, factories were run by slave labor. More than that, the southern states, which had always felt themselves different from the northern states, had found in slavery their self-identity. They were aggressively slave holding and they saw no incompatible status between slavery and democracy.

In fact, many of them like Jefferson Davis, learned it in the classics, said the great republics of Greece and Rome rested upon freedom as well as slavery. The Athenians defined freedom as their freedom to rule themselves and their freedom to rule over others. These learned southerners, again like Jefferson Davis, who with his second wife in the evenings, used to read Latin to each other, said Aristotle proclaims that slavery is part of nature. Some men are by nature slaves and others are by nature, like the Greeks, free. Cicero talks about slavery as being part of human law and talks about the justice necessary to a slave, but never condemned slavery. The Bible, which we rank even higher than the classics, Davis would tell you to read the Ten Commandments—what is the next paragraph after the last of the Commandments dealing with? It deals with how to treat a Hebrew slave. The Old Testament condones slavery and Paul does not tell a slave to run away from his master, does not tell a slave owner that slavery is wrong. Paul tells him to be a good slave.

The South hardened its attitude about slavery. In 1860, if I were a professor at the University of Georgia, I could lose my job if I allowed a class even to discuss slavery. Again, this is just to see it in the viewpoint of 1860, but many southerners would tell you that slavery was simply a matter of choice. They did not necessarily want to argue with you about whether slavery was moral or immoral, but it was their choice whether or not to have slaves. It was legal under the Constitution, it was legal under the state law of Alabama or Georgia, and if you want to get down to morality, slavery is condoned by Cicero, Aristotle, Moses, and Paul. You tell me Mr. or Mrs. Massachusetts abolitionist, who are you to come down here to Georgia and tell me that I am immoral to have slaves? It is what I choose to do and it is legal; therefore, the nation had split.

All of this quoting of Cicero and Aristotle seemed very silly to an Illinois lawyer, Abraham Lincoln. No, he had not gone to Harvard, but he had had no more than one year of formal schooling. He had read and studied and turned himself into a lawyer and had become prosperous. He had lost one election to Congress when he had opposed the Mexican War because it was not only immoral, not only unjustified, but he saw it purely as a war to expand slavery. By 1856, Abraham Lincoln had become utterly convinced that the slave holding states did not want tolerance for this immoral institution. These states and the southerners would not stop until the whole Union was a slave holding empire. Indeed, southerners dreamed of that, of a tropic empire of slavery. In fact, they even believed that the teachings of figures like Charles Darwin and his recently published work *On The Origin Of Species* proved that the survival of the fittest required that they own slaves and that this was a sign of their fitness. They were terrible ideas, but taught even in the universities of the South.

To Abraham Lincoln, this was nonsense. In his debates with Senator Douglas who was going to be senator of Illinois, Abraham Lincoln had asked Douglas, quite innocently it seemed, "Senator Douglas, you say that each territory ought to decide for itself whether or not it is going to have slaves. It ought to be a matter of local choice. Is that correct?" "Yes. Yes it is." "Senator, are you a Christian?" "Why, why, why of course I am a Christian," Douglas had to say. "Senator, what does the golden rule say?" "Do unto others as you would have them do unto you." "Would you want to be a slave, Senator Douglas?" "Well, no." "Then why would you want anybody to be a slave? All of this is nonsense and no God that taught us the golden rule would condone slavery." Lincoln lost that election, but then came the election of 1860 and there the Democratic Party was hopelessly splintered. There was one faction that said we are pro-slavery. There was another faction of the Democrats that said we are opposed to slavery, and there was one that said we will just ignore it and it will go away. Abraham Lincoln, losing very strongly in the popular vote, won the electoral vote and as a minority president was elected in 1860.

The London newspapers said it was typical and characteristic of the political immaturity of the North American Union that at such a critical moment in their destinies, they would entrust their fate to a backwoods solicitor. That is what Abraham Lincoln was. His cabinet thought they were so much smarter than Lincoln and thought that they would run the war. In fact, Lincoln, from the beginning of that war, was one to retain the Union and to, if possible, get rid of slavery. Even in his first inaugural address, Lincoln approached it very cautiously. He promised not to interfere in any state, in any county, in any way with slavery. "We are one people," he said and, "We can solve this by our Constitution." He recommended calling a constitutional convention, but the war came and the war was longer and bloodier than anyone had imagined it would be. The casualty list piled up and up. There were battles like Antietam, still the bloodiest single day in American history, far bloodier than D-Day. There were 23,000 casualties at Antietam in one day and the war showed no signs of ending. It seemed as though the South would win.

What is on the seal of the Confederate states of America? It is George Washington and the legend, the words, *Deo Vindice*—God Will Vindicate Us.

Robert E. Lee's father had been one of the greatest of the Revolutionary generals, Light Horse Harry Lee. Robert E. Lee's wife, Mary Custis, was the granddaughter of George Washington. Robert E. Lee, there at Gettysburg, carried in his vest pocket the watch of George Washington given to him as a wedding present. He looked out upon the federal line with a spyglass that had once been carried by George Washington. For Lee, David and the Confederate soldiers, who fought from 1861–1865, were fighting because of the American Revolution. The second American Revolution, they had done nothing differently than their forefathers. They had declared their independence from a country that had become tyrannical wanting to interfere with their, as they saw it, fundamental right to property. That was their ideal of liberty, democracy, and slavery.

Those who fought for the Union listened evermore to the song that sent them into battle, The Battle Hymn of the Republic.

> I have read a fiery gospel, ridden rows of burnished steel:
> "As ye deal with my contemners, so my grace with you
> shall deal; Let the Hero, born of woman, crush the serpent
> ['neath] his heel, [His truth] is marching on." In the beauty
> of the lilies Christ was born across the sea, There's a glory
> in His bosom that transfigures you and me: As He died to
> make men holy, let us die to make men free.

Abraham Lincoln, as this war had grown more and more bloody, began to believe that he had been so wrong at the start in thinking it was somehow possible to save the Union and let slavery continue. He became more and more convinced that God had sent this terrible war upon our country for this original sin of slavery. His own little boy died of illness in the course of the war and Lincoln became to see that as a punishment sent by God to him to make him realize that all of these losses in battle, all of these casualty lists were not numbers; they were somebody's little boy. God had taken his little boy to understand that slavery must end.

In late June of 1863, Robert E. Lee had crossed the Potomac River. He had met with the Confederate cabinet and described a bold strategy by which he would capture the Pennsylvania capital of Harrisburg. He would entrench in the high ground which he had done so often and so successfully, force the army of the Potomac to come against him on that high ground, destroy the army of the Potomac in one more great battle and then sweep down upon Washington, capturing the city of Washington and bringing the British and the French to the aid of the of the Confederacy. In fact, as he crossed the Potomac, he carried in his pocket a letter from Jefferson Davis, president of the Confederacy, to be laid upon the desk of Abraham Lincoln dictating terms for the recognition of the independence of the confederacy. He was reckoned in Europe as well as in the north as the greatest general of his day, worthy to rank with Alexander, Julius Caesar, and Napoleon. Battles that he had fought like second Manassas, Fredericksburg, and Chancellorsville in May 1863 resound still through the annals of military history.

Hardly less remarkable than General Lee were the men who followed him, the army of northern Virginia, the army of cavaliers and crackers, of gallant knights in butternut gray. One observer watching them march through Maryland and Pennsylvania on their way to Gettysburg said, "We could literally smell the rebels coming before we saw them. They were a most ragged and hungry pack of wolves. No two of them had uniforms alike and they were so dirty that the only things clean about them were their guns and their teeth from their constant diet of apples and corn on the cob. But, somehow they carried themselves with a panache that was lacking in far better equipped and far more numerous Union troops."

Many of these rebels came from the Deep South and they spoke a dialect we could barely understand; they were profane beyond all belief. These were the men that Lee lead to Gettysburg. He had not wanted that battle, but it came. He had never left the field in the hand of the enemy and he would not do so now. "The enemy is there," he said, "there on the hills of Gettysburg and there we shall strike it!" He was worried though; there had been change after another in the Union commanders, the most recent one General Joseph Hooker, who was a total fraud, absolutely defeated by Lee at the Battle of Chancellorsville. But, on the eve of Gettysburg, Lee was alert that there was a new Union officer, General Meade. When he was told that, he immediately said, "Is that George Meade?" "Yes, general." "He was my student when I was commandant at the academy. He is the most capable officer." That was the highest accolade Lee could give. "He is the most capable officer, he will not make a mistake, and he will take the utmost advantage of my mistakes."

The first mistake had come on that first day of July 1st when Lee's orders had not been explicit and harsh enough to his generals that they should seize that high ground on which the Union forces were already digging in. The second day, once the Union occupied that high ground stretching all the way from Cemetery Hill to Little Round Top, Lee had sought to break the Union left flank. There was assault after assault after assault, but the Union held good. On the night of the 2nd and early morning of the 3rd, Lee faced his decision. Should he withdraw? It was very dangerous to do; he had come up through narrow mountain roads to withdraw. To turn his flank and rear to the Union forces was to invite disaster. Moreover, "there was nothing," he said. "My men cannot do if they were properly led."

He decided on this assault on the 3rd across three-quarters of a mile of open ground into the Union, guns to break the Union center and to roll up the Union Army. The same tactics had worked in the last great battle fought in Europe, a battle closely studied by Lee. That was the Battle of Solferino in Italy, between the forces of France and Italy against the Austrians, in which a heavy bombardment by the French and Italians had been followed by direct frontal assault on the high ground of the Austrians and the Austrian center had broken. At 3:06 in the afternoon, Lee rode by his troops and they started moving forward mostly from Virginia and North Carolina. The overall commander of the assault was General George Pickett, not the brightest star at West Point academically, but a hard, tough fighter. Most of his troops were fresh. Pickett said, "Up and to your posts, men," Pickett said, "and never forget today that you are from Ole' Virginia." The North Carolinians under

General James Kemper, very distinguished graduate academically of North Carolina, started out. "Forward men for the honor of the old north state."

As they began to move forward, at first, the Union guns were silent, almost in awe of these 17,000 men marching in close order, their battle flags waving. They passed by a group of Union surgeons who were taking care of wounded Confederates, as well as Unions. The day before, they had heard these surgeons say, after the failure of different attacks, "This rebellion is pretty much played out." The Confederates said to these surgeons, "Here is your played out rebellion for you," as they marched forward. Then, the great cannons of the Union side began to open up. Huge gaps were torn in the Confederate line, but they kept on coming dressing their lines, moving closer together. They reached the road that ran to Emmitsburg, Maryland and the picket fence. When I take my students there they mock at a little rail fence while I try to get them to climb over it and see what that would be like, rifle fire beginning to hit you. By the time they start up that slope that looks so small from the road, but after you have been under fire and start going up it, it is a very steep slope. There, before them, the Union line watching these ferocious figures coming up waving their battle flags, they begin to yell.

The Union line is just about to break as on the Confederates come and there is one battery at the center of the line where the Confederates are focused, New York battery. Its soldiers are just about to turn and run, but the officer commanding them has just graduated from West Point that June, Lorenzo Cushing. There he is commanding the battery and he says, "Boys, hold, give 'em one more blast, give them a great shot for me!" They turn to say no and they see that he is holding his intestines in his hands. They give one more blast and the Confederate line begins to fall back. As they retreat back across that open ground, fire still pouring among them, Lee rides out taking full responsibility saying, "It is all my fault boys, it is all my fault, no one could have fought more bravely than you!" All that next day, he waits hoping that General Meade will launch a counter attack, but Meade is too smart for that. In a driving rain on the night of July 4th, the Confederates said they were "following the will of God, following the path of George Washington." On July 4th, God has given his answer, as Lee understood, and the Confederates began their long retreat.

The cause of the Confederacy was now dead. Britain and France would never recognize it and only the military genius of Robert E. Lee and the loyal devotion of his soldier to him kept the cause alive until that Palm Sunday of 1865 when Lee surrendered. Lee thought that slavery was a great moral wrong. He never owned a single slave. He never owned a foot of ground in Virginia, but he believed that to allow the federal government to usurp the right of the state about slavery would be to create a despotic central government. He wanted slavery ended, but by each state individually. That would never happen. It required a war, the Civil War, which ended slavery, ended secession, united this country under a truly moral Constitution, and gave this country the ability, as Winston Churchill said, to "become the bastion of freedom." If the South had won at Gettysburg, all of history would have been different.

Adam Smith (1776) versus Karl Marx (1867)
Lecture 23

> Today, we judge institutions almost purely in terms of the economy. A university is judged to be great on the basis of its endowment, on the success of its fundraising ability. A political candidate is judged first and foremost not by ideas, but by how viable he or she is in terms of being able to raise money. Economics determines every aspect of our society.

The founders of the United States understood the importance of economics, but their overriding concern was political freedom. Throughout much of the 20th century and into the 21st, our overriding concern has become economic freedom or the lack thereof. This shift can be traced back to Adam Smith and *The Wealth of Nations*.

Smith was skeptical of the reigning economic idea of his day, mercantilism, according to which the wealth of a nation lay in its accumulation of gold and silver. Mercantilism also advocated national self-sufficiency in manufacturing, supported by the government. In contrast, Smith believed that the productivity of a nation was a sign of its wealth, not its accumulation of gold and silver. He further believed that the market was guided by an "invisible hand." If the government allowed the economy to operate freely, the market would regulate itself.

For Smith, the capitalist was the true hero of society. This is a person who accumulates and invests capital and wins out over competitors by producing the best product and selling it at an appropriate price. The capitalist also takes over other businesses that are not as efficient and increases employment through greater division of labor. Smith's vision of the unlimited potential for wealth production from the capitalist dominated 19th-century political thought.

The view of Karl Marx about the results of **capitalism** was radically different. Like Hegel, Marx believed that history progressed through a process in which conflicting ideas—he used the terms "thesis" and "antithesis"—produced a synthesis. In the 19th century, according to Hegel, the conflict between unrestricted freedom and absolute despotism had spawned the synthesis of liberty under the law. Marx, however, believed that the struggle between those ideas had created a synthesis that was based on the economy.

Marx lived in a time when the golden view of Adam Smith seemed a terrible lie. Europe had witnessed a significant expansion in the factory system, but the workers were increasingly oppressed. In 1848, Marx wrote *The Communist Manifesto*, using the term "communism" to mean a system in which the freedom of a class of people as a whole takes precedence over the freedom of the individual. Marx called on the workers of the world to unite against their oppressors.

Both Marx and Smith believed that the true value of a product is derived from the labor that goes into it; thus, the laborer is the real creator of wealth. For Marx, the role of the capitalist is simply to exploit the labor of the worker.

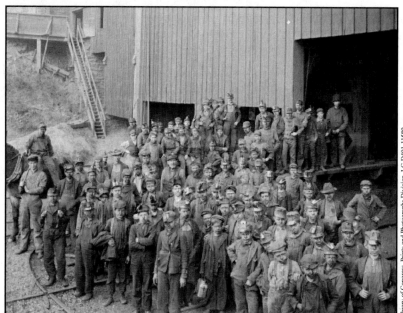

Marx and Smith agreed that a product's value was derived from labor.

He came to see all of history as a struggle between the classes based on the mold, or method, of production in a society.

Marx foresaw a situation in which the working class became so oppressed and the factory owners grew so greedy that the capitalists would begin to devour their competitors and form monopolies. The wages of the workers would be so low that they could not even form a consuming society to buy goods, and the capitalists would have to turn to other markets. The result would be imperialism. Marx also predicted that the workers would finally come to understand that their loyalties should lie with their class and would revolt. They would establish the dictatorship of the proletarian, expropriating the wealth of the capitalists and abolishing the evil of private property. All need for government would disappear, and a golden age of the worker would emerge. ■

Important Term

capitalism: Economic system based on private ownership of the means of production, the setting of prices by the free market, and the accumulation of capital and wealth in the hands of private individuals.

Suggested Reading

Heilbroner, *The Worldly Philosophers*.

Marx, *Capital*.

Smith, *The Wealth of Nations*.

Questions to Consider

1. Do any aspects of Marx's communist system appeal to you? If so, what are they?

2. Reflecting on the teachings of Adam Smith, do you think the United States should buy all its military equipment from foreign countries if they can produce it more cheaply?

Adam Smith (1776) versus Karl Marx (1867)
Lecture 23—Transcript

Our theme in this lecture is the publication of two great books that forever changed history, *The Wealth of Nations* by Adam Smith in 1776 and, almost a century later, *Das Kapital* by Karl Marx in the year 1867. These two books established immediately the importance of two views of capitalism that are with us still today. These are two books written, that everyday somewhere in the world, are still quoted. They reverberate with us today every time we hear a discussion in the news media, every time we hear a politician talking about words like Socialism and the free market. These go right back to Adam Smith and to Karl Marx. It is the publication of these two books that concerns us, their ideas, and above all their impact. Not always exactly what Adam Smith or Karl Marx said made the difference; it was how people interpreted them. Both of these works are seminal works in creating our own age of economic man and woman. That's a term I'm going to use—economic man and woman.

Writers like Aristotle and indeed the code of Hammurabi that we discussed in our first lecture all understood the code of economics. The founders of our country most certainly understood the importance of economics. But, for the founders of our country, the overriding ideal, the overriding value, was political; it was political freedom. Today, early in the 21st century, as throughout much of the 20th century, the overriding ideal has been economics and economic freedom or the lack thereof. Today, we judge institutions almost purely in terms of the economy. A university is judged to be great on the basis of its endowment, on the success of its fund raising ability. A political candidate is judged first and foremost not by ideas, but by how viable he or she is in terms of being able to raise money. Economics determines every aspect of our society. That great shift from the idea of political freedom to economic freedom as being all important goes right back to Adam Smith and the publication of his *Wealth of Nations* in the same year that The Declaration of Independence was written. It was not a coincidence; both were fundamental testaments and statements of the ideal of freedom, political freedom for The Declaration of Independence and economic freedom for Adam Smith.

Smith was a man whose whole life was successful and in this way he was totally different from Karl Marx. Adam Smith was born in Scotland. At a very early age, he had graduated from Oxford and had a very good appointment at the university in Scotland to teach moral philosophy. His first book was about moral philosophy, *The Theory of Moral Sentiments*, in which he argued that the best moral system arose when everybody looked after themselves—self-interest. Each man and woman, Smith argued, is the best judge of his or her self-interest, and when everybody acts out of self-interest, the result will be a whole society that works harmoniously. It won him great fame; he was discussed not only in Britain, but in Europe. It won him the friendship of Charles Townsend who was the British Chancellor of the Exchequer. He much admired Adam Smith, and looked to Adam Smith for some advice on how to deal with the American colonies. Smith told him—and wrote in fact in *The Wealth of Nations*—that a huge debt of the kind Britain had incurred as a result of the war with France from 1756–1763 would destroy Britain. A way had to be found for the American colonies to pay their share of the taxes, Smith advised Townsend. Townsend asked him for specifics and Smith suggested a tax on molasses and a stamp tax. The American Revolution began with some extent with the ideas of Adam Smith, some of his less successful ideas.

But, Townsend was so taken with Smith that he made him the offer that Smith would take charge of his son and take him on a grand tour of Europe. He agreed to pay him 300 pounds per year for the rest of this life. He would pay all expenses while the grand tour was in place. The amount 300 pounds would be very much equivalent to about $200,000.00 today. This would make Adam Smith independent for the rest of his life and all he had to do was take this teenager around the sites of Europe. His current income from teaching at the university in Scotland was only 170 pounds, which he collected from student fees. Smith said that the reason the Scottish universities was better than the English universities was because in England universities the professors drew a salary, so they did not care whether they taught or not. In Scotland, the whole income of a professor came from his teaching fees, what the students paid. The more students that thought they learned something in his class, the higher his income would be. When Smith decided he was going to leave the university, he announced to his students that he was going to refund their money and they unanimously, "No, you don't have to, Professor; we've already learned enough from him." What a wonderful tribute that was.

The tour ended when one of the accompanists was murdered in the streets of Paris, but Smith came back to England and was able to continue his life with this huge pension. Later on he got a sinecure that paid him another 600 pounds a year, so he never had to worry about money. Instead, he worried about the economy and he worried about what made a nation wealthy. Smith was very skeptical of the reigning idea of his day, which was mercantilism. That was the idea that lay at the base of how France, one of the great powers of Europe, tried to finance its designs to rule all of Europe. Mercantilism believed that the wealth of a nation lay in its accumulation of gold and silver. The more gold and silver a nation had, the more powerful it was. That was basically the idea of the Spanish Empire to accumulate as much gold and silver as they could from the New World and they would be a great power. Smith saw this was faulty because Spain had declined and he believed that France was also in decline.

What was the reason for it? Mercantilism also taught that one of the best things you could do was to foster your local national industries. In other words, make your country self-sufficient independently. Produce all of the iron necessary to build the weapons needed for war, and foster your own wool industry; avoid, as much as possible, importing any items from any other country, so that there will be no outflow of your gold and silver. Smith found that completely false. The more he pondered it, dictating it day after day, standing against the fireplace and rubbing his head so much that the grease he put on his hair left a splotch upon the marble fireplace, pondering and lecturing to the person he was dictating to, he came to the conclusion that the true productivity of a nation was the sign of its wealth. The more a nation produces, the greater its wealth, not the accumulation of gold and silver.

How does a nation produce? With that Smith came to the revolutionary idea about the market and the law of the market. For Smith, market had almost a theistic approach; it was something more than human, this invisible hand of the market. The invisible hand of the market, the law of the market, meant that there would always be the right amount of goods produced at the right price. The best thing a government did was not try to foster industries, not try to accumulate gold and silver, but basically stay out of the economy altogether to let the market operate freely, the free market. Government should defend the country, protect against crime, enforce contracts in a court of law, and see to it that the currency was sound. Other than that, government had no role whatsoever in the economy.

Smith used ideas and examples from his own day; they are as valid today as they were then. We could talk about oil, for example. Smith would tell us that there is a great demand for oil obviously. When that demand for oil outstrips the production of oil, then prices rise. Oil gets evermore expensive, and more and more people want to make the profits that come from that oil. More and more people will go into the oil business. More and more students will go into petroleum engineering. They will go into what is called land management and become people who buy up leases for oil drilling. The price of oil will get higher and higher until suddenly people say it is too high and I am not going to drive a car that guzzles too much gas. I am going to buy a small car; I am going to cut back on all of my consumption of oil. Then, suddenly there is an overproduction of oil. There has been an overproduction of the various rigs that are used to drill oil and then the price collapses. Then, all the people who work in the oil industry, many of them find themselves without jobs. The situation will stay until the price of oil collapses far enough, until people finally say I do not have any problem driving a big car now; I am going to increase my use of oil. Then the price will go up again; people will go back into the industry. And so it will happen with every possible product you can imagine; the market is self-regulating.

In Smith's own day, beaver hats were popular and the poor beaver had been hunted to extinction in Scotland where it once lived, and Siberia, and the last place the beaver was found plentiful was in North America. Prices for beaver furs skyrocketed. Men would comb the Rockies looking for beaver furs to bring to a big rendezvous. People would pay these men big sums of money because there was an insatiable demand for beaver fur. They would then be sold and turned into hats and coats. There seemed to be an inexhaustible need for beavers. Then, one day in China, a wealthy aristocratic lost his beaver hat, could not find anyone to make him a beaver hat, had a silk hat made, brought it back to England, the Prince of Wales fell in love with it, started wearing silk hats, and nobody wanted beaver hats anymore. One day out there in the Rockies, these men of the mountain were told that there was no more demand for beaver hats and they had to find another livelihood. So it will always be that the market will regulate itself.

Of course, Smith said, there will be hardship as a result of all of this. All of these people who have made their living out of one kind of industry, let us say making shoes, when suddenly the demand for shoes decreases and there's a huge demand for gloves, the people who have been making shoes will suffer. They will not be able to feed as many of their children. They will have to change their trade and start making what is wanted by society. Yes, there will be suffering, but there will be a boom again and every time there is a boom, everybody all through society, gets a little better off. Step by step, we progress, Smith assures us.

It is an idea of the economy that is based upon a notion of progress, as long as the market is left alone. What an idea for the businessman because, for Smith, the capitalist is the true hero of society. That is a person who accumulates capital, who invests that capital, who wins out over competitors because the capitalist produces the best product, and sells it at the appropriate price, carefully regulating that price so that he makes enough profit, but does not make the price so high that he can no longer sell it. That capitalist not only accumulates and reinvests, but he takes over other factories that are not working. If you have a series of banks and some are failing, Smith would say do not step in and give them any aid from the government. They deserve to fail. Let the banks that are successful, who have been lending money according to the proper rate the market sets, not the Federal Reserve—Smith would be utterly opposed to the Federal Reserve setting interest rates—but the rates that the market approves of, that bank has profited and let them take over all the other banks. The capitalist is the true hero. Smith sees a really unlimited future for wealth production from the capitalist because one of the main results of capitalism is greater division of labor, greater division of work, so that somebody working on the assembly line is dependent on so many other people for the clothes that they wear, for the food that they eat, so jobs keep being created.

Such was the rosy picture of Adam Smith. In the 19th century, this ideal dominated political thought. The great nation of England was the superpower of its day, based upon this ideal of capitalism and the free market economy of laissez faire economics—let us alone to do the job. Government stays out of business. This was the belief of Winston Churchill. In fact, early in his career at the turn of the 20th century, he left the conservative party, which had been the party of his father, and joined the liberal party because the conservative party was determined to establish tariffs. Tariffs are absolutely opposed to the idea of a free market economy. Churchill, all through his life, believed in the teachings of Adam Smith.

The view of Karl Marx was radically different about the results of capitalism. Marx had a very different life than Adam Smith. He was born in the city of Trier in what we would call Germany today. His father was an attorney who had converted from Judaism to the Lutheran faith. Marx went to university, but almost immediately was attracted to the teachings of Georg Wilhelm Friedrich Hegel, the most influential philosopher of the entire 19th century. Hegel taught, and Marx came to believe, fundamentally that the whole of the world's ideas were made up of the conflict between a thesis and an antithesis. Out of these two conflicting ideals came a synthesis. On the one hand, Hegel taught, there is the idea of absolutely unrestricted freedom. On the other, there is its counterpart, the idea of absolute despotism. In our own age in the 19th century, Hegel said, we have seen these come together, fight it out, and then create the synthesis, which is of liberty under law. In fact, the whole view of Hegel was one of progression of ever growing liberty. The more Marx pondered this, the more he thought that Hegel had gotten it wrong; he had turned it on his head. Yes, there was a struggle that created a synthesis, but it had nothing to do with those ideas. It was all about the economy.

Marx lived in a time when it seemed as though the progressive golden view of Adam Smith, of capitalism and ever greater progress for the working man, was a terrible lie. Europe had seen, in the first part of the 19th century it seemed, the explosion, the huge development of the factory system. It had seen the workers instead of ever getting wealthier or enjoying more and more privileges in society, being in the viewpoint of Marx, ever more oppressed. They began to develop a true working class mentality in which for ordinary workers there was a constant struggle against those who owned the factories where they worked to oppress them. It found its statement in 1830 and in 1848.

In 1848, Marx wrote his first important essay, "The Communist Manifesto." He was using the term communism to mean a system in which it is not the freedom of the individual that is all-important, the way Smith had taught, but rather it is the freedom of a class as a whole and the individual is utterly subordinate to the class of which he lives. Let the workers of the world unite, Marx wrote in this fiery essay of 1848, in the aftermath of a collapse of the working revolution. Let the workers unite; they have nothing to lose but their chains. He was a newspaper editor who could not keep a job; he could not get a position in the university because of his radical teachings. The various newspapers that he started in Germany and France collapsed because nobody would pay for advertising.

But, Marx had formed a very unlikely friendship with a very unlikely partner, Friedrich Engels. He was a German like Marx, but the son of a very wealthy family, who himself played the stock market and was a very respected member of the stock market. But, like Marx, he shared this belief in the evils of capitalism. Capitalism must be overthrown and a true workers' state must be established. Only there lay justice and ultimate freedom. He wrote checks on a monthly basis to Marx. Marx moved to London, the one place where he could carry out his writing in safety with full tolerance. He was spending day after day in the British museum, while he ponderously wrote a thorough going examination, as far as Marx was concerned and as far as many people would believe right down until today, a thorough going critique and destruction of the idea of the benefits of capitalism.

He shared some of the same ideas of Adam Smith. For example, they both believed the true value of a product is due to the labor that goes into it, the Labor Theory of Value. Gold in itself is worth nothing; it is good for nothing other than filling a tooth. But, gold represents the labor of all those hundreds of men and women who search for gold, but only one finds it. Then, all the labor of refining and marketing that gold, that is why gold is valuable and every product represents the labor that has gone into it. That means that the laborer is the real creator of wealth. For Marx, the role of the capitalist is simply to exploit the labor that is put into it by the worker.

Marx was a very thoroughgoing student of history. Adam Smith used history and he would dip richly into history for various examples to illustrate his ideas of the free market economy, but Marx was a philosophical historian. He sought for the laws of history, and he found them in the economy and in class struggle because the whole of history was struggle between the classes based upon the mold of production of a society. It was the mold in which goods were produced that determined what kind of society it was.

In the early history, in the time of the birth of civilization, the time of Hammurabi, right on through the time of Cicero, Julius Caesar, and Augustus, right down to the fall of the Roman Empire in the 5th century A.D., all that vast 3,500 years of society had been determined by slavery as the mold of production. The two classes were the slave and those who oppressed the slave. By the 5th century A.D., the oppressive class had come to the understanding for a variety of reasons that more money was to be made by not having slaves, instead of reducing free individuals to the status of serfs. The great period of history from 476 A.D. right down to until about 1500 A.D. was the age of serfdom, in which feudal lords lived on their lands, and again coerced oppressed men and women to work that land and pay a large portion of the produce of that land to the feudal lord who did nothing, but take his money and squander it or buy more land so that he could buy more serfs.

These oppressors are smart and crafty. By about 1500 A.D., there had come to be in Europe a whole new class, the bourgeois, what we would call the middle class. At least that's how the Marxists sometimes use the term—the bourgeois, the middle class. The middle class had come to the understanding that you did not even have to fool with land; wealth was portable. Wealth was gold and silver and the way you invested it in banking accounts. It was not property and land, but property and money and all of the other objects that were a symbol of capitalism. So arose this merchant class. They accumulated capital and began to invest it in various factories and devices that made a factory operate, like a steam engine. Instead of having to pay enormous sums of money to keep serfs in their place, now they could invest in factories, use a steam engine, and instead of having serfs or slaves, they had workers, who went down, dug out the coal, and put it into a steam engine. Then they developed assembly lines.

All the time, the capitalists got more and more wealthy. If you had a slave, you had to pay to feed that slave. If you had a serf, you had to allow them to take some of that produce. But, the worker, this proletarian, was paid nothing and there seemed to always be more of them available than there were jobs. They were paid an absolute subsistence wage and then all that accumulated over that, they had to work six hours to make a subsistence wage, but in the lack of any labor laws you could force them to work ten, eleven, or twelve hours. All those hours of profit that came out of that, over their subsistence wage, you could keep. If they did not like that, working six more hours than they needed to, you could fire them because there were plenty more to take it. There would always be enough workers to work at subsistence levels because the humans themselves kept reproducing and reproducing.

Marx said we will reach a simple situation in which the working class is so oppressed, in which the capitalist has grown so greedy, that the capitalist will begin to devour their own competitors. Great monopolies will be formed. The workers have been so oppressed and their wages have been kept so low, that they cannot even form a consuming society to buy these goods. The capitalist will have to turn to other markets. Marx already foresaw and his disciple Vladmir Lenin understood thoroughly that imperialism would result from capitalism. The capitalist society of Britain would have to occupy India in order to have new markets for all the produce that was being generated out of the cotton system of Britain.

Capitalism would have cycles of great boom, when it seemed as though the workers were getting enough to eat and maybe rising a little bit, but the devouring of the capitalists upon one another, creation of great monopolies, would bring about another cycle of absolute despair. Capitalism would breed depression and war. Out of a great war over markets and out of the depressed state of the worker, would come the Revolution. The workers would finally understand that their only loyalty lay to their class. They would rise up and break those chains, and with violence pull down the whole of the capitalist structure and create the dictatorship of the proletarian, expropriating forever the wealth of the capitalist, abolishing forever what was the fundamental evil of private property. Then, in that glorious dictatorship of the proletariat, all need for government would disappear and a golden age would emerge, a true workers' paradise. That idea shaped the 20th century. It is still the governing ideal of China and Cuba, even as capitalism is the guiding ideal of Europe and our own country.

Charles Darwin Takes an Ocean Voyage (1831)
Lecture 24

Darwin understood that there could be a kind of bird that lives on cows and eats their insects. The insects are food for the bird [and] the insects annoy the poor cow, so ... the cow and the bird live together. But if another kind of bird arrives that also needs those kinds of insects, and there are not enough cows and insects to go around, then they will be involved in a struggle for life and death. Nature, as Darwin described it, was not harmonious.

Two days after Christmas in 1831, Charles Darwin sailed from England on a small ship of the royal navy, the *Beagle*. For the next five years, he would travel as the ship's naturalist, examining and cataloging all the plants and animals discovered on the voyage. Almost 30 years later, in 1859, Darwin would publish his groundbreaking book, *On the Origin of Species.*

Darwin's thesis was quite simple: All life has evolved, perhaps even from one form. He believed that species mutated and that it was sometimes hard to distinguish the difference between an actual species and a variety of a species. Darwin went on to argue that species evolve through a form of selection, as farmers, ranchers, and even pigeon fanciers understand. But how does this selection operate in the world of nature?

Darwin viewed the origin of species as a many-branched tree of life. Species came into being; some of them mutated into more successful forms; and others proved to be unsuited to survive. He noted that variants occur in nature, similar to what we might find in domestic pigeons or cows. If the variant provides an advantage to the organism in which it arises, such as a long beak that enables a bird to get more bugs to eat, then the variant will survive, and a new species will be gradually produced with only that variant.

The question about the struggle for survival that Darwin introduced disturbed his contemporaries. Given that only a limited amount of food is available to two or more closely related species in an ecosystem, a species that has an advantageous adaptation will gradually force out a similar species without the adaptation. This struggle for life is more severe among closely related creatures than among those that are far apart.

Darwin's ideas were not completely new. The idea of evolution was present in a number of areas in the 18th and 19th centuries, as we've seen, for example, with Adam Smith's evolutionary view of capitalism and Karl Marx's evolutionary view of history. Even religion was seen to have evolved from animism to monotheism. Darwin himself pointed out that the debate over whether a divine intelligence had created the world or whether the world and its inhabitants had evolved from lower forms could be traced to classical Greece. Darwin's theory of evolution also fit in with contemporary work in biology and geology.

Charles Darwin (1809–1882).

It was not the evolutionary character of Darwin's views that excited controversy among scientists but his idea of natural selection, which was still debated well into the 20th century. The distinguished American naturalist Asa Gray was an early supporter of Darwin, as was Thomas Huxley. Gray wrote, "I believe deeply in God, but I believe that natural selection and evolution is the *modus operandi* by which God has brought this variety into the world."

Some politicians and economists accepted Darwin's ideas because his work furthered their own agendas. The capitalist Andrew Carnegie, for example, developed the idea of social Darwinism, according to which great capitalists, such as himself, were the result of survival of the fittest. In Germany, the professor Ernst Haeckel used Darwin's theory to support his idea that the races of the earth were involved in a struggle for existence in which one must triumph. That perverted form of Darwinism became the national philosophy of Germany in the Third Reich and was used to justify unfathomable evil in the first part of the 20th century. ■

Suggested Reading

Barzun, *Darwin, Marx, Wagner.*

Darwin, *The Origin of Species* in *From So Simple a Beginning.*

Hodge, *The Cambridge Companion to Darwin.*

Questions to Consider

1. Are you surprised that Darwin's theory of evolution is still so divisive?

2. Do you agree that DNA is our modern version of fate in Greek tragedy?

Charles Darwin Takes an Ocean Voyage (1831)
Lecture 24—Transcript

Our theme in this lecture is Charles Darwin and the publication of his book in 1859, *On the Origin of Species*, and his theory of evolution by natural selection. This book published approximately 150 years ago is still the subject of discussion in school boards, in Congress, at universities, and in small and large churches all around our country.

To understand why the publication of this book was an event that changed history, go back with me briefly to two days after Christmas in the year1831. Sailing away from England is a small ship of the royal navy, the Beagle. It carries with it, a young—in his 20s—naturalist, Charles Darwin. His father has not wanted him to make this voyage and undertake this responsibility as the zoologist, the naturalist, for this scientific expedition, but his professors at Cambridge have urged him to do it. His father has reluctantly given in; after all, the boy Charles has already rejected his father's advice to study medicine. He has spent much of his time at Cambridge listening to the few lectures that are available on biology and working to some extent in laboratories. He has been recommended to the ship's captain, Captain Fitzroy, as the naturalist to carry out the careful examination of all the plants and animals that they will discover in the course of this expedition that is to go all the way around the world, all the way down the coast of South America. It's a huge five-year long expedition to carry out topographical studies, geological studies, plant and animal studies, as well as studies of the politics of South America and other areas that are touched upon. He has not only been recommended as a competent naturalist who can do the job of classifying and describing the plants and animals, but also a companion because that is what Fitzroy wants because he cannot spend all of his time talking to the sailors. He wanted someone he could have gentlemanly conversations with.

They set sail, his father heartbroken with not being able to see his son for five years and really not being able to communicate with him except for letters that will take weeks to arrive back in England, but the boy will come back safely in just a little under five years. He will ponder and begin a career as a distinguished naturalist. Then, in 1859, germinating all of these years since the voyage of the Beagle, Darwin will publish his book *On the Origin of Species*.

I want to step back for just a moment. In our Lectures 19, 20, 21, and 22 on the Spanish Armada, the Battle of Vienna, the Battle of Lexington, and the Battle of Gettysburg, we explored battles. These were great events that have shaped the modern world. In our Lectures 23, 24, 25, and 26 we want to examine the ideas, the intellectual achievements, the scientific achievements, that have shaped our world. We have already discussed the economic ideas of Adam Smith and Karl Marx. Those ideas retain their vigor and import us. We study now the theory of evolution, this book by Charles Darwin that still resonates today. We will go on and look at modern medicine embodied in the noble figure of Louis Pasteur, and in the conquest of the sky, conquest of distance, first inaugurated with the flight of the Wright brothers. When we discussed Confucius and Buddha, we talked about the Jewish prophets, talked some about Socrates, we call that era—the era from Buddha to Socrates from around 600–400 B.C.—the axial age. This is a well-known term because it describes the idea that the fundamental and spiritual concepts that arose in that period still form the axis around which the spiritual life of much of the world still revolves.

We could also employ the term axial age to describe that period from 1776 on down into the 20th century. In 1776, The Declaration of Independence, our nation and that part of the world that lives in freedom still revolves around that great declaration of the Constitution, which followed. All through the latter part of the 19th and 20th centuries on into the 21st century, the ideas of Marx and Adam Smith have shaped the way the world's economy revolves. Adam Smith, in following his ideal of the free market economy, many men and women fought strongly against child labor laws. For the government to regulate child labor laws was to interfere with the market. Meat packers fought in the name of Adam Smith against pure food acts. If you ate meat that had spoiled in the can, if you got botulism and died, that was just the market working. You should then, or whoever is left over from your family, exercise your right not to buy that brand of meat anymore. But, the government should not in any way interfere with the meat packers' right to pack that meat any way they saw fit. In the debate over medical care today, there are those who say that this is interference, if the government gets involved with the medical care, with the working of the free market. But, any harm done by Adam Smith is miniscule compared to 50 million people who died in the gulags of the Soviet Union, or the 50 million who died in the camps of torture racks of Mao Zedong, or 2 million who died in Cambodia, so that the ideas of Karl Marx could be put into practice.

Darwin is a far less harmful figure than Karl Marx, yet his ideas still resonates with us today. What are the ideas embodied in that book, *On the Origin Of Species*? Let's take its exact title. It was a product of long thought by Darwin; in fact he was finally rushed into publication by the realization that another naturalist working in Borneo who had corresponded some with Darwin, Alfred Russell Wallace, was just about to bring out a book on the theory of evolution as it was recognized in the biological world. Darwin pondered over, he cogitated about the lessons he had learned, the elaborate journals he had kept during his voyage of the Beagle, and the book, when it came out, was entitled very carefully: *On the Origin of Species by Means of Natural Selection, or the Preservation of Favoured Races in the Struggle for Life.*

Darwin's thesis was quite simple; all life has evolved. Indeed he believed that all life had evolved perhaps even from one form. He believed that species mutated; they were not set down for all time, but they mutated. He believed that it was very hard sometimes to distinguish between what was an actual species and what was just a variety of that species. Darwin went on to argue how do species arise? It is a very long and carefully argued book. If I were a facetious person, which I am not, I would have to say that this is one of the greatest books never read. That's because everybody who quotes Darwin, I think of those numbers, very few of them have actually made it all the way through the book. It is written in fairly clear, good English prose and it is one long argument about the role of natural selection in the way the various species, plants and animals, have evolved.

Darwin starts by making a very common sense point, in the first chapter, about the way that every serious farmer, rancher, and even those people who take pride in raising beautiful prize pigeons, all of them understand that species evolve and they do so by a form of selection. Darwin says, "You want to raise pigeons." I didn't know this until I began to look into this whole issue. I had never imagined how many people get excited by pigeons and all the different pigeon shows that exist, certainly in 19th-century England. I didn't know about all the varieties, like varieties of dogs, that arise. How carefully, these pigeon fanciers love their creatures and try to create a perfect pigeon in particular category—a racing pigeon or a pigeon with a special kind of big beak, a pigeon with a little beak, or a pigeon with a fan tail or a pigeon of a particular color, Darwin says that these breeders know very well that you take a pigeon that has this color and breed it with another pigeon that has that color, and pretty soon you arrive at that perfect color pigeon.

He said, also, every pigeon fancier knows that sometimes a variety just appears out of nowhere, the same way that there might appear out of all these calves that are born with long horns one with little bitty short horns. If this is not a desirable variant, then the little creature lives out its life, you don't allow it to mate, and it goes away. If you are a rancher worried about getting caught on long horns of cows, then you might take that one little cow, breed it with a regular cow, hope that out of the calves that arise there will be another, maybe two, with these short horns, and pretty soon you have short-horned cows. Darwin says that we all understand that. The question, then, is how does natural selection operate—not in the world of domestic pigeons, but in the world of nature itself?

Darwin then goes on to argue about how species arise. For Darwin, the tree of life was a many-branched vehicle. That is to say, species came into being, some of them changed into more successful forms of different species, and others proved to be unsuited to survive, so they were like the dead branches of a tree. Species went on and turned into entirely different species. He said, for example, traveling in South America, on one of the islands there were three different species of mockingbirds. But, I also saw species that were absolutely unique to one locale like the great turtles of the Galapagos. What was the origin of the species?

Darwin went on to say that in nature these same variants occur that we observe in domestic pigeons or cows. Darwin never truly understood how or why the variant occurred, but it does occur. He says, if that variant that appears in a bird is a great long beak that enables it to deeply into a tree to get more bugs to eat, then it will have an advantage over all of its fellows of that species who have little short beaks, and so it will survive and gradually produce a whole new species that has only this long beak.

That all seems calm enough, but this question about this struggle for survival, there Darwin went more deeply into ideas that would disturb his contemporaries. This is because all of nature, as he said in his title, is involved in a struggle for life. There is only a limited amount of food available to one species or closely related species in one terrain, in one ecology, one ecosystem. That species, let's say a bird, that has an adaptation like the right form of beak that enables it to get more of the food, it will gradually force out and exterminate the other similar species. Darwin believed that the struggle for life was more severe among closely related creatures than among those that were far apart. For example, Darwin understood that there could be a kind of bird that lives on cows and eats their insects. The insects are food for the bird, the insects annoy the poor cow, so they let the cow and the bird live together. But, if another kind of bird arrives that also eats those kinds of insects, and there are not enough cows and insects to go around, then they will be involved in a struggle for life and death. Nature, as Darwin described it, was not harmonious; it was red and tooth and claw.

Darwin saw other means of selection. He wrote briefly, and he would develop it more in his book *On the Descent of Man* published in 1871, about sexual selection. There were variants in nature like the tail of a peacock. What possible purpose did the tail of a peacock serve? Darwin said it is the means of attracting a female. That variety, which proves irresistible to the female peacock, will propagate more and those with the little tiny, ugly, scrawny tails will be driven out in this struggle. This was Darwin's book. When it was published, it sold out rapidly. It was not just a huge bestseller because the original runs of the book were not enormous, but it was read and it immediately began to be discussed.

But, his ideas were not completely new. In fact Darwin was but the embodiment of the evolutionary ideas of the 19th century. The 19th century was the great age of evolutionary though in all areas of ideas. We have already seen that Adam Smith, writing in 1776, has an evolutionary view of capitalism, and by evolutionary I mean every progressing upward. Many of the Greeks had thought of the world as being in cycles. In fact much of the intellectual ideas of Greeks had gone into the idea of how humans had fallen from the golden age down to the level of iron in which we exist today, creatures with lead or wooden feet. There was a collapse of the human race, but Adam Smith said, "The economy under capitalism in the free market will always have ups and downs but the trajectory is upwards." Karl Marx taught an evolutionary view of economics and an evolutionary view of history, from slavery to serfdom to capitalism to the workers' paradise, the progress of history was upwards and could not be stopped. It was an iron law that the evolution of history and the economy would be towards the total abolition of human property and worldwide socialism.

In history, the teacher of Marx, Professor Hegel, taught that the evolution of history was towards ever-greater freedom and liberty. Books were written in the 19th century even before Darwin, long before Darwin, on the evolution of European morals. It was believed that human beings had evolved from being cruel and vicious and brutal to understanding sympathy for other people, that kindness was a characteristic that could be acquired. Over the generations we have taught our children to be kind to others, to do unto others as you would have them do unto you, and this quality of kindness could be transmitted by inheritance. I know some of this sounds crazy, but that's alright; these were the ideas of the people and we must understand them. Darwin himself believed in some of these acquired characteristics. Kindness could be taught and the evolution of humanity was towards ever-greater morality.

Economy, history, morality, and religion—the human race in its primitive stage—that was a term that was used in the 19th century—had been animists. They had worshipped maybe a rock or an ancestor and then they had come to see the noble gods and goddesses of Greece; they had advanced to polytheism. They understood that this rock was nothing more than a symbol for the god Mars, let us say. Then they advanced in figures like Epictetus and Seneca to monotheism. Then came Christianity. There's the upward evolution of religion from animism to monotheism. Evolution was part of the 19th-century idea; there was nothing unique there in what Darwin had to say. It was not even unique in terms of describing the natural world in those terms.

In fact Darwin's own grandfather, Erasmus Darwin, had believed that life had evolved. As Darwin himself pointed out, this debate over whether there was a divine intelligence creating the world or whether the whole of the world including the human race had evolved from lower forms went right back to classical Greece. The philosopher Anaxagoras, the friend of Pericles in the 5th century B.C., taught that the whole world had come into being through *luz*—divine reason. The whole of the universe was intelligently designed. The philosopher of the same period Anaximander said that this was just nonsense. He studied fossils and he said it was quite clear that lower forms of life evolved at the higher forms of life. I don't see anything about gods involved in this. It was also true that church fathers like St. Augustine had warned against too literal of an interpretation of the book of Genesis. It should be interpreted in an allegorical fashion. In the late-18th, early-19th century, along with Erasmus Darwin, the most famous naturalist of the period, John Baptiste Lamarck, had described the course of life on earth as an evolutionary process. He believed that characteristics were inherited and that these acquired characteristics like kindness could be inherited.

Darwin's theory of evolution fit into what was being said about biology and also geology. In fact when Darwin got on board the Beagle in 1831, one of the first things that his captain, Captain Fitzroy, did was say, "I'd like to loan you this first volume of Charles Lyell's *Principles of Geology*." Darwin was so absorbed in this *Principles of Geology*, which had just come out, that he got the second volume sent to him when he was in South America. Lyell, who would gone on to become a very influential supporter of Darwin, traced that geology itself was a result of evolution. The earth had evolved and that was in quite distinct contrast to those who taught that it was a result of catastrophes like the flood. There was a gradual evolution of the earth itself. The more that Darwin studied strata, as he made his way on this great voyage, the more he became convinced that Lyell was right.

In geology, biology, history, ethics, and religion, evolution was there. It was not the evolutionary character of Darwin's views that most excited controversy except among some religious people. Where it excited controversy among scientists was not evolution—most were willing to accept that—it was this idea of natural selection. That, it was thought, was dubious. These variants worked in such a way that a favorable variant lead that species to survive. There it was debated well on late into the 20th century and it is still debated by some biologists today. The evolutionary part did arouse violent opposition from some religious figures—not all of them. Fundamentalist Protestants were more outraged, but there were men in the Church of England who said, "God works through natural selection."

The distinguished American naturalist, Asa Gray, was one of the earliest supporters of Darwin. Already in 1860, he wrote: "I believe deeply in God, but I believe that natural selection and evolution are the *modus operandi*, the mode of operation, by which God has brought this variety into the world." The student of anatomy and somewhat self-educated Thomas Huxley declared himself as Darwin's bulldog and began a series of debates with some of the religious figures who disputed evolution. These debates were carried on at a very low level. One person asked Huxley, "Was it your grandmother or your grandfather that was a descendant of a monkey?" But, working class lectures held to working men and women centered upon this question of evolution and the idea of natural selection.

There were debates in the scientific community, but there was also reception of these ideas because of specific political and economic agenda with which Darwin had no real connection. Darwin must not be blamed for some of the misuse of his ideas. A great book like *On the Origin of Species* is successful immediately because it tells a great many people what they already believe. A great many people believed in evolution, but also saw in this struggle for life a political and economical idea. The great capitalist, Andrew Carnegie, would take the idea from Darwin as it filtered down through these various popular forms, and proclaim the idea of social Darwinism. Great capitalists like him were the survival of the fittest. Capitalism fostered that the best capitalist, the best factories, survived and all the others were squashed out by the competition, the same way that unfavored species lost out and died away.

It was the moral duty of a capitalist like Andrew Carnegie to give away some of the money that he had accumulated; he was not stingy. He was proof that the best triumph in the world in which the market is left alone.

That was a perfectly good way of viewing the economy, but there were more dangerous ways in which Darwin was taught. One of his concluding sentences, changed a little bit in later editions, described the marvel, the wonder, that out of war and famine and death came the highest of all objects: Higher animal life. In other words, the war and death that was carried on in nature eradicated what should not survive and allowed only the best to survive. That's there to be read in that last sentence. You can interpret it differently, but that's how it was read.

Some of the strongest supporters of Darwin were in Germany. There was a distinguished professor of biology, Ernst Haeckel, who in the latter part of the 19th century put forward a view that the races of the earth had different origins. He said that black, Caucasians, as they were called in those days, to use their terms, Oriental, to use those terms, all had evolved into separate races based upon language. They were involved in a struggle and a fight for existence in which one must triumph. The most favorite of these races, to use the term in Darwin's own title, Haeckel pronounced was the German, the Caucasian. That perverted form of Darwinism became the national philosophy of Germany in the Third Reich. In Darwin, they read that in order to survive for life those who pulled down these favorite races must be removed. Darwin himself had said that one of our acquired characteristics is kindness and sympathy; therefore, even though people with learning disabilities may be a drag on society—that's horrible, but that's what he said—nonetheless they will be kept alive. This was not so in the Third Reich of Hitler. People with epilepsy or learning disabilities were marched into the gas chambers.

Darwin's book, still discussed today, the source of much intellectual stimulation, and contrary to the will of Darwin, reverberating through much of the first part of the 20th century to do untold evil.

Louis Pasteur Cures a Child (1885)
Lecture 25

Epidemics, surgery at its most horrifying—that was medicine in 1842, '43, '44, when Pasteur began his chemical studies. There was no understanding whatsoever that diseases were caused by germs.

In the summer of 1885, a French peasant woman came to the laboratory of Louis Pasteur, asking for help for her son, who had been bitten by a rabid dog. Pasteur was not a medical doctor, but he was persuaded to test his experimental rabies vaccine on the boy. The boy was given a series of injections and survived. Later, Pasteur's treatment of rabies would cure many more of its victims, and the Pasteur Institute would be inaugurated in honor of this achievement.

Pasteur was born in simple circumstances in 1822. When he began his studies in chemistry in the early 1840s, the science of medicine was still archaic. Ether had been used by a country doctor in Georgia but was not widely recognized as an anesthetic. The medical profession as a whole was totally unconcerned with hygiene and had no understanding that germs cause diseases. In fact, there was vigorous support for the idea of **spontaneous generation**, that is, that diseases began spontaneously, in much the same way as life itself.

Pasteur did not start out to transform medicine but to study crystals. His superb work earned him a position first at Strasbourg, then at the University of Lille. There, he was asked to research the spoilage of milk, beer, and wine in conjunction with studies of problems that affected the local economy. Pasteur concluded that certain microbes in beer and wine caused spoilage, but if the original liquid could be purified, it wouldn't spoil. Systematically, he then set out to prove germ theory: that there is no such thing as spontaneous generation; instead, germs cause infection. Other doctors, including Joseph Lister in England, were working along the same path.

After he developed the process of pasteurization, Pasteur was appointed professor of chemistry at the University of Paris. There, he studied silkworms to determine how to eliminate microscopic parasites that killed them and recommended a proper nutrient mix to silkworm farmers. Pasteur was then asked for assistance with an anthrax outbreak among sheep. Veterinarians believed that whatever caused anthrax was spontaneously generated and then dug up by animals, but Pasteur had confidence in the germ theory. He believed that he could create and administer a weakened form of a disease in a vaccine that would be far less dangerous to the patient and would promote immunity. In a public demonstration, Pasteur's vaccine proved overwhelmingly successful.

> **The germ theory of disease revolutionized surgery and the treatment of all manner of illnesses, but it was just the beginning.**

Pasteur lived a long life filled with honors, but he lost three of his five children, two from typhoid fever. For us, Pasteur serves as an exemplar of the man or woman of science who understands that science itself is but a means to help humanity. The germ theory of disease revolutionized surgery and the treatment of all manner of illnesses, but it was just the beginning. In the 20th century, following the intellectual currents unleashed by Pasteur, Lister, and others, medical science would recognize the therapeutic values of penicillin and drugs derived from sulfa. Jonas Salk would develop the polio vaccine. Today, heart and other organ transplants extend the lives of thousands. But these advancements are not without cost. In Athens of the 5th century B.C., scientific medicine as developed by Hippocrates was available to all citizens, regardless of their ability to pay. The heights that medicine has reached today raise for us a fundamental question that will be debated for years to come: Should medical care be an absolute right of everyone? ■

Important Term

spontaneous generation: The theory that a living organism can arise from nonliving matter.

Suggested Reading

Debre, *Louis Pasteur.*

Dubos, *Pasteur and Modern Science.*

Questions to Consider

1. Pasteur's lesson for life was "Will, work, success." Do you agree?

2. Do you believe that every citizen in a democracy has the right to the best health care available?

Louis Pasteur Cures a Child (1885)
Lecture 25—Transcript

The subject of this lecture is Louis Pasteur, as the embodiment of all that is best in modern medicine and the transformation, the way that the modern medicine of the 19th and 20th and our own 21st century, the way that it has changed history and changed the life of every man, woman, and child who walks the earth. We can still find great spiritual nourishment in Confucius and Buddha. We read Thucydides and understand the lust for power, the corruption of power, was the same in 5th-century Athens as it is today. But, medicine is what has lifted the human race to an entirely different plane of existence. Louis Pasteur embodies all of the pioneers who created our world of health today.

To understand that, go back with me to July the 6th, a summer day, the year 1885, in Paris. A woman comes into the laboratory of Dr. Pasteur. From her dress, it's immediately clear that she is what was in those days called a peasant. She has very little money. She has with her a child, who's seemingly alright. But, she says, "*Monsieur l'docteur*, my little boy has been bitten by a mad dog. The physician in our little village says he will die a horrible death, that nothing can be done for him." It is a horrible death, lingering day after day, the patient collapsing into dementia, foaming at the mouth—the horror. Pasteur said, "Why did you come to me?" "I came to you because our doctor says there is nothing he can do, but you are a genius." "Madame, I am not even a medical doctor, *Je suis désolé*, I am so sorry. There is nothing I can do."

"You do not work with rabies?" "Yes, your doctor is very well informed. I have been working for some time trying to develop a vaccine to prevent rabies." "I don't know what you're talking about. Can you help my little boy?" "Madame, even if I could, I would not be allowed to by law. I am not a medical doctor. You don't understand this. I would have a malpractice suit." "Doctor, will you let him die?" "No, I will not let him die. Prepare and let us start giving him injections. Over a series of days, we will give your boy injections. We will watch him and we will see if this vaccine will not only prevent, but cure the rabies once it has gotten into the body. Let us see."

His assistant said, "We've barely tried this on dogs." "Let us try it. I won't allow this child to die in agony, if there is any way I can help. If you're afraid to help because of legal consequences, I will do it alone." "No, Monsieur le Doctor, I will help you," says the assistant.

The child would survive. Pasteur would treat another and another and another. Such would be public celebration of this cure for the horrible disease of rabies that the Pasteur Institute would be inaugurated. There, Louis Pasteur, this great scientist, would be buried in a magnificent tomb, and all above him would mosaics celebrating the achievements of this man of science.

You know that little boy, Joseph? He went on to become a custodian there at the Pasteur Institute, earning a small income, locking up at night, cleaning the floors. In 1940, the Nazis came into Paris. Some German officers strolled over to the Pasteur Institute and said, I read in the guidebook about those mosaics of Louis Pasteur. They told the custodian, "Open those doors." The custodian said, "I can't. They're locked." "Get the key." "I don't have the key." "You're the custodian and you don't have the key?" "No, I don't." "We're coming back tomorrow and you're going to have that key. Do you hear us?" The little boy that Pasteur had saved from rabies, grown up now, went home and committed suicide, rather than allow the Nazis to defile the resting place of the great Pasteur.

Who was this man who inspired such devotion? He was born in simple circumstances in 1822. To understand what he achieved, this son of a man had been a soldier in the army of Napoleon, who the father was a tanner, a very modest occupation. To achieve what this boy born in such modest circumstances achieved, let's look at the state of medicine in 1842, '43, '44, when he began his studies in chemistry—for he was a chemist, not a medical doctor—at the *Ecole* Normale Superieure in Paris , the best university in France of its day.

In 1842, for the first time, and hardly recognized at all, ether was used by a country doctor, Crawford Long, in a small town in Georgia. But, all through the 1840s on into the 1850s, as way back to the time of Hippocrates and back to Hammurabi, if you were going to operated on, it was in excruciating pain.

They might give you a drink of alcohol. If you were a soldier, you might bite upon a bullet. But, the pain was absolutely unbearable. Many died of the shock of the pain. There was no way to ease your pain in the midst of an operation. Had the hygiene of the medical profession, doctors in Boston, the best hospitals, would go from treating a patient with a fever, into delivering a baby, never washing their hands. Why, in fact, they were outraged at the thought that they might be dirty.

During the Crimean War, that noble, wonderful woman, Florence Nightingale, went all the way to Turkey to witness the agony caused by the British soldier through medicine, not through the Turks and the Russians. The Russians whom they were fighting against are not caused by any specific thing in Turkey, but by the horrible doctors who were British, doctors who allowed an open sewer to flow right where the sick were being supposedly treated, lying there in their own filth, attended by filthy male nurses. A bullet wound was almost a life sentence. Gangrene filled the halls of every hospital in the world, the stench of decaying flesh. Ask one of the well-paid doctors of the time, why it's a miasma, he'd say. That's what causes gangrene; bad air causes gangrene.

There was a fear you had for your child. Go through the cemeteries of prairie towns, outlying farm districts of this country, and see tombstone after tombstone—June 1st, June 2nd, June 3rd, June 3rd, June 3rd, 1825. There were five or six of your children dead of a fever and you buried them with your own hands. Even if you find the doctor, he doesn't know about the fever. He can't treat it any more effectively than Hippocrates could treat the great Plague.

Bloodletting—let's take an example of a doctor in the early 19th century in America, one of the founders of our country, Benjamin Rush, a very great man and the most distinguished physician of his day. Do you know what his favorite treatment was in 1800? It was bloodletting. You have yellow fever? Let some blood. You have a cold? Let some blood. "Never be too cautious," he said, "In using the knife to let blood." George Washington, slightly earlier on his deathbed, was being bled by leeches. He said, "Please, just let me go." Benjamin Rush either let blood or gave you a laxative. He was a big believer in laxatives, as were most of his colleagues. He developed his own medicine, mercury pills. "That will purge you," he said. Thomas Jefferson thought so highly of Benjamin Rush that he sent Meriwether Lewis to study under Rush in a crash course in medicine, before Lewis led the great expedition. Rush taught him some useful things about setting bones and this sort of procedure. But, the main prescription is to purge them. He gave Lewis this huge box of these mercury tablets, these thunder balls, as Rush called them. Still today, we can locate camps where Lewis and Clark stayed because of super abundant deposits of mercury in their soil.

Epidemics, surgery at its most horrifying, that was medicine in 1842, '43, '44, when Pasteur began his chemical studies. There was no understanding whatsoever that diseases were caused by germs. In fact, there was a vigorous support by the medical profession of the idea of spontaneous generation. Life began just spontaneously and somehow spontaneously, perhaps, these whatever it was that caused gangrene arose.

Pasteur did not start out to transform medicine. He started out to study crystals. That was the topic assigned him by his professor. He studied them superbly. He took his thesis to his professor in 1847. The professor began to cry as he read the thesis. Pasteur said, "*Monsieur l'Professeur*, what have I done? What is making you cry?" The man said, "I love science so much and this is a perfect work of research." He had studied and solved this problem in crystallography, but he came upon the idea of asymmetrical crystals. Such was that mind always probing that from that moment on, Pasteur believed the universe is asymmetrical. But, that clashes with everything that physics tells us. I believe that the universe is asymmetrical. I was enlightened to learn that only a couple of years ago, the Nobel Prize was awarded in physics to three physicists on the ground of their theory of an asymmetrical universe.

He took up a position based upon very sound recommendations, first at Strasbourg, and then at the University of Lille, in the northern part of France. He was given a pretty good laboratory for the time to work in, a good salary. He had married. But, the director of the university came to him and said, "We're not going to force you into any research you don't want, but this is a new university, a new Department of Science, and we think it would be a wonderful step if you would study problems that affect the local economy. In particular, there is the problem of spoilage, the spoilage of milk, the spoilage of beer, and even the spoilage of wine. Pasteur could have said, "I'm a pure research scientist." But, he understood the best kind of research is what can be applied.

He set himself to the study of what causes spoilage in wine, beer, and milk. He found that there was yeast, of course, in wine. But, in wine that had spoiled and in beer that had spoiled, there were also these microbes. Using the microscope, there were also these microbes. He began to work his way towards the theory that these microbes were what caused the spoilage. If you could so purify the beer, or the milk, or the wine, so that none of these microbes were present, it would not spoil. Systematically, he set out to prove the germ theory, that there is no such thing as spontaneous generation, that germs produce other germs and that they are what infects, and that you can pasteurize.

Louis Pasteur was not so smart that he didn't think he could learn from ordinary housewives. Since 1810, canned products had been produced in France. In fact, Napoleon had given a prize to the first man who showed how you could preserve food in cans. It was done by gentle heating. Pasteur developed the idea of gently heating milk, until there were no microbes present, beer, and yes, even the wine that he loved so much, terrified that it would spoil the wine. But, in fact, it saved the French wine industry. He developed his own flask, the swan necked flask. One of the great exhibits at the Pasteur Institute used to be broth that Pasteur had boiled to the right point, had completely sealed away from the oxygen, and remained pure, unspoiled all those years.

The germ theory was developed. There were other minds working along that path, like the great surgeon Joseph Lister in England. Lister became of Pasteur's most fervent admirers. A lot of scientists and a lot of doctors thought this was absolute nonsense. Even the ancients talked about spontaneous generation. That is how anything came into being. But, no, Lister knew that Pasteur was correct. He began to study ways in which you could purify an operation from germs coming from the air—a solution of carbolic acid, strong enough to kill the germs, but not too strong to hurt the human flesh. Lister began the process by which every operation began with sterilizing the patient, in those days with carbolic acid, carefully spraying the instruments, and even spraying carbolic acid in the air while the operation is being carried out. Lister could show his reluctant colleagues mortality rates from operations dropping from 80 and 90 percent down to 5 percent. Pasteur, out of the practical need to prevent wine and beer and milk from spoiling, had given to the world the germ theory, which would transform medicine and transform all of our lives.

He then, celebrated for his scientific genius, was appointed professor of chemistry at the University of Paris. He had a poorer laboratory there than there than he did in Lille, but he was at the very center of scientific research. Once again, it was his aptitude for carrying out practical research that brought so much good to the world.

The French silkworm industry was being destroyed. The silkworm industry was a very important part of the French economy. Whole regions of France were absolutely dependent upon it economically. The silkworm people went to the government. One of the ministers of the government was an admirer of Pasteur and he came to him and he said, "Doctor Pasteur, we want you find out why the silkworms are dying." Pasteur said, "I don't know a thing about a silk worm. I'm not sure I would know a silk worm if I saw one." "Please?" He lent his skill. Once again, what made him so great was careful experimental research, never to stop thinking about a problem. *Il faut travailler*; that is what his father had taught him. You've got to work. He taught his students: Will, work, success, determination, hard work, and you will succeed."

He studied over and over again what was wrong. He used his microscope and he realized that there was a parasite killing these silkworms. He found a way to get rid of the parasite, but the worms still died. He went back to the drawing board all over again, and came to the conclusion that the parasites' work was helped along by poor nutrition. The farmers did not really understand what was essential to the best nutrition of their little silkworms. He tried all manner of nutrients until he created the right mixture of nutrients, removal of the parasite, and then, in clear and simple language, explained to the silkworm farmers how they were to build the proper kind of hothouses, how they were to take proper care of the silkworms.

I know you don't care about silkworms, but what makes Louis Pasteur to me so remarkable is that we have, in this man of science, the idea of treating the whole patient, whether that patient is a silkworm, or you, or I. He's not a technician that you come to see because you have a bad knee and you want it replaced, and he does the knee operation and doesn't look at anything else. Maybe you have a cancer. Pasteur said, "This has to be looked at in a whole fashion." The silkworm industry was saved.

The ministry came again to him. He'd like to get back to some pure research, but here was the ministry saying, "We've got this terrible anthrax outbreak. The sheep are dying all over France. All the best specialists of the age say there is nothing can be done about it." "Why is this?" Pasteur says. "Read their papers on anthrax. They say it is a result of spontaneous generation. That is to say, whatever causes the anthrax is in the ground spontaneously generating, and the animals dig it up." "Don't they learn from the germ disease?" "That's why we come to you, Doctor Pasteur." "Alright, I'll study anthrax."

Once again, every veterinary doctor was after him, all except for a few wise and good veterinarians. He was challenged to a public demonstration because he had developed a vaccine. Vaccines had been known since the latter part of the 18th century. In fact, one of the heroes of the Battle of Bunker Hill was Joseph Warren, the most successful doctor in Boston at the time of the American Revolution, who chose to be a patriot, rather than going to Britain and making a fortune, and who had used the smallpox vaccine. The other doctors in Boston refused to use what had been developed in England. They just didn't think it worked. He did and none of his patients died during the smallpox epidemic. But, it had to be transferred directly.

Pasteur began to develop the idea that you could create a weakened form of a vaccine, in this case for anthrax, and it would be far less dangerous to the patient to administer it. He developed his vaccine and he took on these challenges. "I will, in a public display, give my vaccine to 50 sheep. I will not give it to 50 other sheep. Then, I will inject all of these sheep with a live anthrax." It was done. When they came back at the appointed time, Pasteur was worried. "I've put my whole scientific reputation on the line. I'll be the laughing stock of France of the scientific world." But, as his carriage drew closer, he heard the excited talk of the crowds that had come. There were all the poor sheep that had not been vaccinated lying dead, and all the ones that he had vaccinated, even though they had been injected with the disease afterwards, the vaccine had saved them and they were quietly munching or whatever sheep do.

Then, the Ministry of Agriculture came to him again and they said, "We've got a chicken cholera outbreak. You've got to save the poultry industry of France." He did it, once again with a vaccine against the chicken cholera. By now, the awards were pouring in upon him—awards from France, like the Legion of Honor, from Britain, and even from Germany. He began his work with rabies, developing a vaccine for this dreaded disease. And so it would be in 1885, in our July day, that he would save young Joseph de Meister.

He lived a long life, a life filled with honors, but a life that was truly sad as well. He loved his little children and three of his five children died. Two died within a short time of each other in 1868. They died of Typhoid Fever, one ten years old, one two years old. The pain that Pasteur felt, the greatest scientist of the age, the man people came to with their medical questions, the savior of the silkworm industry, could not save his own little children. So stressed was he—not by the work, he loved his work—but by the loss of his little children, that he himself had a stroke. For the rest of his life, he would walk with a limp. But, he never stopped working—*il faut travailler*. As he lay on his deathbed, honored throughout the world of science, the last words of this good man were, "*Il faut travailler*," you have got to work.

Louis Pasteur is for me the paradigm of the man or woman of science who understands that the science itself is but a means to help suffering humanity. The germ theory revolutionized surgery. It revolutionized the treatment of all manner of illness. But, it was just the beginning. Someone scolded me for mentioning this at one point in a lecture I gave. But, in 1924, the son of President Calvin Coolidge, a young man of great vitality, the darling of his father's eye, was playing tennis one day at the White House. He got a blister; he didn't take proper care of the blister and it became infected. He died of that infection. Here was Calvin Coolidge, president of the United States, with the best medical care in the world at his disposal, and his child could not be saved because there was no antiseptic. There was nothing like, to use a brand name, Neosporin—antibiotics, is what I mean. There were no antibiotics. They had not been developed. Pasteur thought they were there and began research on them. But, antibiotics, like penicillin, a simple dose of penicillin could have saved that boy. As Coolidge said, "All the power and all the glory of the presidency passed away with the death of my son," simply testifying all the pain that has been felt through the ages.

In 1928, again, carrying on with a path of the intellectual currents unleashed by men like Pasteur, Robert Koch, and Joseph Lister, Alexander Fleming would notice the therapeutic values of penicillin. But, he couldn't find anyone who could purify it enough for him. By the 1930s and on into the 1940s, wounds that would have been fatal began to be cured. There arose the whole set of drugs derived from sulfur. In World War II, American troops went into battle with little kits filled with packets of sulfur drugs and the admonition to sprinkle that on any open wound. The mortality rate from wounds dropped enormously.

On and on this upward goes this progress of medical science. Those in their 60s now remember as children, kids in their class walking with heavy braces on crutches, doomed to this lifetime of disability by polio. Parents were terrified to send their children to public swimming pools in the summers of 1950 and '51 because of the fear that polio would strike their child. Then, the genius of Jonas Salk would banish forever that terror, walking in the steps of the great Pasteur with his vaccine.

The miracles—and that's what they are—continued to multiply. Heart transplants bring you back from the dead. There's a range of drugs that can take a person suffering from depression and make them whole again. But, with it has come a price, a cost. In the Athenian democracy of the 5th century B.C., where scientific medicine as we saw was developed by Hippocrates, the medicine available was far better than it ever existed before. The ability of a doctor to help you was far greater in the Athenian democracy of the 5th century B.C. than it had ever been before. In their democracy, in their belief in the greatest good for the greatest number of citizens, the Athenians also developed the idea that every citizen has the right to the best medical care available, whether they can pay for it or not. The very heights that medicine has reached raises for us the most fundamental question that we will debate for years to come: Should medical care be an absolute right of every citizen of our country? Pasteur's legacy echoes still with us today.

Two Brothers Take a Flight (1903)
Lecture 26

Learned newspapers from New York, even *Scientific American*, were talking about the foolishness of the idea of flight. It was said in an authoritative media source: "If a million men ... work for a million years, flight might be possible."

At the time of the founding of the United States, travel had not changed much since the days of Cicero or Julius Caesar. In 1828, Charles Carroll, the last surviving signer of the Declaration of Independence, laid the cornerstone of the Baltimore and Ohio Railroad, launching our conquest of distance. Seventy-five years later, the conquest of air would be undertaken by two entrepreneurial brothers, Orville and Wilbur Wright.

The Wright brothers were born in modest but reasonable circumstances—Wilbur in 1867 and Orville in 1871. In 1890, at the height of the bicycle craze, the brothers opened a bicycle shop. In addition to fixing and selling bicycles, Orville and Wilbur devoted time to their interest in flight; they studied the flight of birds and followed the news about attempts at glider flight.

The young men realized that certain elements were required to produce a vehicle that could fly: wings, an engine, and most importantly, the ability to control the craft. Initially, they constructed a glider, aided by research materials they received from the Smithsonian Institution. They learned from the Weather Service that one of the best places to practice gliding—in terms of wind and other factors—would be Kitty Hawk, North Carolina. They spent the summer of 1900 in Kitty Hawk, working on their glider and making attempts at flight. After a winter in Dayton, the brothers returned to Kitty Hawk and continued their work, although their efforts were largely unsuccessful.

The brothers faced the challenge of overcoming yaw, pitch, and roll during glider flight. They hit upon the idea of constructing the wings in sections that could move separately and be controlled by a set of cables.

This breakthrough allowed them to achieve success with their glider. A mechanic friend then built for the brothers an 8.5-horsepower engine out of aluminum.

On December 17, 1903, Orville made the first flight in front of a small group of witnesses at Kitty Hawk. The two men took turns flying throughout the day, with Wilbur finally covering more than 800 feet after almost a minute in the air. Afterwards, the brothers returned to Dayton and continued to work on their invention, guarding it carefully from the public eye. The press, particularly the French press, was skeptical about the claims of these Americans that they had been the first to fly, but reporters and the aviation community were convinced when the Wright brothers gave a demonstration in France in 1907.

In 1912, Wilbur died of typhoid fever. Orville lived until 1948. For the remainder of his life, he continued his interest in aviation and defended the truth that he and his brother had been the pioneers of flight. At the outset of World War I, both sets of European powers saw the potential for the use of aircraft in reconnaissance. Later, planes were fitted with machine guns to engage in air battles, and by 1918, strategists developed the idea of using planes to drop bombs. When World War II began in 1939, the invention of these two bicycle shop owners became the most devastating power the world had ever seen. Then, in a very short span of

The Wright Brothers: Orville (*top*) and Wilbur (*bottom*).

years, men would walk on the moon. All this would emerge from the first flight of the Wright brothers on December 17, 1903. ■

Suggested Reading

Evans et al., *They Made America*.

Tobin, *To Conquer the Air*.

Questions to Consider

1. This lecture calls the Wright Brothers "entrepreneurs." We have also used that term for Columbus. How do you define an entrepreneur?

2. The airplane provides an example of an explosion of technology once the basic concept is proved. Can you think of other examples?

Two Brothers Take a Flight (1903)
Lecture 26—Transcript

Our theme in this lecture is Orville and Wilbur Wright, the two brothers who made the first flight in a heavier-than-air craft propelled by an engine. The first flight was the beginning of the conquest of the air.

When we talked about Louis Pasteur, he did indeed give full reign to the germ theory of disease. But, had he not discovered the germ theory of disease and proven it, someone else would have. In the case of even Adam Smith and *The Wealth of Nations*, had he not written that book celebrating the market, someone else, perhaps not as well, but would have written it. In the case of Charles Darwin, we have seen how much evolution was already in the air in the mid-19th century. Had he not written *On The Origin of Species*, someone would have written a similar book, and in fact did. These are but embodiments of ideas that were changing history. So too, the Wright brothers, if they had not made that first flight, as they very well knew, somebody else was going to do it.

Remember also our story about Christopher Columbus, when he sailed to America and then returned to Spain, he was sitting around the table having dinner with Spanish Grandees. They were jealous of him, suspicious of the fact that he was a foreigner. They began to say, "Why anybody could have sailed westward and found whatever you found." Columbus said nothing for the moment. He simply took a boiled egg that is part of the menu, and handed it to one of them, and said, "Make it stand on its end." Then the next, and the next, nobody could. Then, Columbus took it, remember, cracked it on its bottom, and it sat up on its own. "Sure," he said, "once a genius shows you the way, any fool can follow." The Wright brothers were those geniuses who pointed the way to that conquest of space.

We pictured the beginning of medicine with Louis Pasteur in the 1840s. Picture this: When the Constitution was signed, the signers of that Constitution had gotten to Philadelphia, wrote back home, communicated back home, in exactly the same way that Cicero or Julius Caesar did. That is to say, they walked it, it was sent by horseback, or it was carried by sail or human power rowing. It took as long to communicate as it did in the days of Julius Caesar. It was a long, arduous trip from Georgia to Philadelphia. In fact, the constitutional convention was eleven days delayed in starting because the delegates had so much trouble getting there.

But, in 1828, the last surviving signer of The Declaration of Independence, Charles Carroll, had lived long enough to lay the cornerstone of the Baltimore and Ohio Railroad. With the railroad, with the use of the steam engine, already earlier in the steamboats in the very beginning of the 19th century, distance began to be conquered. But, there was still the air, the mystery of the birds. That would be conquered by these two American brothers, Orville and Wilbur Wright—true examples of the entrepreneur. It's a term we use a lot today. There are schools that teach entrepreneurship. It's part of business courses at great universities. We speak easily of an entrepreneur, but it's a noble word. I told you Columbus was an entrepreneur, and so too were the Wright brothers, and so too were many, many Americans who settled this country.

First of all, you've got to have a passion to be an entrepreneur. There has got to be an idea you want to achieve. For those entrepreneurs who were the Pilgrim Fathers, it was the right to worship God as they chose. For Columbus, it was sailing to India by going westward. It was the passion to give his family a better life that led a farmer to take his wife and children from a settled place in Ohio out to the prairies of the Dakotas. The Wright brothers had the passion to fly. Then, you've got to be willing to take risks. Columbus risked everything, his life, by sailing westward. That farmer who took his children out to the Dakota Territory risked famine and disease to create a better life for them. The Wright brothers risked their fortune, a steady income, and their necks in trying to fly.

The passion, the willingness to take risks, and then the belief that while this is in your own self-interest, it will also leave the world a better place. In crass terms today, we say it generates wealth, but it means to leave the world a better place. Certainly, that farmer who settled Dakota left the world a better place. For all the trouble that flight has caused, its use in warfare, all the inconvenience it causes each of us every day, the Wright brothers left the world a far better place.

They were born in modest, but reasonable circumstances—Wilbur in 1867, Orville in 1871. Their father was a churchman. They grew up in the Middle West, primarily in Ohio. He was not a minister who preached. He was a director of the Church of the United Brethren and had a reasonable income. He was an educated man who had a very good library. He taught his boys enormous self-reliance. "Milton Wright," Orville always praised him as did Wilbur, "he gave us the right start to life. He taught us to work hard." It was, of course, the hope of the father Milton and the mother that Orville and Wilbur would go to college. But, one was injured very badly in a sports accident. The other dearly didn't want to go to college. Both of them just decided together, as they did so much in their lifetime, after arguing about it, they would open up a bicycle shop. They did this at the very height of the bicycle craze in the early 1890s in this country.

Bicycles had been around for a number of years, but they had been, up until 1885, very cumbersome, one huge wheel and one little wheel, very unwieldy. But, in 1885, the first safety bicycle, as it was called, was put out. It provided a very cheap and quick and not very tiring form of transportation. Many roads in this country were first paved in response to the use of bicycles. It was a booming enterprise. There in Dayton, Ohio they set up a bicycle shop and became very good mechanics, working with their bicycles and a lot of satisfied customers. They could, of course, just gone through life opening up branches of their bicycle shop, maybe spreading to other towns in Ohio, but the two brothers were fascinated by flight.

In fact, both of them would lie on their backs for hours just watching birds fly and trying to understand from that how the bird soared, how he maneuvered, what the movement of his wings told them. They were fascinated by attempts at glider flight. Germany was one of the leading centers of glider pilots. The two brothers, Orville and Wilbur, became extremely interested in the deeds of Otto Lilienthal. These were carried in the newspaper, as he would make ever bolder glides. Then, in 1896, he fell and broke his neck. Rather than being concerned about the death of a glider pilot, the two brothers decided instead that if he couldn't conquer air, Lilienthal couldn't, they would.

They began their focus. They understood from the start that there are the following elements required in producing a vehicle that can fly. You've got to have the right wings. You've got to have an engine because they were going to start with gliding, but they were determined to build a craft that would fly through an engine, fly through the air, comparable to an automobile of their time. Then, you've got to control it. Others working along the same idea in Italy and France, in England and Germany, tended to focus on the engine. But, the Wright brothers believed the first real step was control. By 1900, they were fully on their way to develop a glider and how to control it.

The first step was to learn as much as they could about gliding and any ideas that were held about flying with an engine. They wrote off to the Smithsonian Institute. They found out that one of the officials of the Smithsonian Institute, the secretary Samuel Langley, was very interested himself in flight. They were sent back this huge packet of material with works, and books, and essays going all the way back to describing Leonardo DaVinci's ideas for flight. They made themselves fully up-to-date, which is what you ought to do in any entrepreneurial enterprise. Make yourself fully up-to-date with what has been already done. Then, they began to construct their glider. Once they had the basic idea of how to do it, constructed their model, they wanted a place to fly it. Once again, with thoroughness, they wrote to the American Weather Service. All this time, they were still running their bicycle shop and they lived on a very tight budget. They wrote to the Weather Service. They came back with the answer that there are these various places where it's probably in terms of the wind, in terms of soft landing, the best place to practice gliding.

One of these was Kitty Hawk, North Carolina, so they wrote to the postmaster there who also owned the little general store. They got back a letter saying, "I'd be glad to help you, so come on out." The first step when they got there was actually to find Kitty Hawk because the people on the shore really didn't know much about where this Kitty Hawk was. But, after a harrowing trip by boat, nearly getting sunk, they and their glider equipment arrived. They had brought everything with them to make the correct glider, except the wood. They assumed that without having to transport that and spend the railroad fare for it, they could buy it. But, they needed 18-foot long spars and 16-foot was the best they could find. They didn't give up; that's what they made do with. Working alongside the general store keeper, who became fascinated by what they were doing, they began to build their glider, construct it, and to try attempts at gliding, to learn how to control the craft.

They came back to Dayton for the winter and went back again in 1901. That was the low point for them, the period in 1901 in the summer and early fall, because the glider really just wasn't doing anything. One of their flights ended in almost death. As they were going back one said to the other, "Men may fly some day, but not in our lifetime." Learned newspapers from New York, even *Scientific American*, were talking about the foolishness of the idea of flight. It was said in an authoritative media source: "If a million men," let's say men and women, "work for a million years, flight might be possible." The secretary of the Smithsonian, Samuel Langley, had become a laughing stock. He had convinced the army that he could build an aircraft that would fly with an engine that could be used for reconnaissance purposes by the army and for dropping bombs. They had paid him, the army had given him, $50,000. There was a public demonstration of his aircraft, which was going to be catapulted into the air. The news media was all around it on the Potomac, and off it went, catapulted, and went right into the Potomac, sinking, as one of the reporters said, like a handful of wet mortar. This made it even clearer to the media and to the army that nobody was going to fly for a very long time.

But, the two brothers didn't give up. They got over their gloominess. They started there in Dayton again, working in their bicycle shop. They had a very good assistant, Charlie Taylor, who was a superb mechanic. They said, "We've got to find out why we can't control our glider." Why does it do three things that are still fundamental to flying and airplane in solving? Why does it pitch? Why does its nose and back go up and down? Why does it roll, turn over and over like this? Why does it yaw? Why does it go side to side? Once again, they studied birds to see why they didn't roll, and yaw, and pitch. They came upon the idea of studying the way wind works by putting a wheel on the top of the bicycle they rode on, on the handlebars, and watching how it responded to the wind at different speeds.

Working together, both contributed the equal amounts, and they used to argue all the time. Their house was run by the sister Kathryn. She, time and time again, at the end of one of these arguments during the dinner hour, would say, "I am leaving this house, once and for all, and getting married." The brothers said, "You can't get married. We can't live without you." She would say, "Then you've got to stop this arguing." Sometimes their arguments would take the following form: Wilbur would be insisting on one particular point about the construction of the wing, how long it had to be. Orville would be insisting it had to be a different length, eight feet versus six feet. Then the next morning, Orville would come down and say, "You were right, Will." Will would say, "No, you were right." They would get into another argument over it.

They became convinced that they could control these specific problems by a set of cables that enabled one part of each wing, the furthest part of the wing, to be pulled by those cables, and thus move separately, and then, a frontal elevator, and then a tail. Working these together, the yaw, the pitch, and the roll could be controlled. When they flew their glider the next summer of 1902, there at Kitty Hawk, when they achieved real success in that glider flight, that was the breakthrough. Now they came back home ready to build the engine. They had control down. They had furnished their ideas, had honed their ideas about the shape and size of the wing. Now they had to have the engine. They said to their mechanic, "Charlie, can you make us an engine that will work?" Charlie said, "Sure, I'll do it, Wil and Orville." He used aluminum, a bold brilliant idea to make it light, and came up with about an eight and a half horsepower engine. He said, "That will work for you, boys."

They went back to Kitty Hawk in the fall, continuing to work and think these problems out, waiting for just the right weather. On December the 14th of 1903 it came, but the flight that they launched was about two seconds, not worth counting. Then came Sunday. They would not work on a Sunday. Their father had taught them that. Then, the next day just wasn't a good weather day, but the 17th dawned. The wind was right, the sky was right, and they were right. The owner of the general store was there. A local boy was there to help and be witnesses. The first of the flights was undertaken by Orville, lying down, flying just a short distance, staying up just a short time, but he had flown. They flipped a coin and Orville had won it for the first one, then Wilbur. He flew a little further. Then Orville again, that same day, just a little bit further. It was getting late in the afternoon, about five o'clock. It was a cold day and darkness was falling fast. Wilbur said, "Let me try one more time up." Up he went, higher and higher. For almost a full minute he had flown and over 800 feet. That sounds like nothing to us today, but when he came down in that soft sand, he had done something no one had done since the beginning of human history. The brothers had done it together.

They had flown and that had been their passion, but they wanted to be recognized for what they had achieved. They hadn't invited reporters. There was a lot of skepticism about what they had done. They didn't go back to Kitty Hawk. They continued to refine their ideas there in Dayton, working out in a local cow pasture. But, they took the view that people should have to pay to see them fly. There were too many entrepreneurs looking around for the secrets of how they had done it. Time and time again, the army would ask, "Show us a demonstration of your plane and we'll be willing to pay you." The Wright brothers would say over and over again, "No, you pay us first, and then we'll fly. You give us a contract. You insure our patent that we have taken out, that it won't be infringed, and then we will show you."

Newspapers ran stories like "Flyers Are Liars, the Fraud of the Wright Brothers." The French, in particular, were very skeptical about the claim that these Americans had been the first to fly. If the first person to fly would be successful, it would have to be a Frenchman. The debate went on, and others began to fly just a little bit. The Wright brothers kept their counsel, continued to refine their plane, and then by 1907, these *bluffeur Américain*, as they were called by the French press, were ready to demonstrate. There, when they flew for the first time in France, the acknowledged aeronautical experts of the day, men who themselves had flown after the Wright brothers, had said, "We are all children in the hands of the Wright brothers." The two brothers won the acclaim of the French, flying in circles, in perfect figure eights, something no other flyer could do. They even impressed the United States Army, which in 1909 gave them a contract. They had gained their glory and their claim to be the first to fly was acknowledged all over the world, except at the Smithsonian Institute, where the secretary, Samuel Langley, maintained his hatred of them and insisted that they had been pre-dated.

Then, in 1912, Wilbur went to a restaurant in Boston, ate seafood, and died of typhoid fever. Wilbur Wright was a man of destiny, as was Orville. The man or woman of destiny, as we have defined them, is that person who has one specific destiny, one mission. Blessed are you if you find the one thing you are meant to do. What both Wilbur and Orville Wright were meant to do was to fly. Having done that, everything else was an anti-climax, so he died. Orville spent of the rest of his life, down until his death in 1948, fighting patent suits, starting an aircraft company, but not really being interested in it, and living a fairly retiring life, in a mansion that he built there in Dayton. He had fallen out with his sister. She had married a professor from Oberlin. He never spoke to her again, except one more time in his life. But, there he lived, continued his researches into aviation, and fiercely defended the truth that he and his brother were the first to fly.

When the Smithsonian continued to deny this claim, Orville gave their permission to put up the reconstruction of their first flyer to a museum in Britain. It wouldn't be until after World War II that the Smithsonian would claim its right and proudly display the Flyer Number One of the Wright brothers. The world had been given flight. In a great display in 1909, celebrating the anniversary of Henry Hudson sailing up the Hudson River, the brothers flew their plane around the Statue of Liberty. Orville was of course alive, and Wilbur was still alive, and they flew their plane around the Statue of Liberty. The crowds were just wild with delight at this proof of American ingenuity. In fact, even the foreigners were just so amused when the plane landed and the brothers turned to their old friend, Charlie Taylor, who had made the engine for the first plane, and Wilbur said, "It flies pretty good, don't you Charlie?" "Yeah, Wil, she'll do alright," a typical American understatement.

But, watching that display of flying was a German military attaché. He said: "This will be decisive in the next war." And so it would be that within eleven years after this first flight on December the 17th, 1903, the aircraft that armies had eagerly bid for and which was rapidly being developed in Italy, Germany, France, Britain, as well as in this country, had far more than commercial value. It became crucial to war. At first, in 1914, the generals weren't quite sure how to use the aircraft. Many of them were still tied to the old idea of cavalry, and the idea even of cavalry as a means of reconnaissance. But, the airplane was used for reconnaissance already very early in the war. The pilots fought at one another, a German pilot firing his pistol at a French pilot, and the French pilot firing back, and both of them dropping large metal spikes down upon the heads of the enemy troops. Soon, the inventive mind of man found out how to fit these planes with machine guns and the great air battles of the sky were fought out. Heroes like the Red Baron rose to prominence. By 1918, the strategy had been developed to use the plane, the aircraft, now capable of dropping bombs in close coordination of the newly developed tank, and close coordination with infantry attacks, to bring the planes into battle to destroy the enemy forces and then grind them down with the tanks, and let the infantry pour through the gaps. By 1919, the allies had very large numbers of planes outfitted for just this kind of warfare and large numbers of tanks.

But, the war had ended. On November the 11th, 1918, the war had come to an end, but the strategists continued. B. H. Liddell Hart, the great British strategist, Charles de Gaulle, making himself hated by the French High Command for portraying how in the next war tanks and aircraft would be the absolutely decisive weapons. In this country, in the 1920's, Billy Mitchell, destroying his career, proving that aircraft could sink the most powerful of battleships. A corporal in the First World War, Adolf Hitler, all through the 20's pondering this question of how to restore what he saw as the honor of Germany. When he became chancellor of Germany, immediately seeking out those young officers who understood with him the concept of blitzkrieg, lightning warfare.

When the next war began on September the 1st, 1939, the invention of these two bicycle shop owners, these American entrepreneurs, Orville and Wilbur

Wright, became the most devastating power the world had ever seen. The aircraft would drop the atomic bomb. Then, in a very short span of years, men would walk on the moon. The flight of the Wright brothers, December the 17th, 1903—the world has never been the same.

The Archduke Makes a State Visit (1914)
Lecture 27

In the mid-1860s, Austria restructured itself. ... Austria began to restore its finances and to modernize its army. Franz Ferdinand was determined, when he became emperor, to continue this process by restructuring the Austro-Hungarian Empire politically. His ideal was a forerunner of the European Union of today.

O ur theme in this lecture is a terrorist attack that killed the heir to the throne of the **Austro-Hungarian Empire** and set in motion World War I, a war that resulted in the deaths of 11 million men and brought down the Austrian, Russian, and Ottoman empires. It propelled America to superpower status, ended the imperialism of Britain and France, and made possible the Russian Revolution. The legacy of World War I is still with us today, in unsolved problems in the Middle East and in Kosovo, where the conflict began.

On June 28, 1914, the city of Sarajevo in the Austrian province of Bosnia was preparing for a state visit from Archduke Franz Ferdinand. Some decked the city with flags, while others, members of a terrorist organization called the Black Hand, prepared to carry out the visitor's assassination. Until this day, Europe had been experiencing a summer of peace and prosperity. The countries of France, Britain, Germany, Australia, Canada, and the United States were all united in a free-flowing global economy, and many believed that war was a thing of the past.

Still, the countries of Europe maintained huge standing armies and were divided by various alliances, and a warped sense of nationalism pervaded the continent. Countries were believed to have the divine right to bring under their borders all those who shared a common ethnicity and to drive out those who did not. The south Slavic ethnicity was frustrated from expressing itself by the Austro-Hungarian Empire, which had prevented the independent country of Serbia from annexing Bosnia, Croatia, and Slovenia. Franz Ferdinand presented a danger to Serbia because he was a farsighted, capable statesman who was determined to revive the empire and form a strong union

The arrest of Gavrilo Princip, the assassin of Archduke Franz Ferdinand.

of its diverse ethnic groups. The Black Hand was formed by officers in the Serbian military who were in favor of an independent Serbia and opposed to Franz Ferdinand's ideas.

By coincidence, the archduke's visit was scheduled for the anniversary of a battle that had taken place in 1389, in which the Serbian army had been destroyed by the Turks. Security for the parade was slim, despite the fact that the Austrian secret service had learned of the possibility of an assassination attempt on the archduke.

As the motorcade progressed, a bomb was thrown that injured several people but not its intended target. In the ensuing chaos, the archduke proceeded to the town hall, then headed for the hospital to see those who had been wounded. En route to the hospital, his car stalled in front of a delicatessen where one of the Black Hand conspirators was eating a sandwich, having given up the attempted assassination. He walked out of the delicatessen and shot both Franz Ferdinand and his wife.

The Austrians saw the assassination as justification for destroying Serbia. Harsh diplomatic communications were sent to the Serbian government, and the other powers of Europe grew tense. Russia decided that it must support Serbia and called on France for its support in the event of war. Germany declared that it was behind Austria, while Britain vowed to protect the neutrality of Belgium if the Germans approached. A month after the assassination, Austria declared war on Serbia, and the other powers of Europe joined the fray. What had been predicted to be a brief conflict dragged on until November 11, 1918, and left millions dead. ∎

Important Term

Austro-Hungarian Empire: The designation from 1867 to 1918 for the empire combining Austria and Hungary, as well as other political entities, under the rule of Franz Ferdinand as emperor of Austria and king of Hungary.

Suggested Reading

Donia, *Sarajevo*.

Tuchman, *Guns of August*.

Questions to Consider

1. Did World War I settle anything? Can you think of any war that did? (I can.)

2. World War I led to major advances in medicine, air travel, and many other areas of science and technology. How can war be said to be the mother of progress?

The Archduke Makes a State Visit (1914)
Lecture 27—Transcript

Our theme in this lecture is a terrorist attack that changed history forever, the terrorist attack that killed the heir to the throne of the Austro-Hungarian Empire, Franz Ferdinand and his wife, and that set in motion World War I.

Without that terrorist attack, World War I may never have come. World War I had the most immediate impact upon 11 million men who died fighting in his trenches on untold millions who were wounded or suffered as a result of losses in the war. It brought down three great empires: the Austrian Empire, the Russian Empire, the empire of the Ottoman Turks, and let's add to that a fourth empire because it caused the Kaiser to flee from Germany. As Winston Churchill said, the victors won at a cost so high as to the indistinguishable from defeat. England and France would never recover their greatness.

The war propelled America into the status of a superpower. The war flamed the fuel and fires of nationalism that would bring about the end of the colonial empires of Britain and France. The war made possible the Russian revolution and all the suffering that came from that for almost a century. The First World War led directly to the Second World War, in which 50 million died. The First World War is still with us today. It left behind unsolved problems in the Middle East, where American troops are stationed and fight and die. In recent years, American troops have gone to Kosovo, where the whole business began. If you want an event that changed history forever, it's World War I.

Go back with me to June the 28th, 1914. It's a beautiful summer day in a really beautiful summer throughout Europe. We are in the city of Sarajevo, a beautiful, multicultural diverse city that is in the Austrian province of Bosnia. The citizens of Sarajevo, like all the citizens of Bosnia, are subjects of the emperor of the Austro-Hungarian Empire. The city is beautifully bedecked on this day. Flags of the Austrian empire with its double-headed eagle fly everywhere because the city is expecting, and many of the citizens are looking forward to, a state visit from the heir to this great empire, Franz Ferdinand, and his wife, Sophie.

But, there are others who are not so happy about this. The city of Sarajevo was also crawling with members of a terrorist organization, the Black Hand, as they call themselves. This terrorism is one of the small blips on what is otherwise a Europe of peace and prosperity. In fact, Europe would almost need two generations before it would recover the peace and prosperity of this summer in 1914. In fact, you can have professors tell you in this summer of 1914, let's say in June, early June of 1914 that Europe and in fact the whole world was moving to a new plane of prosperity and peace. There would never be another major European war. Why is this you would ask that professor. One, the professor would say, because we are united in a global economy. The products of France, of Britain, of Germany, of Australia, Canada, the United States, they all flow in a free market economy. We are so joined together that business itself would not allow another war to break out. Also, 1914 is the heyday of our laissez-faire economics, the ideal of Adam Smith.

Two, wars in the past have broken out because there was a lack of communication. Today, in this modern era of 1914, we have the telegraph. We can immediately communicate and the misunderstandings that brought about wars in the past because diplomats took so long to communicate back and forth are gone forever. We have communication, the global economy, and technology. The people of the world today can travel. There's even air flight, as we know from our study of the Wright Brothers. There are very fast moving boats that can go across the Atlantic in three days. There is so much communication between the various people of the world that they will not have misunderstandings. Moreover, mankind has progressed. Remember our evolutionary theory that the human race was moving ever and ever higher towards a new morality. The weapons of war would now be so terrible like airplanes that it would just be such a destructive event that the human race and all of its evolutionary beauty would not allow to occur. That was our Europe in 1914.

But, diplomats and military men nonetheless had prepared for war. All of Europe was armed to the teeth, huge standing armies that came about because of drafts and all of the great nations. Europe was divided into alliances: France, Britain, Russia all allied, in fear of Germany. Germany was in fear of France. Britain and Russia had allied itself for Italy. There were the large armies in place. There was a technology that would make a war terrible.

There were also ancient hatreds and passions that had only been submerged. This is because right along with those professors who taught how there would never be another European war, there were professors of history, of political science, even professors of biology who saw in the teachings of Charles Darwin the proof that out of war and disaster came an ever stronger race. War was an essential part of this survival of the fittest. One race, like the German race, must of necessity fight and destroy the French race if Germany was to have its place in the sun. The world, just like the world of nature described by Darwin, was limited in its resources. War was an essential part of the struggle for survival. In fact, even Darwin had pointed out that the most closely related species fought most savagely against each other. Darwin had foreseen that the Europeans would exterminate ultimately those who did not have European civilization. War, nature, red in tooth and claw, that too was one of the ideals of Europe in 1914.

Then, there were ancient ethnic hatreds. Nowhere did this hatred simmer more seriously than in Bosnia and in this city of Sarajevo. For the 19th and early 20th century was the great age of nationalism. It was the age of ethnic identity. It was an age that believed every single nation has a unique language. Out of that unique language comes unique ideas, unique art, unique music, and unique science. There was German art, German science, and German literature, stamped indelibly with the nature of the unique nature of the German race. There was Italian literature, Italian art, and Italian science, stamped in this nonsense view but people accepted it. It was stamped with the indelible character of the Italian race. There was a unique southern Slavic ethnicity, a unique art and a unique literature that bound itself inextricably with the soul of the south Slavic people—countries we would call Croatia, Serbia, Bulgaria, Bosnia. It was the divine right of each of these nations, like the Germans, like the French, to bring under the borders of one country all of those who shared this common ethnicity and to drive out those who did not have this ethnicity. To create following the perverted teachings that they had taken from Darwin, perverted from Darwin, following the need for every race to be pure.

But, the south Slavic ethnicity, what would ultimately find its statement in the old country of Yugoslavia, meaning the country of the South Slavs, this south Slavic ethnicity was hampered, prevented from expressing itself because of the Austrian-Hungarian Empire. It was Austria that had prevented Serbia from annexing Bosnia. It was Austria that prevented Serbia from annexing Croatia. It was Austria that prevented Serbia from annexing Slovenia. Serbia was an independent country. It had won its independence against the Turks in the 19th century. But, it had to be a greater Serbia in the mind of its national heroes and patriots. Austria was the block to all of this. The greatest danger from Austria came in the form of Franz Ferdinand because he was a farsighted, capable statesman, who was determined and had very good ideas about how to do it to revive the Austro-Hungarian Empire as a great new nation.

Just about the time we were fighting our Civil War, Austria had reformulated itself. The old Holy Roman Empire had been ended by Napoleon in 1806. In the mid-1860s, Austria restructured itself. The Austrian emperor was also king of Hungary. Austria began to restore its finances and to modernize its army. Franz Ferdinand was determined when he became emperor to continue this process by restructuring the Austro-Hungarian Empire politically. His ideal was a forerunner of the European union of today. It would be a federal union of the Austro-Hungarian Empire in which the numerous ethnic groups that made up this empire would each have their share of political power and would have ethnic autonomy, in the sense of using their languages in the schools, in the universities, of being able to use their languages in the courts—even adapting the laws of the Austro-Hungarian Empire to suit the traditions of the ethnic groups that made up this diverse ancient land.

The Germans were of course among the most important of these. But, the Bohemians, what we would we would call the Czechs, the Slovaks, the proud Hungarians, the Slovenes, the Croatians all along the coast of Dalmatia, and yes, the Serbs, who lived within the border of the Austro-Hungarian Empire, all of these would be represented in the parliament and all would have these various aspects of autonomy. To those Serbs who dreamt of a greater Serbia, this was such a good idea, this was so likely to win support from thoughtful and peace-minded Serbs that it would destroy forever the hope of a gigantic powerful Serbia. At the head of this terrorist organization, determined to destroy the Austrian attempt at revitalizing itself, was the Serbian military. Leading officers in the Serbian military formed this terrorist group, the Black Hand. Their agents moved not only all through the Balkans, but in France, in Britain, even coming to this country, the United States, to gather funds from Serbian immigrants for this terrorist set of operations.

One of their most trusted agents in Serbia itself was Danilo Ilić, a schoolteacher. It was frequently in the person of schoolteachers that the most violent Serbian nationalism was to be found. He taught his students over and over again that there was only one destiny, for Serbia to become a great nation and for each of them to devote his or her life to fighting and dying for Serbia, and for killing, murdering, assassinating anyone who stood in the path of a greater Serbia. I know these ideas sound crazy today, but you must remember that it hasn't been more than a decade ago that these same ethnic ideals led to terrible massacres there in the area around Sarajevo. Ethnic hatred dies hard. In 1914, it was in full bloom.

Then, came the news that the heir to the throne of Austria, Franz Ferdinand, was coming to Sarajevo. He was going to observe Austrian military maneuvers. He was bringing his wife with him. The two were deeply in love. She was not of the highest nobility. She was a Bohemian countess. The uncle of Franz Ferdinand, the great old last European monarch, France Josef, had not approved of their marriage. In fact, the children born of that marriage would not be allowed to come to the throne of Austria. But, they were so deeply in love and she went with him everywhere she could. He had brought his beautiful wife with him, both of them now content in middle life, and they were going to come on June the 28th. They arrived and there was a six-car procession. Franz Ferdinand wanted the top down and wanted to drive at no more than about ten miles an hour because he wanted to be able to see the city and to wave to the crowds. There were large crowds there. Many of the inhabitants of Sarajevo were German and they were waving frantically. There were Austrian citizens who spoke German and they were waving frantically. Other citizens of the empire were there waving, but there were also some rather sullen faces.

Franz Ferdinand turned to the governor of Bosnia who was riding with him and said, "Count, some of these people look so angry." "I know," the count said, "there was a slip-up in the planning for this, your Royal Highness. That is to say, do you know what day June the 28th is?" "No, not actually. What's June the 28th?" "Yes, but it is the anniversary of the Battle of Kosovo Polje, the Battle of the Field of the Blackbirds in 1389." "Now that does ring a bell, yes. That was when the Serbian army was destroyed forever by the forces of the Turks, and it is a day of ill omen in Serbia, and it is also a day in which they dream again of the greatness of Serbia." "Your coming here on June the 28th really looks like, how should I say it, your Highness, thumbing your nose at them." "Why couldn't we have done it on the 29th or the 27th?" "I don't know, just as I say, it was a scheduling mistake." "Do you think we're going to be all right?" "Yes. How many security agents do you have with us?" "Just two or three, but that'll be plenty." "Are there troops in the city in case these angry looking people get out of control?" "No, there are not, but we've got part of the Austrian army." "Yes, but we looked into this, this morning as a matter of fact, and the troops don't have their dress uniforms with them. We thought it was probably not a good idea to bring them into the city." "We have almost no security?" "No, we don't." "Do you know anything else about this?" "I don't want to spoil the day for you; everything's going to be fine." "Please," and he's waving to people, "is there anything else?" "No, not really, your Highness."

But, in fact there was. The Austrian secret service had learned from very authoritative sources that there might likely be an assassination attempt on the archduke. They even had sources that reported, again authoritatively, that some six terrorists had been ferried across the river into Bosnia by Serbian boats; these terrorists had been armed with Serbian pistols and with Serbian hand grenades. These terrorists, who were Serb nationals, five of them Christian Serbs, one of them a Muslim, had a specific plan organized at the very highest level of this terrorist organization, this widespread terrorist organization, to kill Franz Ferdinand. Yes, social security slip-ups happen again and again in history.

As the motorcade made its way down, one of these terrorists stepped forward to throw his hand grenade. But, he got afraid and didn't do it. But, as the procession went on, a second one did throw a bomb and it blew up injuring several people in the procession, not hurting the Archduke and his wife. But, he was outraged and he leapt out and tried to take care of the people that had been wounded. They were rushed off to the hospital. Franz Ferdinand said, "What are we going to do? Should we continue with this procession?" The governor said, "I don't know. It'll look so bad if you turn around and go back. That had to be just an isolated incident." "Somebody throwing a bomb is an isolated incident?" "Sure, they're always crackpots." "I don't know, but when I get to the town hall, I'm telling the mayor off."

Sure enough, they arrived. Franz Ferdinand stormed out of his car, not even waiting for the driver to open the door officially. He stormed up to the mayor who began to read his proclamation of welcome. Franz Ferdinand, resplendent in his uniform as a general in the Austrian cavalry with a huge green plumed hat said, "Shut up. Is this how you welcome your visitors? They threw a bomb at us. Friends of mine have been wounded. This is a schrecklick, it's an outrage!" "Would you like to see the rest of the sights, your Highness?" "No! We're going to the hospital right now to visit the wounded. Tell the driver we're off to the hospital."

The driver didn't have one of these little systems you have today where you poke stuff into the computer and it tells you turn left at the next roundabout, that sort of thing. No, and he really wasn't all that familiar with Sarajevo so he started off going by what he thought was the most direct route. Then, the Archduke said, "Go faster!" He said, "Maybe I can take this side street." He turned down the side street and suddenly realized that was going in the wrong direction. Franz Ferdinand said, "Does he know what he's doing?" Just as it stopped and the driver began to put it into reverse, an old-fashioned car with a clutch, what they always do, it stalled. Then the gear locked up on him, so he was trying to get it unlocked, get the car started back up. There on the corner where the car was stalled, a lot of people now milling around, there was almost no security whatsoever. There were a few police and more police had been called out after the bomb, but still not nearly enough police.

As the car was stalled there, there was sitting inside a delicatessen, Schiller's Delicatessen, having a sandwich, Gavrilo Princip, one of these six conspirators. After the bomb had failed to kill the archduke and the archduke was said to be going off towards the hospital, he'd given up the idea and was going to have lunch. There was the car. He put down his sandwich, walked out, and fired two shots. The first one hit the archduke, and the second one, his devoted wife, as she threw her body across him. "Live for our children," he said. "It's nothing. I'll be fine." Then, he died and she died.

This terrorist organization had achieved its goal because of security mistakes, a laxness in security. But, the Austrians had been waiting for just such a chance to attack Serbia. Of course, they didn't want it to be this assassination of the heir to the throne, but this was one final proof that as an English newspaper actually said, "If the whole country of Serbia were towed out into the sea and sunk, the air of Europe would be cleaner." Serbia was an outrage to Europe. The Austrians were determined to use this assassination once and for all to destroy the Serbs.

The Austrian diplomats immediately began to draw up a note, an ultimatum, to be sent to the Serbians. At first throughout the capitals of Europe, yes, there was shock at this assassination, but surely it had been the act of a random fanatic. Surely the Serbian government wasn't behind it. Surely Serbia would cooperate with the Austrians in an investigation. The summer would go on and English diplomats could go off to their summer homes. The French diplomats could summer on the coast of Normandy. German diplomats could go to the spas. But, the note that the Austrian sent, the ultimatum, was very strong.

One of the articles insisted that Austrian policemen carry out the investigation within Serbia. The Austrians were convinced that the Serbs would reject that complete infringement upon their sovereignty. But, the note that the Serbs wrote back was very, very subservient. They even offered to give arbitration to the international court at The Hague to this question of the Austrians conducting the investigation. "Absolutely unacceptable," said the Austrian ambassador. By this time, the czar in Russia and the kaiser in Germany, and the diplomats in London and in Paris were beginning to get worried. Russia decided that it must not fail to support its one strong ally there in the Balkans, Serbia. If the Austrians choose this opportunity to destroy the power of Serbia, Russia would be in grave danger.

They began to communicate with the French. They said, "If the Austrians march into Serbia, we will have to take this as an act of war against Russia. You have an alliance with us in which you promise to go to war if we have to go to war." The French wrote back and said, "We accept this obligation." All along the time there in the embassies and various parts of Europe, the French diplomats began to think, "Austria's not behind all of this; it's the Germans. It's the Germans who are pushing the Austrians into this war on Serbia, so that they will have an excuse to attack us in France and attack the Russians."

The Austrian emperor, Franz Joseph, wrote to his old friend, the kaiser of Germany, Kaiser Wilhelm, and said, "Will you stand by Austria?" The kaiser wrote back, "We give Austria a blank check. Do whatever is necessary and Germany will be at your side." "What are we British going to do?" "I don't know; we've kind of got understandings with France, in particular. But, I think that's only if there is an actual attack upon France. It's not absolutely clear what our foreign policy is. Even some of the high ministers of state weren't allowed access to some secret treaties that had actually been made between France and Britain." "But, one thing is sure," the British said. "If the Germans march through Belgium, which is a neutral country, guaranteed in this neutrality by us, then we will have to go war."

The days ticked on. On July the 28th, one month to the day, Austria declared war on Serbia and began its invasion. On August the 1st, the kaiser was telegraphing frantically back and forth to his cousin, Nikki, the czar of Russia, Czar Nicholas. He said, "Can we not avoid this war?" Nicholas said, "I want to avoid a war, but my general's telling me that you're mobilizing." Willie says, "Yes, yes, we have to mobilize in case you attack us." "We have to mobilize in case you attack us." "Tell them both to stop mobilizing." "My generals," Nikki says, "telling me that they can't stop mobilizing." "What do you mean they can't stop mobilizing?" "They've got the trains going and the troops going. We just can't stop; it'll be chaos." "My general's telling me the same thing."

And so, war came. No one, except a very few fanatics had wanted it, but it came. The Germans believed that their only hope for victory in a war on two fronts against Russia and France lay in crossing into Belgium. They broke the neutrality of Belgium. By August, Russia, France, and Great Britain were at war with Germany and Austria. The military men promised a quick war, but it would drag on until November the 11th, 1918. That evolutionary apex of human society and civilization, that ordinary soldier who was reduced to wearing metal helmets, like the Middle Ages, crouching and crawling through the mud of trenches, with a gas mask on his face, armed with a rifle, and a knife with a serrated edge and brass knuckles, and dying by the millions, just to kill his fellow man.

World War I came as a result of a terrorist attack, and the world has never been the same.

One Night in Petrograd (1917)
Lecture 28

> The Gulag system began to expand. The czar had his Siberia and he had had his prison camps, but they were luxury resorts compared to what the Soviets put into place. ... Monasteries were transformed from places of worship and spirituality into the most brutal kinds of prison. It is only by terror, Lenin insisted again and again to his comrades, that we will establish communism.

With their seizure of power in Russia in November 1917, the **Bolsheviks** set out to create the first communist state. The Russian Revolution and the establishment of the Soviet Union would bring death to millions over two generations, but it would also make the Soviet Union one of the two superpowers of the world. Still today, Russia bears the imprint of its long years of communism, and the ideas of the Russian Revolution are still the official doctrine in China, North Korea, and Cuba.

In 1917, the Russian Empire possessed vast resources of oil, enormous mineral wealth, and rich soil, yet it was also a land in which workers lived in subhuman conditions and peasant farmers often fell victim to starvation. Vladimir Lenin was among those who sought to change the empire with the ideals of **socialism**. Lenin was a devoted student of Marx, but he believed that Marx had not explored the final step to achieve a communist state. Capitalism would not just collapse on its own accord. When the circumstances were right, a small, dedicated, hardened group must take power and force the masses to realize that it was in their own best interest to become a communist nation.

With the outbreak of war in 1914, Russia valiantly fulfilled its promise to its allies to slow the German advance. But the Russian army was poorly equipped and incompetently led; ordinary Russian soldiers suffered terribly and died in the millions. In the spring of 1917, Russian soldiers began to simply leave the trenches, while Germans poured across the frontier. Now armed, the Russians were determined to better their living conditions at home. Bread riots broke out in major cities, and the czar was forced to abdicate; he was succeeded by Alexander Kerensky, a brilliant lawyer and socialist. Kerensky insisted that Russia should remain in the war, but the Germans hatched a plan to import terrorism to Russia to spark a revolution that would take the Russians out of the picture. That terrorism arrived in April 1917 in the person of Vladimir Lenin.

Over the next few months, Lenin began to acquire followers, promising bread, land, an end to war, and power to the civic committees of Bolsheviks (called "soviets") throughout Russia. In Petrograd, on the night of November 7, the communists and their armed supporters seized the major instruments of communication and the power plants. When the city woke up the next morning, the Soviets were in power.

The communists set about creating a workers' paradise but became embroiled in a civil war with the remaining forces of the czar. Over the course of two long years, 20 million Russians died, either of starvation

Vladimir Lenin gained support by promising the Russian people bread, land, and an end to war.

or as a result of the war itself. Meanwhile, the hold of the Bolsheviks tightened, and Lenin embarked on a program of terror. Social democrats and other dissenters were imprisoned or shot by the thousands. Lenin made a humiliating peace with Germany to concentrate on his internal enemies—the opponents of communism.

Lenin died in 1924 and was succeeded in 1929 by Joseph Stalin, who continued and extended Lenin's rule by terror throughout the 1930s. Nevertheless, when Hitler invaded the Soviet Union in 1941, the Russian people rallied to defend their nation. They saw Stalin as the only man cruel enough to beat the Nazis, and he did. From that point on, the Soviet Union would emerge as one of the two superpowers of the 20th century. ■

Important Terms

Bolshevik: From the Russian "majority party." Self-designation of Vladimir Lenin's faction of the Russian Communist Party in 1917.

socialism: Economic and political concepts based on the ideal that the welfare of society as a whole is more important than the freedom of the individual members of society.

Suggested Reading

Wilson, *To the Finland Station*.

Wolfe, *Three Who Made a Revolution*.

Questions to Consider

1. Winston Churchill deplored the refusal of the British government in 1919 to intervene and overthrow the Bolsheviks. Would you have agreed with Churchill? Would you agree in retrospect?

2. Why has Russia chosen despotism over freedom?

One Night in Petrograd (1917)
Lecture 28—Transcript

Our theme in this lecture is the seizure of power by the Bolsheviks, the communists, in Russia, in November of 1917—the Russian Revolution. It changed history forever. With that seizure of power in November of 1917, the Bolsheviks set out to create the first communist state, the realization on earth of Karl Marx's dream of a workers' paradise. The Russian Revolution and the establishment of the Soviet Union would bring death to millions over two generations, but it would also make the Soviet Union one of the two superpowers of the world. Under the strength of communism and its dictator Stalin, the Nazi threat to Europe would be broken. Still today, Russia bears the strong imprint of its long years of communism. The ideas of the Russian Revolution are still the official doctrine of the power of China, North Korea, and Cuba. They have shaped ideas about economics, society, and politics throughout Europe, Asia, Latin America, and even in our own country.

The Russian Revolution changed history forever. To understand it, go back with me to the night of November 7th, which will turn into the morning of November 8th. The year is 1917 and we are in the city of Petrograd with a hardened band of terrorists—terrorists who are devoted to violence and to the establishment of a communist state by terrorism and ruled by terrorism. The head of this band of terrorists is Vladimir Lenin. Even the name is not really his. He took it from the River Lena where he was in exile in Siberia during the days of the Czars. His mother and father might not have seen him as a potential mass murderer on a scale surpassing even Genghis Khan. In fact, his father was a fairly nondescript civil servant. He was raised in good middle-class surroundings, rather prosperous. But, when he was a teenager, his brother was involved in terrorist activities.

The Russian Empire was a vast empire stretching all the way from Vladivostok to Finland with vast resources of oil already being exploited, enormous mineral wealth, and rich soil. It was counted to be one of the superpowers of Europe. It had been Russian troops who had played the major role in crushing Napoleon. Yet it was a land torn by deep social hatreds. The poor of Russia were indescribably poor—the workers of Russia working in subhuman conditions, the peasants frequently starving in a year of famine, with no government relief coming to them.

There were those who sought to change this decrepit Russian empire by terror. They had various names, even various philosophies, but it all came down to socialism. This is the idea that the root of Russia's problem—the root of the problem of the whole world—was private property. Once private property was utterly abolished, then a paradise would dawn. These people saw themselves as believers in democracy, but not our idea of democracy where the individual is supreme. No, it was an ideal democracy in which the individual is intended to be utterly subordinate to the group as a whole—communism.

The brother of Vladimir was involved in terrorist activities. He was arrested by the Czar's secret police and hanged.

Thereafter, Vladimir developed a hatred for this system and a determination to overthrow it. He studied. He was caught reading Marx's books and expelled, but finally allowed back into university where he graduated with a good degree as a lawyer. He devoted his life, starting in his late teens, to communism and to creating, in Russia, a communist revolution. Like the Wright Brothers, but in a very different and far more terrible way, Lenin was a man of destiny. He had one mission in life, and he set out to achieve it. He mastered completely the teachings of Karl Marx. But the more he read, he realized that Marx had not taken the final step. Capitalism would not just collapse on its own accord. The circumstances had to be right. When the circumstances were right, a dedicated, small, hardened, and utterly amoral party of terrorists must take over power and force the masses to realize that it was in their own best interest to become a communist nation.

He lived from hand to mouth. He married. His wife was devoted to him and a devoted communist. They argued frequently over small points of Marx's doctrine. He became one of the leaders of the international communist movement—in many places, completely outlawed. He certainly could not live in Russia where he was known well to the secret police who had sent him to Siberia on at least on one occasion. No, he lived in Switzerland. You can still visit and see the plaque on the house where he lived in Switzerland. At times, he became despondent. He thought that we will never live to see the revolution.

But, in 1914, the war came—the war for Russia. Russia nobly and valiantly fulfilled its promise to the French and the British. It sent its troops already in August of 1914 into Germany to slow up the German advance enough so that the French could rally. The Russians suffered defeat time and time again. It had a vast army, but many of their soldiers were wearing their first pair of boots. They had their first overcoats. Some of them didn't even have rifles in major engagements. They would wait around for one of their comrades to be killed and then pick up a rifle. The Russian artillery was formidable on paper. But, much of it was old fashioned. Far more worse, much of the ammunition was bad. Corruption was at every level of Russian society and huge government contracts were given because of bribes. Worst of all, the Russian generals were incompetent. The ordinary Russian soldier, worker, and peasant, abused and spit upon by his officer, died in the millions. He suffered terribly in the cold, suffered from disease, and suffered from incompetent surgery in the field hospitals.

Worst of all was the Czar Nicolas, a weak willed man utterly in the grasp of his wife, a domineering woman who said Russia needs a strong ruler. He took over command of the army. At the critical points, as starvation began to break out in cities like Petrograd, he was far off at the front doing a very bad job of leading the army. In fact, he would get up late in the morning, have an English style breakfast, consult a little bit with his generals, take a nap, take a walk, then go to bed and read novels while he sat up in bed having a little late night wine.

The Russian army collapsed, until finally in the early, early spring of 1917, the Russians did what every army in these trenches dreamt of doing. They just went home. They just crawled out of these muddy trenches, at first one or two, and then platoons and then squads, divisions, whole armies just left. The Germans poured across the frontier. But, these Russian soldiers kept their rifles. They kept their machine guns. They were determined to go back and gain bread and land. Therefore, the revolution really began with the Russian army.

The situation collapsed so rapidly that there were riots in the streets of the major cities over bread. Finally, the Russian parliament simply came to the conclusion that the Czarist government had to fall. A deputation went out to the front line where the Czar was and his private train and said you must abdicate. "Oh," he said. "All right." He wrote his name. "What is the date by the way?" "March 15th." "Ah, yes, March 15th. And I am also going to abdicate for my son." "But, we thought your son would take over." "No, no, I don't want him to be Czar either so we're abdicating." The 300 year dynasty of the Romanovs was no more. Russia became a constitutional democracy.

Almost immediately to the fore came a brilliant orator, a lawyer, a socialist but most certainly not a communist—Alexander Kerensky. He tried to form a European style parliamentary democracy. There were numerous different political parties constantly quarreling among each other—from people who wanted to restore the monarchy through people who believed in an English style of liberalism and a laissez-faire economy and limited government intervention, down to people who wanted a socialization of Russia, but one that came about constitutionally. Kerensky was the leader.

The foremost question was one, what kind of constitution would Russia have, and then two, what to do about the war? The Russians were suffering disastrous defeats. Those parts of the army that were still in the field were being overrun and had no supplies. Germany was penetrating deeply into Russian territory. Kerensky insisted and the parliament went along with him—that the honor of Russia demanded that they continue the war. What also helped in this decision were the vast sums of money poured into the hands of Russian politicians by the British and French to bribe them to stay in the war. The people were not getting their bread and they were not getting their land. The war went on and on and on.

It was at this moment, in a determination to get Russia out of this war, that a German diplomat came up with a scheme. He had gone through the police files of the German secret police, finding the name of Vladimir Lenin, living there in Switzerland, carefully going through his dossier, and interviewing people who knew Lenin. He came up with the idea of sending Lenin and a few of his close associates in a sealed train—as though they were bacteria—through German territory to Russia, and let Lenin spark off a revolution that would take Russia out of the war.

In April of 1917, Lenin arrived at the Finland Station, that station in St. Petersburg that was closest to the territory of Finland. The crowds were there to greet him—a small but powerfully built man, a brilliant orator, and completely bald as though the very brains had pushed out his hair. There he began to speak. "I promise you—all power to the Soviets." These were the committees that in the name of the Bolsheviks had sprung up in cities, towns, and villages all over Russia. "All power will go to the Soviets and thus all power to the people because these are democratically elected. I promise you bread, I promise you land, I promise you an end to the war." Bread, land, peace proclaimed over and over again.

Then, there were long debates with other communists over questions like, should we immediately seize power? There the doctrine of Marx was brought up. Karl Marx says that there must be a bourgeois state first before there can be a communist state. Russia is just really emerging—remember our terms from our lecture on Marx—it is just really emerging from serfdom. I am not sure we have had a bourgeois state. Lenin said, we have got one now, do we not? Is that not what you call that parliamentary democracy? That is a bourgeois democracy. Yes, yes it is. Then let them govern for a short time and then we will overthrow them. Let them continue to hang themselves with this war. The moment will come and it will come, comrade, soon. It had come already by November.

People were still starving and the Russian offensive was in utter disarray. By the night of the 7th, the Bolsheviks, this hardened band of terrorists—because Lenin was convinced revolution could be carried out only by a small group of utterly dedicated, utterly amoral individuals—was ready to seize power. They had all of the capable soldiers in the city of Petrograd and in certain other vital Russian cities under their control. The fleet at Kronstadt there outside of Petrograd was armed and fully devoted to the communist cause.

129

Large numbers of policemen were on the side of the communists. During that night, the major instruments of communication, like the telegraph office and power plants, were seized by the communists and their armed supporters. When the city of Petrograd woke up the next morning, all power had gone to the Soviets.

Alexander Kerensky tried to rally the army behind him. He was a pitiful figure, fleeing the city of Petrograd in an automobile, stopping from time to time at the various armed camps all around the city of Petrograd trying to use his brilliant oratorical skills—and just about being killed every time by the soldiers who had come to hate him and hate this form of democracy so much. Kerensky would flee to the United States. He would live to be an old man telling over and over again how he really could have beaten the communists.

Now all power was with the Soviets and Lenin. The communists set about to create that workers' paradise, but it was a struggle. The forces of the Czar had not yet been defeated. For two long years, Lenin and his allies, like Comrade Stalin and Comrade Trotsky, would fight a brutal, savage civil war. According to some estimates, 20 million Russians died either of starvation or as a result of the civil war itself in which armies loyal to the Czar, the whites, would ride back and forth across Russia. The red armies would rally and drives them back. Foreign armies intervened. The French sent some troops, British sent some troops, and Japanese sent some troops. Even Americans sent some troops to Siberia. Winston Churchill insisted, in Parliament, that if the British would send one well armed division, the Bolsheviks could be defeated and destroyed. But, that was just one more of Winston's crackpot schemes. It was Russia's business. If they wanted a communist government, then let them have it.

Civil war and starvation came. Comrade Lenin showed himself to be supremely adaptable. The people had to eat. He was willing to make compromises with fundamental aspects of Marxist doctrine such as not carrying out a collectivization of the farms and allowing individual peasants to produce their own food. Step by step, the hold of the Bolsheviks tightened. The very word Bolshevik is a term that came from the early party days when at a brief moment Lenin had a majority of the communist party. Thereafter, he called his faction the Bolshevik faction. By now, they were communism in Russia, these Bolsheviks. They had originally disagreed with their political opponents on the question of the use of terror.

Terror was introduced by Lenin in a systematic way. The prisons were filled up with anyone who dissented, anyone who taught socialism that was not communism. In fact, the social democrats—those who believed that Russia should have a government such as now exists in states like Germany in which there was private property, but there was welfare, social security, free healthcare, and free universities—were the most dangerous. They were shot down by the hundreds and then by the thousands. Anybody who was an aristocrat was suspect. In the old Winter Palace that had been stormed by the Bolsheviks on the night of November 7th, November 8th, young officers—who were there in the palace trying to defend it—were taken one by one in the grand ballroom of the Winter Palace. Their heads were crushed like walnuts on the coming down of a grand piano smashing its lid down upon them—terror.

The Gulag system began to expand. The Czar had his Siberia and he had had his prison camps, but they were luxury resorts compared to what the Soviets put into place. Far off Siberia filled up. Monasteries transformed from places of worship and spirituality into the most brutal kinds of prison. It is only by terror, Lenin insisted again and again to his comrades, that we will establish communism. But, peace came to Russia in its foreign war. Lenin insisted that the Russians make a very humiliating peace with the Germans, signed at the city of Brest-Litovsk in 1918. This brought an end to the war, giving up large amounts of Russian territory. It brought foreign peace to Russia, to concentrate on the true enemy—the internal enemies, the opponents of communism.

Lenin was still a relatively young man—only 50 years of age in 1921. But, he had been shot on more than one occasion by attempted assassins. Then he suffered a stroke. The severity of that stroke was kept hidden. Though in very feeble condition, he continued to guide the Soviet Union. The jockeying among his followers, to see who would succeed Lenin, became intense. Lenin in fact had become the new Czar. He was as absolute a despot, as brutal, as Ivan the Terrible. When he died in 1924, Lenin left behind a testament in the possession of his devoted wife. In it, he went through and discussed the closest associates, those who had shared power with him, those who were at the very top of this Soviet government, what was called the Politburo. He discussed each of their characteristics like that of Trotsky and Zinoviev, figures now long passed into history.

He also mentioned Comrade Stalin. He was, of all the leading Bolsheviks, the only one who was really the son of a worker. He had been a convinced communist from his early teenage years. He had organized for the party. He had written important memos for Lenin on the nationality problems in Russia, the ethnic groups. But, Comrade Stalin, Lenin said, "is too rude, too coarse, ever to inherit my position." But, Comrade Stalin was one of the craftiest men who ever lived. Step by step, after the death of Lenin, Comrade Stalin, from 1924–1929, carefully orchestrated his seizure of complete power. By 1929, Joseph Stalin was a despotic Czar greater than Ivan the Terrible had ever been.

He was born in Georgia. It was part of the Russian Empire. At the end of his life, he could, if he wanted to, speak with a heavy Georgian accent. His father had been a cobbler. His mother was absolutely devoted to her son and saw to it that he got an education and studied for the priesthood. He was thrown out of the seminary for reading Marx's books. But, until the end of his life, he had great admiration for the priests who taught him there at the seminary because of their expert ability at ferreting out suspicious students and using students to inform upon one another. He also picked up an oratorical ability that always enabled him to speak almost as though he were singing a mass. He was a devoted communist.

When he became absolute ruler in 1929, he continued and even elaborated upon Lenin's rule by terror. All through the 1930s, there would be periodic purges of the Communist Party, the Red Army, and workers in factories. You would be sitting at your desk one day and suddenly the—they had various names, but call them the KGB, the Secret Police—they would show up in your office and tell you that you were under arrest as a German saboteur and collaborator. After all, these great communist projects, these five-year plans that were supposed to quintuple the production of wheat, never worked. There had to be a reason and it couldn't be that communism didn't work; it had to be that there were people sabotaging the work of steel production and wheat production. So, you're called a German collaborator. You say, but how can you say that? The KGB reaches into your desk and they pull out a pamphlet written in German. Yes, the party sent me to school to learn German so I could read these technical treatises. Are you saying that the party is at fault? Because remember, the party can never be wrong.

That's another thing thing that Stalin admired from his reading about Jesuit Priest—the teaching that if the Jesuits tell you that black is white, you not only believe that black is white, but you are utterly convinced that black is white. Therefore, the party can never do wrong. So, are you saying that party is wrong? No, no, I'm not saying that. Then, you'd be brought before a judge. There, if you pleaded guilty on the spot, you'd be sent off to Siberia for 10 years—but, at least you didn't get beaten and tortured. If you said, I'm innocent, you would then be beaten and tortured in the most savage way by the Secret Police until you finally did sign any confession that was put in front of you. Then, it was off to Siberia. There was no comfort in the fact that you were one of only millions who, in one year, would be arrested and sent off to Siberia. Maybe 25 percent of you would die on the way of cold and starvation. There, if you were still alive, you would be worked on a diet of about 1,400 calories. You got slim fast. You were sent out in temperatures of 49 below zero. What made it all the more terrifying to those who were left at home is that it was all random.

Yet, when Hitler invaded the Soviet Union on June 22nd 1941, he thought that the communist system would collapse and that the people would revolt against Stalin. They did not. They rallied not behind communism, but behind holy Mother Russia. They saw Stalin as the only man cruel enough, mean enough, and hard enough—after all, the name he took meant man of steel—to beat the Nazis; and they did. At Stalin's own town of Stalingrad, the Russian army was crushed.

The Communist Revolution with which Lenin seized power found Russia using wooden plows—a decrepit third-rate power in Europe, with its people receiving no medical care if they were poor, and no job security. Under Joseph Stalin, the Soviet Union would emerge as one of the two superpowers of the world. It would gain an empire that stretched all the way into Germany and controlled China. It was an atomic power. People had a level of social help and welfare that many in Russia today look back upon with great fondness. The Bolsheviks changed history forever.

The Day the Stock Market Crashed (1929)
Lecture 29

[Stock] does not go up 10 percent on a regular basis. It is not a CD that pays you 6 percent and is guaranteed. It is a piece of paper. It is speculation, and the whole country went wild with speculation in the 1920s.

The stock market crash of 1929 set off a worldwide depression and raised the specter of social revolution. It led to the dictatorship of Adolf Hitler and the election of Franklin Roosevelt. Moreover, the Great Depression illustrates the truth that history does not repeat itself, but men and women repeat the mistakes of history. A careful study of the crash of 1929 reveals chilling similarities to our own economic crisis of recent years.

After World War I, many young men returned home, got married, and settled down into jobs and family life. In the early years of the 1920s, these young men began to buy homes, often with mortgages they couldn't quite afford, and to make other purchases on installment plans. They also began to invest their savings in the stock market, buying on margin—in essence, borrowing money from a broker. The stock market and the economy as a whole seemed to be booming.

In the summer of 1929, the stock market grew 25 percent in three months. In September, it experienced some ups and downs, which were said to be the result of "market correction." Then, on October 24, the market began to crash. Panic selling set in, with millions of shares being traded. At noon on that day, the great banking houses decided to step in and provide organized support. The market held on for a few more choppy days before collapsing on October 29. Every stock fell; the great crash had come.

The most educated voices of economics said that this was just a temporary correction. The market would soon turn around and productivity would increase. Yet goods piled up on shelves, American workers lost their jobs, and farmers had no one to buy their crops. Household appliances and cars bought on credit were repossessed and homes were foreclosed. Some families had to split up to live with relatives, and others began moving from town to town, looking for work. How had the nation reached this point?

First, it's important to realize that a stock is not an investment but pure speculation. It is worth nothing in and of itself; it is worth only what someone is willing to pay for it, which means that it must have a buyer. In the 1920s and in more recent times, people forgot that simple fact. The 1920s were also a period of weak federal regulation of the market and weak monetary policies. Easy credit was available to almost everyone. Margin buying further contributed to the crash. When brokerage firms called in their margins, those who had borrowed to buy stock found that they had to sell at a loss and couldn't pay the margin. With everyone using leverage to invest in the market, stocks ceased to be related in any way to the profitability of companies. At the same time, the business world saw a number of scandals, in which CEOs were discovered to be embezzling from their companies. The speed of communication meant that once the collapse began, it set off a panic around the world.

First, it's important to realize that a stock is not an investment but pure speculation.

One of the greatest economists of the 20th century, John Kenneth Galbraith, said that all it takes for one disaster to occur is for all those who experienced an earlier similar disaster to die off, as most of the adults of the Depression generation have. We are now learning the frightening similarities between the collapse of 1929 and our own current economic situation. ■

Suggested Reading

Alter, *The Defining Moment*.

Galbraith, *The Great Crash*.

Manchester, *The Glory and the Dream*.

1. Does the financial crisis that began in 2007 resemble the financial crisis of 1929?

2. What do these two depressions tell us about our collective failure to learn from history?

The Day the Stock Market Crashed (1929)
Lecture 29—Transcript

Our theme in this lecture is the Great Stock Market Crash of 1929, an event that changed history and reverberates still today. The Stock Market Crash set off the Depression that in this country lasted 10 years and is the most severe depression in our country's history. It led to a worldwide depression. It affected 25 percent of the American workforce in the most immediate fashion. They were out of work. It brought misery and humiliation to millions of Americans. It raised the specter of social revolution in this country. It led to the dictatorship of Adolf Hitler in Germany and to the election of Franklin Roosevelt in this country. The Great Depression, set off by the Stock Market Crash, led to social security, welfare benefits, and all manner of social entitlements that we still have today. It leads us to contemplate the uniqueness of America because Germany's way out of the Depression was an Adolf Hitler. Ours was a democracy under Franklin Roosevelt. I will tell you one more thing. The Great Depression of 1929, studied carefully, reinforces once again that history does not repeat itself; men and women repeat history. The more carefully you study the Crash of 1929, you will see its chilling similarities to what happened in our country in recent years.

Let's go back to October 29th, 1929. You are you, only living back in 1929. You come home that afternoon, from your job where you're an engineer with a large firm. You come in and your wife says, "What's wrong?" "We're ruined," you say. "We are ruined." "What do you mean, we're ruined?" "I mean we've lost everything. We've lost all of our financial security. If I don't keep my job, we won't even have enough to eat. I'm not sure how we're going to pay for the car. We're ruined. We've got two kids about ready to go to college, how are they going to go?" "I don't know what you're talking about." "The stock market, don't you keep with things?" "I heard something about it on the radio. I don't understand all of those things. Is that why you've been so worried the last few days?" "Yes!" "Why did you ever get into it in the first place?" "Because everybody was getting into it. But, I don't know, I'm going to go over and talk with Fred. He's the one who originally suggested that I go into the market."

You go next door to your neighbor and he says, "Listen, everything's going to stabilize. Just think back to five days ago. The banks are going to be bailed out. They're going to give an organized support to the market. The only people who are going to lose in this are those who sell now." You just follow old Fred's advice. You go back not as worried as you were and you do think back five days ago to October 24th when the market had also dropped sharply. At noon on October 24th, the leading bankers like JP Morgan's firms, began to buy stocks and stabilize the market.

How had you gotten here in the first place? You had graduated from one of our great American universities, let's say in the heartland, Minnesota, University of Nebraska. You were class of 1917, the first of your family to go to college. You got your degree in engineering. You were looking forward to a solid financial future and raising a family in prosperity. But that April, shortly before graduation, President Wilson had led our nation—"this great and peaceful nation" as Woodrow Wilson said—into war. America tried to stay out of the war for three long years, be "neutral in thought and deed" Woodrow Wilson had told us. He was reelected in 1916 on the platform that he will keep us out of the war. But, events had moved too fast—sinkings of ships like the Lusitania, telegrams deciphered in which Germany was trying to get Mexico to attack us, reports of German saboteurs operating in America and above all, Wilson's idea that this was a war to make the world safe for democracy, to stop the militarism of the Prussians.

You had a professor. You admired him tremendously. He was a powerful speaker and he addressed your class day after day in the lecture course. No matter what he was talking about, whether he was talking about the Peloponnesian War or Alexander the Great, he always brought it back to a final line—I want each one of you boys to enlist. Your girlfriend had said, "I'll wait for you." The employers that you had been talking to, interviewing with, they said, "We want a man who fights for his country. That job'll be waiting for you when you come back."

Off you went. You joined millions of your fellow countrymen in the Rainbow Division. You fought in France, you fought gallantly. You were in the trenches of France in the mud. You learned from the French soldiers how to survive machine gun fire of the Germans, how to survive an artillery barrage. You were in the muse Argonne offensive, fighting in desperate hand-to-hand conflict with the Germans. You won the croix de guerre. You prayed over and over again that your boy would never have to go through what you went through in the Argonne. Then came November 11ᵗʰ 1918, the armistice. You were one of those who were waiting to see who could fire the last shot—not really realizing that if you fired one second before the 11 o'clock hour of the armistice, you might kill somebody. Your group didn't get off the last shot, but nonetheless you had been among the last shots.

Then you came home and you marched down the streets of New York. You went back home and your girl was waiting for you. You got married and you got a good job. America had come out of that war and above all, the sordid negotiations at the Versailles Treaty. You were absolutely disgusted with Europe and feeling that all of war was just a "grand illusion" as a popular movie proclaimed it. We wanted nothing more to do with Europe, no war ever solved anything. You were going to take care of your family.

You began to make money. 1919, 1920, '21, '22, '23—you were putting away some real money. You were buying things for your family. Your parents had always rented a house. Now that seemed foolish because you could get a mortgage at a good rate from the bank. In fact, the people at the bank were your friends. When you went down to get your mortgage to buy your house in 1920, the man who was going to write out the mortgage for you, the mortgage officer, looked at your financial reports. He said, "You know, your salary's not quite large enough to buy this house you want, but I'm going to let you have it." Then, suddenly, his boss came in and went over the form and said, "That man can't pay for that house." The mortgage officer turned to his boss and said, "Look, that man was in the Rainbow Division with me. He went to the Argonne the way I did. He's good for the money." You got a house that maybe you couldn't quite afford, but it was a nice big house—two bathrooms even.

Then your wife wanted a refrigerator. She was tired of the old icebox. You were tired of that melted ice running over the floor. You said, "I don't know, my salary's okay but we got the house to pay for." She said, "How about the installment plan?" Installment plan, that's it! What a marvelous invention! I don't have to buy the whole refrigerator. I don't have to pour out $300. I can just put down $10 and then pay a small amount each month. Sure, we can buy a refrigerator, the best one they've got.

Oh, how about a car? I don't know, I ride the streetcar to work and the groceries are delivered. Yeah, but we could take Sunday drives. Yes, dad, yes, dad, we want a car, we want a car, we want a car! All right, so buy a car on the installment plan. That Henry Ford, he was a genius. He had utterly refuted Karl Marx who said that the working man and woman will never be paid more than a subsistence wage. Henry Ford realized you pay your workers a good salary and then they can buy your cars. Cars were available, they were a good price. You bought a Ford car. That was the best you thought. Once again, you bought it on the installment plan. You're getting just a tiny bit worried, but the payments you could meet and you were getting raises in your salary. Then, we want a radio, dad! A radio, sure. Radios in those days were the equivalent to plasma TVs today. They were these huge expensive monstrosities of furniture that you put in the middle of the room and everybody sat around. We could listen to the programs together on it and get the news off of it. Sure, we'll buy a radio. You bought your radio.

Here you are—you have come back from the great war, you have married, you have a lovely family, and you're living a life of luxury that your parents could not have imagined. There is, of course, Sunday dinner at home. I mean turkey, roast lamb, big fine meals, and then a drive out into the country. Dad and mom come over. Dad says, "Putting away a lot of your money, son?" You say, "Well, I'm saving some, Dad." "Well, how do you pay for all this stuff?" "The installment plan." "Yeah, I've heard about that. I think you ought to buy things with cash. That's how I always did, and if I couldn't afford a house I just rented it." "Yeah, Dad, but that is so old fashioned." "Boy, I'm telling you it's not a good idea." "Dad, talk about things you know about, don't talk about this modern economy we live in."

It's 1926 now. You're out one day mowing the lawn with the lawn mower that you bought on the installment plan as well. Fred from next door comes over and says, "Well, what do you think of the market? It just keeps going up, doesn't it?" "What market, the food market?" "No, not the food market where you buy your groceries. The stock market!" "Oh, I don't pay much attention to that." "Well, you must make a pretty good salary." "Well, I do all right." "Well, what do you do with your savings?" "Well, I do what I did even during the war—I buy what we used to call liberty bonds, savings bonds, US bonds. They pay a good rate of interest, 6 percent, and you know, I'm investing in my country." "What you are is a sap," Fred tells you. "Six percent? That's nothing. Do you know how I bought a vacation home in Florida?" "Uh-uh." "Just skimming the cream off the market. Why, do you know just one of the stocks I've bought over the last several years has gone up 600 percent! 600 percent! Have you—yes—have you seen what GE is selling for, Westinghouse, Bethlehem Steel? They're just going through the roof and you can still get in on it. Only a sucker buys savings bonds." "Wow, I don't know." "Let me give you some stock tips."

He quotes you about GE and so on. He sits down with you and you figure it up. You say, "Wow, you want me to put 5,000 in the market?" "Sure, but look at this graph right here that was produced by a professor at Yale. It shows you that if you put $5,000 in this market, by the time your kids are ready for college, it'll be worth $80,000." "Eighty thousand dollars?" "That's right. See, the market goes up historically oh 10, 15, 20 percent, and now it's going up higher than that." "Wow, I know, but $5,000—that would take every bit of my savings." "You don't have to spend $5,000. No, no, no, you buy on margin." "You buy on what?" "Margin. That is to say you put maybe 50 percent—$2,500. You can do that. And then the bank just lets you use that money." "They do?" "Sure. Oh, they charge you an interest, but you will make so much profit off that stock. Say you buy, on margin, this stock at $20. And in just a few weeks, it's going to be worth $100." "It is?" "Sure, sure thing. So you can then sell it, pay back the money you borrowed to buy it on margin to the brokerage, and then you still got a profit of $600." "Wow, and this just keeps building and building?" "Well you do, you put your money in the market and sure enough it just keeps going up and up." You're making an ever better salary, the whole country is booming, everybody is driving a car. It's just going to get better and better.

President Calvin Coolidge had said, "The business of America is business." That is to say what we worry about is just making money. Then comes the summer of 1929 and the market just goes through the roof—25 percent in three months, stocks like American Radio selling for $500 a share and never even having paid a dividend. All of the wisest voices, even *Ladies Home Journal,* say the market has reached a new plateau and will never again see a business slump. You keep putting your money in. Then, it gets choppy in September. There's some ups and some downs. Listening to the radio, you hear strange terms like technical correction and market correction. But, the fundamentals of the economy are still sound.

You talk to Fred again. He says, "Remember, the only people who lose are those who sell." You keep it in there. Then, on October 24th , the market begins to crash. A panic selling sets in with millions of shares being traded, more shares than would be traded again—except on October 29th—until the 1950s, millions of shares trading. For some stocks, there are no buyers whatsoever. At 12 o'clock, having met in the paneled rooms in one of the great banking houses, the great banks like JP Morgan and others, decide to step in and give organized assistance, organized support. Calmly, dressed in a dapper fashion—grey suit, highly burnished shoes, a little carnation in his button hole—Richard Whitney, the vice president of the New York Exchange strolls up to one of the counters and says, "Buy 5,000 shares of GE at $200 a share." "But, sir, the current price is 194." "I know, but 200's a better price for it." They're buying it at even higher levels! Then, he goes to station after station—"Buy 5,000 shares of Bethlehem Steel," "Buy 10,000 shares of Westinghouse." The banks are there. They're not going to let the market collapse. You and Fred talk about it that evening over the fence and everything's going to be all right.

Then, there are a few more choppy days. Then comes the disaster of October 29th when the market collapses. The ticker tape that you have followed so actively falls so far behind that it's not until the next day that the full result of the disaster is known around the country. Sometimes, in the giddy days of 1929, in the summer, the ticker would fall behind, but that just meant you had to wait until the next day to learn how rich you were. But, now, thousands and thousands and thousands learn they were ruined. It was already clear to you that afternoon of the 29th, the way it was collapsing. Every stock was falling. The Great Crash had come.

"Oh," your boss told you, "This is just a temporary correction. Listen to the president. He says prosperity's just around the corner and, you know, Mr. Hoover's the best educated, best financial mind ever to be president of our country. Look at what some of the big banking houses are saying. The market's going to turn around and our productivity's going to increase. I promise everybody they're going to keep their job." Then, three months later, you go and there in your mailbox is your paycheck with a pink slip— the last check you're going to get. The company where you've worked so long, that has been such an important part of the community, is bankrupt. There's nobody to buy the goods. The goods pile up on the shelves—the refrigerators, automobiles, and radios. All of these that have been produced in such huge quantities are now there on the shelves.

The farmers—there's nobody to buy their crops. You're worried about feeding your children now without a job. Farmers in Georgia are dumping their milk on the ground because there's nowhere to sell it. The very means of communication that Adam Smith had written so glowingly about had broken down. Then the bills began to come in. You owe two months on the radio, three months on the car, and four months on your mortgage. You go down to your old pal who served in the Argonne with you and he's not there. He's lost his job. The bank itself is in serious trouble. We want your mortgage paid or we're going to foreclose at the end of this month. They show up in front of your house. The neighbors watch your humiliation as they drive your Ford car away, carry away your radio, and carry away your refrigerator. Your wife says, "I don't have enough money to buy groceries for this week." "Well, cut back on some of the expenses." "I have cut as far as we can go." Then they take your home. Mom and dad, despite all of his careful financing, they are in very serious economic trouble.

One of your children must be sent to live with your sister and another with your wife's sister. You can't even take care of them. After a while of this, you join millions of other Americans, men and women, and you just say, "I've had it." You leave. You take to the road. You ride the rails. In town after town, you see these signs—"Keep moving brother, we can't take care of our own." The very poorly organized and underfunded systems of local charity had failed entirely. Doctors are bankrupt. They can't give you medical care. They don't have the money even to keep their offices going. Bread lines—did you think when you were fighting in the Argonne that you'd see Americans lined up to get a bowl of thin soup and a couple of slices of bread? Is that what you had fought the war for? Is that what democracy was about? Why had this come about? Why had this come about?

One is speculation. A stock is a speculation. It is not an investment. It is pure speculation. It is worth nothing in and of itself. It is worth only what somebody wants to pay you for it. There must also be a buyer for the stock you have. People had simply forgotten that—as they forgot it in more recent times. It does not go up 10 percent on a regular basis. It is not a CD that pays you 6 percent and is guaranteed. It is a piece of paper. It is speculation and the whole country went wild with speculation in the 1920s.

There was weak federal regulation of the market and weak monetary policies. It was the great age of the free market economy, the gospel of Calvin Coolidge and President Hoover. Keep the government out of regulating the market, and money supply was easy. It was easy credit. You thought it was easy credit so you thought you could buy your house. It was easy credit so the big banks could leverage and borrow.

Third is margin buying. The federal government had the right, under the Constitution, to regulate commerce. It could regulate the amount of money required to buy on the margin or completely rule out margin buying. That is what wiped out so many Americans—when their brokerage firms called in their margins. They said, you have borrowed 50 percent of what you used to buy that stock. Instead of it going up, it has plunged. You sell that stock at a terrible loss and you can't pay that margin. Therefore, you're bankrupt.

Then there were the new financial instruments. Above all, there was the investment trust. It is the father of the mutual fund, ideally suited to the mentality of the 1920s. This was, I don't know enough about stocks and I really don't have enough money to buy even 500 shares of GE, and why put all my eggs in that one basket? But, you've got a friendly stockbroker. He explains, "Well, you don't need to do that anymore, that's old fashioned. People like you and me, brother, you know, what we do is buy a mutual fund, an investment trust. There we've got the smartest financial minds in the world and they buy a number of different stocks." "Well, do I own that GE stock?" "Well, no, no, you own stock in the investment trust, but believe me, those have been going up 10, 15, 20 percent a year. They make all the decisions so if, you know, GE is a hot stock, they'll buy that. And you know, maybe if bonds are a good idea, they'll buy that, but they'll do all the work for you." "But, how much is that financial instrument, this investment trust worth?" "Well, it's just like a stock." "Okay." "Yeah, yeah, put it on a sort of regular basis and you'll be amazed at how rapid it grows."

Of course, there was that expert advice. The financial instruments were so complicated that only a genius—you know, one of these young dynamos with fire in his or her belly and a number cruncher—they understood it all. You didn't need to. Nor did you need to worry much about this because everybody was a profit of wealth. Professor Fisher at Yale told you that we had reached a new plateau of ever greater wealth. The *Ladies Home Journal* carried an article by Jacob Raskob, a very well known financial expert, who said everybody can be rich. All you have to do is invest $15 a month in stocks, take the dividends, and reinvest them. You'll be a millionaire. Leverage, everybody was using leverage. The big banks were merging with one another, making use of borrowed money. You were using leverage too. You were using borrowed money on margin to buy stocks and you were buying on the installment plan. That was a leverage as well.

What surely should have worried you—as it did real financial experts like Joseph Kennedy—is when everybody started talking about the market. You went to a cocktail party and that's all they talked about was the market. You walked through a museum and even the guards were talking about the stock market. Joseph Kennedy one morning sat down to have his shoes shined and the man shining them said, "What do you think about GE as an investment?" The anecdote is that Kennedy went back to his office, called his broker, and said, "Sell everything."

Stocks had ceased in any way to be related to the profitability of the companies. The stocks were soaring for a company that was barely established. Then there were the serious scandals. The most elevated of the financial and business community, well respected CEOs, turned out to be crooks who had embezzled from their companies. There was a global economy. While that might be a factor for strength, it also meant once the collapse had begun, it struck the entire planet. Then the very speed of communication allowed the panic to set in that set off the spiral of the stock market collapse.

One of the greatest economists of the 20th century, John Kenneth Galbraith, said that all it takes for another disaster to happen is for all those who experienced the earlier disaster to have died off. If you think about it, there is hardly anyone alive today who was about 21 or 22 or 23 years of age—old enough to really understand what was happening—when the Great Collapse of 1929 came. It was a collapse that mirrors in a frightening, but informative way, our own economic situation right now.

Hitler Becomes Chancellor of Germany (1933)
Lecture 30

> **Bank notes in the billions became commonplace for buying food. The savings of millions of thrifty, middle-class Germans were wiped out forever. Small businesses were wiped out, and unemployment began to stalk the land again. Hitler thought that in this desperate economic situation, the democratic country of Germany … could be overthrown by a military takeover.**

Adolf Hitler is, arguably, the single most evil figure in history, rivaled only, perhaps, by Joseph Stalin and Mao Zedong. He was inaugurated legally and constitutionally as Germany's answer to the Depression, just as Franklin Roosevelt was inaugurated in the United States in the same year.

Hitler was born on April 20, 1889, in Austria, to middle-class German parents. He had little interest in school and dropped out as a teenager. As a young man, he drifted to Vienna, where he lived in a shelter and spent his time reading and painting. From that time, he developed a profound anti-Semitism.

Hitler was not alone in his hatred of the Jewish people in the German world of the late 19th and early 20th centuries. Professors at the University of Vienna and elsewhere taught that the Germans were among the favored races and that the German people must be purified by the removal of other races. Hitler also became a fervent German nationalist; he moved to Munich and was living there at the outbreak of World War I. He served bravely in the German army and was energized by the experience of war.

In the spring of 1918, it seemed as though Germany was on the verge of victory. But in November of that year, Hitler was in the hospital recovering from a gas attack when he learned that the Germans had lost. When the German soldiers returned, the myth emerged that the victorious army had been stabbed in the back by Jewish socialist politicians. The Treaty of Versailles stripped away large portions of German territory, saddled the nation with huge reparations, and forced the Germans to admit their guilt in the war. The nation was crushed and humiliated. In that atmosphere, Hitler began his rise to power.

Hitler joined the National German Socialist Workers Party, which had a simple message: All the troubles of Germany are the fault of the Jewish people. Hitler believed deeply in the principles of this party and sought to reorganize it under one leader—the Führer. As the party spread its message, Hitler discovered he had a gift for speaking. By 1923, he believed that the devastating inflation in Germany had paved the way for a military takeover by the Nazi Party. But the party's attempt failed, and Hitler was imprisoned.

Adolf Hitler (1889–1945).

After his release, Hitler returned to the Nazi Party, which had grown into one of the most powerful forces in Germany. The politics of the Weimar Republic was marked by savage partisan infighting and the repeated collapse of the government. The public became convinced that the politicians were scoundrels who would bring Germany to ruin.

Germany had begun a bit of an economic recovery when the Depression struck in 1929. In its aftermath, 30 percent of the German nation was unemployed, and the government took no steps to address the problem. Bloody street fighting broke out between German communists and Nazis. When the situation reached a crisis point, influential business and financial interests decided to step in to prevent a Bolshevik revolution. Hitler convinced these men that his main concern was the preservation of capitalism in Germany, and money and recruits started rolling in to the Nazi Party. Soon, men of all levels of society in Germany were marching side by side into the future, marching toward the election of the Führer, Adolf Hitler. ■

Bullock, *Hitler and Stalin*.

Goldhagen, *Hitler's Willing Executioners*.

Questions to Consider

1. Winston Churchill called World War II the "unnecessary war." What did he mean, and do you agree?

2. Do you agree that Hitler was only made possible by democracy?

Hitler Becomes Chancellor of Germany (1933)
Lecture 30—Transcript

Our theme in this lecture is Adolf Hitler and his inauguration as chancellor of Germany under the Constitution of the German democracy on January 30th, 1933. If you would ask a German celebrating the 50th birthday of Hitler, in 1939—six years after this event—what was the way in which Hitler had changed history? The German would have told you that he brought Germany out of the Depression, he gave work to all Germans, he made our factories some of the most productive in the world, he restored the honor of Germany among nations, and he made Germany a superpower once again. How tragically wrong—for we understand Hitler for what he is. His real role in changing history was to unleash of his own single accord the most destructive war in history, to have upon his hands the blood of 50 million dead, to have perverted the ideals of Charles Darwin so that he killed 6 million people just for being who they were.

He is the most evil single figure in history it can be argued. The only rivals he has for that dubious distinction would be Joseph Stalin and Mao Zedong. He was inaugurated legally and constitutionally as Germany's answer to the Depression. Just as in this country, when Franklin Roosevelt was inaugurated in that same year, Hitler was inaugurated in the depths of a depression that had 30 percent of the German working force unemployed. Within a matter of months, the unemployment problem was solved.

What had brought Hitler to this moment of destiny, as he saw it? He was a strong believer that he had been called by providence to save the German nation. He was, when he was inaugurated, a 43 year old high school dropout. He had been born on the 20th of April in 1889 in Austria, part of the Austro-Hungarian empire of that day. Sometimes people try to tell you Hitler was an Austrian and therefore wasn't a German—that's not how they thought. The German speaking citizens of the Austro-Hungarian empire were some of the most fervent believers in pan-Germanic nationality. They longed for Germany to be united—Austria, as well as the rest of Germany, into one great nation. Many of them were convinced of the superiority of the German race, as they called it. He spoke German as his mother tongue and was thought of by Germans, as well as by himself, as a German.

His father was an older man who had retired. He had gone about as far as anyone could with considerable talents, but not education, in the Austrian civil service. He was a bureaucrat. He had retired on a reasonable pension, and spent most of his time raising honeybees. Hitler's mother, who was much younger than the father, doted on little Wolfie—that was what she called him—just the way Stalin's mother doted on him. Hitler was a loving son. Later on, when his mother was suffering from cancer, Hitler took the most tender care of his mother. She wanted him to be well educated. He was bright enough. You see school photographs of him, but they are already marked by a kind of defiance. That is what his teachers wrote back again and again on his report card—the boy seems to have some intelligence, but not nearly as much as he thinks he does, and he is utterly without discipline. He will amount to nothing unless he buckles down in school.

When he was 16, Hitler came to his mother and said, "Mom, I want to be an artist." He showed her some of his drawings. She said, "Well, what you really need to do is finish school, get your high school diploma." In those days, in Germany, that was fairly close to at least two years of an American college. "Get your diploma and then when I've saved enough money, I will send you to art school, even in Vienna if that's where you want to go." "I don't want to stay in school anymore." Later on in life, Hitler would say, show me a person with a 4.0 GPA and in 10 years, I will show you a failure. Learning in school and making good grades is worthless. All our teachers wanted to do was to turn us into stuffed up examples of themselves, make them into paradigms for us when, in fact, they were just fools filled with useless knowledge.

He dropped out of school. His mother paid for him to go to Vienna, and he showed some of his watercolors. We can still see those watercolors today. They have historical interest, but they are not badly done. They have a good use of color, good understanding of light, good sense of proportion and composition. But, he got very bad letters of recommendation from his teachers at his high school. He did not have a diploma. His work most certainly was not outstanding, and he had no connections. Therefore, he was turned down on more than one occasion from the art school in Vienna.

He drifted there, in Vienna, to a kind of homeless existence. He lived in a shelter. He spent a lot of his time reading and spent some time painting and drawing. With a friend, he would sell some of these watercolors to make a little bit of money. But, above all, he studied and he thought. From these early days, he developed a profound anti-Semitism. It is one of the good things about America that we cannot understand this anti-Semitism. It is a baseless hatred that has caused some of the most evil events in history. We talked about it with the Bubonic plague and the pogroms, the slaughters that were launched of Jewish people.

Lenin addressed it when he said there is no more baseless evil than the hatred of the Jewish people and declared anti-Semitism to be a deviation from party discipline punished by death. Hitler was not alone there in Vienna or indeed in the whole German world of the late 19th and early 20th century in his anti-Semitism. Some of the most influential minds taught anti-Semitism. In the seminars of the University of Vienna, professors taught that the Jewish people were a totally different race from the German people and that all that was good in human history was due to the genius of the German people. Biologists taught that Germany was one of the favored races and that it must be made pure by removing any other races like the Jewish people. Hitler became a convinced anti-Semite, a hater of the Jewish people, and it determined his entire life. As Führer of Germany, it determined his disastrous foreign policy and led the German people into a shame that will endure as long as history is studied.

He became an anti-Semite and a fervent German nationalist. He hated the Austro-Hungarian empire where he had grown up. It was a multicultural diverse empire. He wanted to go where there were only Germans, so he went to Munich. He was living in Munich in August of 1914 when war was declared—war upon Russia, war upon France, and war upon Belgium. A photographer, just by chance, was taking a series of shots of the crowd that had gathered to hear the proclamation of war and there's a shabby looking little man tossing his hat up into the air. It is Adolf Hitler. As he would later write, "That was the liberation of my soul." He loved the Great War.

For many men, unfortunately, World War II or World War I, was the high point of their life. You have to understand it. You had a howling set of children, a wife who nagged you all the time, a boss who picked upon you, and then you were in the war. All of that was gone. All you had to focus on was living from day to day. Hitler was no longer an anonymous figure living in a homeless shelter, scrabbling for money, and wearing shabby overcoats. He was a soldier and he loved the comradeship of the trenches. He loved the sting of battle. He volunteered for the most dangerous of all assignments, a runner. After all, in those days, officers couldn't text message and say, the French are breaking through on our left flank. They had to send runners. Such was the shelling and the machine guns that you might send out 10 runners to carry one message and one messenger would get through; all the rest would be killed.

Hitler would hop from shell hole to shell hole to shell hole, and then deliver the message. He won the Iron Cross, Germany's high decoration for valor. He won it honestly and wore it proudly to the last day of his life. He thought German was going to win the war. In the spring of 1918, it seemed as though Germany was on the verge of victory. German troops were closing in upon Paris, Russia had been knocked out of the war, Italy had almost been knocked out of the war, and the French army had mutinied. Then, suddenly, on November 11th, 1918, Hitler was in a hospital. He had been blinded in a gas attack. The parson came in, the chaplain, and said, "Boys, it's all over. It's all over. We lost." How could we have lost? We were betrayed. The kaiser has been driven into exile.

A group of Jewish politicians, socialists, have taken over the government. They've signed an armistice. Our forces were still victorious in the field. Hitler recovered his sight and came back to a broken Germany. But, it was a Germany that saw its army march back under their own flags—never really defeated the Germans said. The myth grew up that the victorious army had been stabbed in the back by Jewish socialist politicians. The German army was reduced to 100,000 men. The Treaty of Versailles weighed heavily on

Germany, stripping away large portions of what had been German territory and above all, saddling Germany with huge reparations and making the Germans sign a statement that they were guilty of the war. Germany was crushed and humiliated. In that atmosphere, Hitler began his rise to power.

He found the little National Socialist German Workers Party. It had only seven members when he joined, but it taught what he believed in. It had a very simple and evil message—all of the troubles of Germany are due to the Jewish people. Germany must drive out all Jewish people. They are the cause for financial hardship and political disaster. That was what it taught over and over again. The communists are our other great enemy, but the Jews are responsible for communism, this evil doctrine said. Hitler found this to be a party with principles that he believed deeply in, but it was badly organized. He began to organize it under the Führer principle—one absolute leader.

He found that he had a gift for speaking. The first time he went before a crowd, the other much better educated members of the party said, "Do you really think you should give the speech?" They generally spoke in beer halls. "Do you think you should give the speech? You know, you don't have a high school diploma." Hitler said, "You watch me." He describes how he would feel out the crowd—start of slowly, sense their temper, sense what they wanted to hear, and then began to build upon that, keeping very careful eye contact with his audience, and building them into a crescendo until they could not have told you exactly what he said, but it was the force and vigor. Then he said, "Say the same thing over and over again. Do not give people complicated answers for why the economy is bad. The economy is bad because of the Jewish people. Do not give the audience a complicated discussion of foreign affairs. Our only foreign affair is to drive out the Jewish people, bring back Germany, and crush the French. Say it over and over again." "In fact," Hitler said, "You know, if you're going to tell a lie, tell a big lie and tell it enough times and people believe it's the truth."

He was not a cynical, manipulative politician. He believed—that's the tragedy—what he said. He misjudged in 1923. He thought Germany had been made ready for a takeover by the Nazi Party. There had been brought about by the financial debt of Germany its huge trade imbalance—something worth remembering—and devastating inflation. Those early years of the '20s, the German mark dropped to almost nothing. You were an ordinary middle class person—you had a job, you would be paid your salary at 8 o'clock in the morning, and you would be given an hour to rush out and buy bread. You would be paid again at noon. You would rush out and find that the price of bread had gone up 10 times in that morning. Then, you'd be paid in the afternoon and rush out and find that bread had gone up 10 more times. Bank notes in the billions became commonplace for buying food. The savings of millions of thrifty middle class Germans were wiped out forever. Small businesses were wiped out, and unemployment began to stalk the land again.

Hitler thought that in this desperate economic situation the democratic country of Germany—the democratic constitution established at the end of World War I, the Weimar Constitution as it was called—could be overthrown by a military takeover. But, it failed and Hitler was brought into court. Everyone expected him to plea bargain, that's what the judge did. Instead, Hitler got up and said, "I plead guilty. I don't plead guilty just to leading an armed mob, I plead guilty to wanting to overthrow this government. In fact, I will overthrow this government and men like you," pointing to the judge, he said, "your heads will roll when we take power. You are but the symbol of the degradation of Germany." The crowds in the courtroom went wild. Crowds mobbed him when he came out. He was sent to jail, but it was a vacation. He went around in these little short leather pants. Ladies loved him. They found him so handsome. In fact, Hitler said he didn't marry until, of course, the very end of his life, because it was like a movie star marrying—it would make the ladies have a little less attraction to him. They sent him flowers, they sent him candy.

He always had a sweet tooth. Early on, he became a vegetarian. He could not imagine doing any harm to an animal. He loved dogs. He was a vegetarian, did not drink at all, did not smoke. In fact, Winston Churchill once said, "I believe that most of the world's troubles are caused by food fattest [ph]— vegetarians, potato eaters, nonsmokers. I have it on good authority that Adolf Hitler is a vegetarian, that he does not drink, that he abhors smoking, I rest my case." He's a vegetarian and has a sweet tooth. He likes his coffee or tea in the afternoon with whipped cream on a nice piece of cake. He writes his book. What is his book entitled that he writes there in prison? *Mein Kampf*— my struggle. That is not a coincidence. That is a struggle for the survival of the fittest. It is his struggle, struggling for Germany, as he said in one of the subtitles, against lies, treason, and cowardice—my struggle. He profoundly believed in the teachings of Darwin. There was a limited space and Germany must rule it.

He left prison and took back up the work of organization. By the late 1920s, his Nazi Party had grown into one of the most powerful forces in Germany. You must understand that Germany had a parliamentary democracy after World War I. That is, I think, a terrible form of government. It is one in which you do not elect a president on a regular basis to be the chief executive. Our president is the chief executive of our country. He is elected on a regular, four-year basis. He is elected entirely apart from the congressional delegates, representatives. In a parliamentary democracy, the president is a high figure. He doesn't handle the executive business; he's almost entirely a ceremonial official.

In Germany, the main power of the president was to appoint, with advice, the chancellor. The chancellor was like the British prime minister. The chancellor or the prime minister represents the will of Parliament. When an election is held, the party that has the largest number of seats wins the largest number in parliament. They then choose the prime minister to represent its party. When the conservatives have a majority in the House of Parliament, they choose a conservative prime minister. He serves at their pleasure. If they decide to withdraw their support, they can. In governments like the German of the Weimar Republic, there are so many political parties that almost no party ever wins a clear majority. In order to appoint a chancellor, there has to be coalitions. These coalitions are marked by savage partisan infighting and they collapse—so the government collapses. That is what kept happening all through the '20s, right on up through 1933. Government after government collapsed. The public became convinced that the politicians were scoundrels who were using their partisan politics to bring Germany to ruin.

Germany had begun a bit of an economic recovery from the disastrous inflation when in 1929, the Depression struck. Germany was very heavily dependent upon foreign exports, a lot of exports to the United States. When America was no longer able to buy those German products, the Depression turned into severe unemployment. Thirty percent of the German nation was out of work. Families were committing suicide all together because they had grown so hopeless. The government was undertaking no steps whatsoever to deal with this depression. There was partisan politics. There were fights, bloody, murderous fights, on a daily basis throughout Germany between the communists who wanted a communist revolution and the Nazis who hated the communists, but wanted state socialism in Germany and wanted to see Hitler as leader of this Germany. There were fights, chaos, unemployment, and politicians doing nothing whatsoever about it—except holding endless debates while wearing fancy clothes.

The situation reached such a crisis point that very wealthy influential German business and financial interests decided they had to step in. I mean people like the Krupps, the armament manufacturers, the Thiessen family, chemical factories, and others. They decided they had to step in to prevent a Bolshevik revolution. After all, that had happened in Russia in 1917. It seemed to be very likely that the communists would seize power in Germany, put in place the same relentless terror system Lenin had used, break all opposition, take over all private property, and bash the heads of these capitalists in. But, there was one bulwark—the Nazi Party. They hate the communists, they have a very strong public following, and they have an enormously effective leader.

"Adolf Hitler? Why, he doesn't even have a college education." "That's not what we're concerned about." "I know, but have you read his book?" "No, I haven't read his book." "I mean, he talks about terrible things in there. He's going to start another world war, he is going to exterminate the Jewish people." "No politician means what he says, don't you understand that? That's just for public consumption. Let's meet with him."

They do meet with him and they're impressed with him. "Why, he's a very reasonable sounding man." He dresses well, he speaks good German. They invite him to their homes for supper and their wives are much taken with him. He clicks his heel in the German fashion, kisses their hand, brings them just the right color of roses, and speaks quietly.

"Gentlemen, my main concern is the preservation of capitalism in Germany." "It is?" "Yes, of course, I have to say some fairly strong things to get through to the public, but that is my goal—to bring economic stability to Germany, to see that you turn a good profit and to see that the German worker has a good wage with which to buy the products you produce. Oh, I believe so strongly in the system of capitalism." "What about another war?" "No, Germany will gain all that it needs by peaceful means, by negotiation. Germany will retake its place in the world, and I tell you, Heir Krupp, that one of my first goals will be to build more weapons making use of your Krupp factories. I will rebuild the Germany army." "You will rebuild the army?" "Yes, yes I will. Oh, all those guns, oh more than that, tanks, airplanes—a whole depression ended by rebuilding German strength." "Good night, Heir Hitler, I am so pleased we got together."

"Oh, darling, he is such a handsome man, so dynamic, so well spoken. I hope you and your friends will give money to his political party." Sure enough, the Nazis needed funding. In fact, they developed one of the first real campaign machines to raise money for their political activities. They had a whole set of donors. You could be a benefactor, you could be a friend of the Führer—all of these. The money began to roll in and the recruits began to join up.

You were out of work. You had a high school diploma and had graduated from college, but you could not get a job in this Germany of 1930, in this depression. One of your friends said, "Have you thought about joining the Sturmabteilung, the SA, the storm troopers?" "Oh, I don't know what my mom would say about that. Don't they get into a lot of fights?" "Sure, but that's fun, you know, bashing in communists' heads, yeah? Look at my uniform." "Wow, that's swell." "And you have a job. They pay you and they pay you a pretty good salary."

You go home and mom and dad say, "That's a great idea. They're restoring the honor of Germany and I'm listening to this Hitler. He's going to not only get us jobs back, he's going to restore our bank accounts." You get your uniform and grandmother thinks you look handsome too—brown jacket, dark pants, big high boots, brown shirt, snappy little black tie, and your red armband with a swastika in black on a white background. You take to the streets and there's comradeship again. Men of all levels of society in Germany are marching side by side, marching into the future, marching towards the election of your Führer, Adolf Hitler.

[GERMAN SINGING] *The steady step, our ranks tightly joined together, the SA marches forward in firm resolute step.* [GERMAN SINGING] *We will march forward even if everything falls to pieces for Germany is ours today and tomorrow, the whole world.*

Franklin Roosevelt Becomes President (1933)
Lecture 31

Whenever I talk about Roosevelt, ... I will find people who just launch into a savage tirade against Franklin Roosevelt. Therefore, he must have been a very great man to have people still hate him after all of these years. Of course, there are those who still love him. There are many who grew up in the 1930s, '40s, and '50s who remember their parents having a picture of Franklin Roosevelt on the wall of their home.

As we saw in the last lecture, the stock market crash and ensuing Depression left families across America without jobs and without hope. The inauguration of Franklin Roosevelt as president and his immediate actions on assuming office restored confidence to millions of Americans. Some believe that the first weeks of Roosevelt's presidency saved capitalism in the United States and averted a social revolution. More than that, many of the programs he instituted are still fundamental to U.S. political and social order today.

Roosevelt was born into affluence and attended excellent schools, although he was not an outstanding student. After receiving his law degree, he became undersecretary of the Navy in the Wilson administration. Like his cousin Theodore and President Wilson, Franklin Roosevelt believed deeply in the ideals of a progressive form of democracy. At the height of his vigor, he was struck with polio and became permanently disabled. During his convalescence in Warm Springs, Georgia, Roosevelt was confronted with the grinding poverty of many Americans. He decided to return to politics and was elected governor of New York in 1928.

Herbert Hoover had been elected to the presidency by a landslide before the Depression but failed his country utterly after the disaster of the stock market crash. He would be the candidate of the Republican Party again in 1932. Among the potential candidates for the Democrats was Huey Long, the governor of Louisiana, who ran his state on a very progressive platform and seemed to advocate a form of national socialism. When the election came, the American people voted overwhelmingly for Roosevelt.

On the day of his inauguration, Roosevelt made his way to the podium and began his speech: "This is a day of national consecration." Just as Abraham Lincoln had done in his Gettysburg Address, Roosevelt told the nation that we must dedicate ourselves to a great unfinished task. Then, assuring the people that he would speak only the truth, Roosevelt promised that the country would revive and prosper. The new president said, "The only thing we have to fear is fear itself"—unreasoning fear, unjustified fear, fear that would turn every attempt at needed reforms into a retreat. Those words reached into the hearts of Depression-era Americans.

> **On the day of his inauguration, Roosevelt made his way to the podium and began his speech: "This is a day of national consecration."**

Throughout his inaugural address, Roosevelt reminded Americans that, as long as our morals and values remained intact, we would triumph. He laid the blame for the Depression on the nation's business and financial leaders, whose values were self-seeking. The time had come to drive out the moneychangers from the "temple of our civilization" and rebuild it on enduring moral values. Roosevelt further said that all the misery Americans had experienced would be worthwhile if we learned from it certain lessons: that our mission in life is not just to take care of ourselves but to take care of others; that high positions in business and government are not simply a matter of enriching oneself, but they are a public trust and an obligation.

Roosevelt closed his speech with the promise of action, vowing to introduce a series of proposals to Congress that would put people to work and to reevaluate the forms and amounts of charitable assistance the government could provide. All this, he said, would take place under America's traditional form of government—democracy. ■

Hoover, Herbert (1874–1964): President of the United States (1929–1933). Hoover, who was elected during a period of enormous prosperity, was one of the best educated and most successful men to become president.

Suggested Reading

Alter, *The Defining Moment*.

Roosevelt, "First Inaugural Address," in Safire, *Lend Me Your Ears*.

Questions to Consider

1. Who do you think is America greatest president?

2. Is it true that Hitler appealed to all that was worst in his nation and Roosevelt appealed to all that was best in his nation?

Franklin Roosevelt Becomes President (1933)
Lecture 31—Transcript

The theme for our lecture is Franklin Roosevelt, his first inaugural address and the New Deal that he brought to the United States in the midst of a Great Depression. It is a part of a series of lectures that we are giving. We began with the Great Depression and the rise of Adolf Hitler. We will continue through Franklin Roosevelt, the development of the atomic bomb, Mao Zedong and his long march and transformation of China, and John Kennedy and his assassination. All of these lectures have, as their theme, the transformation of history by the Great Depression, World War II, and the Cold War—events that are still with us today, that resonate with us today. I am convinced they will resonate on through the 21st century. There is the unresolved question of the role of Russia, the unresolved question of the role of the European Union, the unresolved question of the power of China, and yes, what is the course that the United States will trace in the 21st century?

To understand that, go back with me to March 4th, 1933. It is a grey, drizzly, and cold day. It is the day that will mark the inauguration of Franklin Roosevelt. Do you remember we talked about you last time—how you had been prosperous in the '20s and suddenly the Great Stock Market Crash took away all your investments? The Depression took away your job and your inability to respond to it. Your sense of helplessness took away your family. You're one of those huddled around a radio somewhere in this vast land listening to this president and wondering, will he be any different than the last president?

He will. He will change history. His inaugural address will restore confidence to you and millions of ordinary Americans like you. But, it is not just his speech; it is the action he takes immediately upon assuming the presidency. You may not agree with every one of these policies, but the government is doing something. You have a president in high office who cares. You believe he cares and he wants to help you. More than that, these policies will continue to shape America—policies like social security are still fundamental to our political and social order today.

There are those who say that the first months of Roosevelt's presidency—in fact, the first week of his presidency—saved capitalism in this country and averted a social revolution. His programs, his image of what makes a great caring president, still shape us today. It amazes me, I have to tell you, whenever I talk about Roosevelt, the feelings he still arouses—above all, feelings of hatred. I will find people who just launch into a savage tirade against Franklin Roosevelt. Therefore, he must have been a very great man to have people still hate him after all of these years. Of course, there are those who still love him. There are many who grew up in the 1930s, '40s, and '50s who remember their parents having a picture of Franklin Roosevelt on the wall of their home.

Franklin Roosevelt and his first inaugural address—who is this man who has come to this moment in destiny, a moment in destiny that will change history? He was born to wealth and affluence. In fact, he was a cousin, somewhat distant, of Theodore Roosevelt. Both came from families that were from New York, had a very great deal of money, and were very, very successful in business. It is interesting that, coming from successful business families, neither Franklin Roosevelt nor his cousin Theodore ever had particular awe before businessmen. They knew businessmen were human, mortal, and very much interested in their own wellbeing.

He went to excellent schools. He went to Groton. He was an athletic young man. He then went to Harvard. He was not an outstanding student at Harvard. In fact, he wanted to go to the inauguration of his cousin Theodore, his inauguration as president. In those days—amazingly enough—for an undergraduate to miss one class, they had to get the personal permission of the president of Harvard University. Roosevelt wrote and said, "Can I go see my cousin's inauguration? I will miss two classes." The president of Harvard wrote back and said, "Judging from your record, you don't do much when you're in class, so I think it's perfectly fine if you go to the inauguration." He's not a brilliant scholar. He graduated, came back, and studied law at Columbia. That was very traditional in his family—to get a degree from Harvard and then a law degree from Columbia so you could be practicing at the bar in New York.

The two sides of the family did not get along very well. Franklin Roosevelt one said, "The only thing that cousin Theodore's family and I agree upon is how not to pronounce our name. Theodore calls himself Roosevelt and I call myself Roosevelt." In point of fact, young Franklin admired his cousin, his bully pulpit that the President Theodore Roosevelt took for the presidency. Theodore Roosevelt was a strong and a progressive president. It was the ideal of Theodore Roosevelt to bring the government back into the hands of the ordinary Americans, to remove all the vested interests that had turned democracy into a charade. Theodore Roosevelt was for more and more democracy. In fact, Roosevelt believed in a referendum on decisions on the Supreme Court. He wanted a constitutional amendment in place so that, if the Supreme Court passed a decision that was unpopular with the people, they could then vote—state by state—and rescind the decision of the Supreme Court. Theodore Roosevelt believed in a strong army, a strong navy, walking softly, but carrying a big stick.

Young Franklin admired Theodore and he admired Woodrow Wilson. In fact, rather than pursuing the law, young Franklin went into government service. He was undersecretary of the Navy during Woodrow Wilson's time. Franklin attended the Versailles Treaty. He met Winston Churchill in those days right after World War I. He believed so deeply in the ideal of Woodrow Wilson, that a League of Nations would prevent another terrible war. Franklin grieved when the Senate rejected Woodrow Wilson's idealism, when the country turned its back on involvement in Europe, and when it seemed that America cared only about making money. Wilson himself died a broken man and a failed president.

Franklin continued on in politics. He seemed to have a very bright future ahead of him, teaching the ideals of Theodore Roosevelt and Woodrow Wilson, a progressive form of democracy. He was a member of the Democratic Party. Then, at the height of his vigor, he was struck down by that terrible disease, polio. We talked about that in our lecture on Louis Pasteur, how millions were in the grip of fear every year that they would be struck down by this disease. He had simply been out swimming with his family. He came home, complained of some cramps, and then the terrible diagnosis was given. He was disabled, disabled permanently, for life. He would never walk again in an unaided fashion without crutches and braces. He could have said, what a cruel blow life has given me. I've got a nice family, I've got a large income, I'm just going to sit around and feel sorry for myself. But, he didn't.

He convalesced at Warm Springs, Georgia. There he became acquainted, in a way he never had before, with the grinding poverty that existed all over our country. Right there in front of him, in Warm Springs, Georgia, was the grinding poverty of the African Americans, the grinding poverty of the poor whites. He was a man of enormous affluence. He asked the question in this land of affluence and prosperity, why do we have poverty?

He made his decision then to go back into politics. He had not had a distinguished record, at Harvard. He had not been a distinguished attorney. He was elected Governor of New York, but he wasn't a particularly distinguished governor of New York. Elected in 1928, one of his main achievements was to regulate a boundary dispute with Canada. But, there was nothing outstanding in his record. People could certainly ask, what has he actually done? The Great Depression came in 1929 and by 1932, as the presidential elections rolled around, a lot of people said nobody can solve this problem. The presidential nomination this year is worth nothing. Many Democrats said, it's probably best if we allow the Republicans to elect Herbert Hoover again and allow the Republicans to dominate Congress. That way, we can continue to blame them.

Herbert Hoover—what a failed president he turned out to be. He was, in fact, probably the best trained man ever to hold that office. He had gone to Stanford. He was a very practically minded man, and a good engineer. He had made a fortune in the mining business. Then, he had turned his services to helping the public. He had served with great distinction and success being in charge of war relief funds for the refugees and starving people in Belgium under German occupation. He was very highly thought of in Europe and brought the skills of an administrator, a practical business man, and a complete faith in the free market economy, laissez-faire economics. Business should have as little to do with the government and government should have as little to do with business as possible. Keep them separate. That was his philosophy.

He was right in step with the times, right in step with his predecessor Calvin Coolidge who had said, "The business of America is business."

But, Coolidge privately had doubts about Herbert Hoover. Coolidge could have won reelection, but he said, I choose not to run. When he was told that Hoover was going to be the candidate of the Republican Party, Calvin Coolidge said, "That man, Hoover, has been giving me unsolicited advice for the last six years—all of it bad." But, Hoover was elected in a landslide. Then came the Depression. "We can do nothing," said Hoover, his advisers, and his cabinet. "We can do nothing to intervene." The few things they did do, like put a new tariff in place, made things even worse. Hoover's main concession to public feeling during this time was to continue to serve seven course meals at the White House where everyone wore white tie and tails and were served by servants in white tie and tails. Hoover believed it would depress the American people if the president didn't live an appropriate lifestyle.

Veterans of World War I came to Washington and set up some shanty towns calling themselves the Bonus Army. They asked that Congress give them their bonus that they had been promised when they enlisted; give it back to them sooner. Hoover sent in troops under General Douglas MacArthur. He tore down their shanty houses, and even took bayonets and jabbed at them. That was his response.

Then, on the other side of the coin, there were men like Huey Long, almost dictator of the State of Louisiana, with his broad social plan. "We're going to soak the fat boys and spread it out thin." He had carried out a very progressive platform in Louisiana with healthcare for the ordinary citizen of Louisiana, building them the best hospitals in the world. Huey Long was proclaiming a form of national socialism. He even had state troopers following him around dressed like Mussolini's Blackshirts.

That was the cry—Huey Long or a Douglas MacArthur who believed in a right-wing tyranny as well. There were those who said, "You know, I've been to Russia, I've been to the Soviet Union. I have seen the future and it works. What we need here is communism. We need a complete abolition of private property and for the workers and farmers to seize the whole of the United States." Nowhere was the depression greater than on the farms—on farms, in the cities, there were millions without work and funds.

The election came. The American people spoke and gave their mandate for change in 1932 with that election. They voted Roosevelt in and they voted the Democrats in with a sweeping majority. They waited. They had to wait all the way from the November election to March, in those days, for the new president to take office. Hoover kept trying to get Roosevelt to work with him, to issue some joint statements, particularly the joint statement that Hoover was most fond of—the fundamentals of the economy are sound and prosperity is just around the corner. But, Roosevelt wouldn't cooperate with him at all and their ride to the inauguration was extremely chilly—and it wasn't just the weather.

Then, Franklin Roosevelt got up. In recent years, there's been a great deal of discussion about whether he tried to hide his disability. Every person in the audience, every person who listened to him, every person in America, knew he had polio. They knew he was, to use the language of those days, crippled. They knew he had to have help as he made his way to the podium—but he made his way to that podium. He would grip a podium so hard as he stood up, using it for support, that sometimes it would crack in his hands. The country knew he was disabled. The country knew he was disabled just the way the country was disabled. Yet, they also knew that he had come back. He had the courage. He had this marvelous gift, this wealthy New Yorker from Harvard and Columbia, of making everyone that cared about him believe that he cared about them. The poorest farmer in a general store in Alabama, the out of work machinist in Detroit, Michigan—all of these listened to these words.

"This is a day of national consecration." As I tell you about Roosevelt's speech, I will adapt it, paraphrase it, and even change it some to suit our circumstances of today. "This is a day of national consecration." Just like the Gettysburg Address of Lincoln, he tells our country that we must consecrate ourself to the great unfinished task that lies before us.

"On this day of my inauguration into the presidency, I am certain that the American people want me to speak to them with all the frankness and candor that our situation impels us to. This is preeminently a time for speaking the truth, the whole truth, boldly. This great nation will endure as it has endured. This great nation will revive. This great nation will prosper. Therefore, let me state my firm conviction that the only thing we have to fear is fear itself. Unreasoning fear, unjustified fear, fear that turns every attempt at needed reforms into a retreat."

"All we have to fear is fear itself." You think of it is a cliché today, but it wasn't then, and it struck your heart. That's what had been wrong all along. You were just terrified. You didn't understand what was happening, nobody seemed to understand the depression. Why had there been plenty of money and plenty of jobs in the summer of 1929 and why had they vanished entirely? You were just afraid that it would never get any better and that fear had gripped you so much that you had quit trying.

"All we have to fear is fear itself. But, at every one of the darkest moments of our country's history, our people have responded to firm, decisive, confident leadership and given the support that is necessary if leadership is to be successful. And I am confident that you will give me that support in the days to come. In this spirit then, we look at the problems that face us. They are grave, but thank God," said Roosevelt, "they concern only material things."

Throughout this inaugural address, he will remind you again and again that, as long as our American moral and values—as long as our American political values—remain intact, we will triumph. "Thank God that they concern only material things, but the problems are severe. Values have sunk to fantastic levels." Roosevelt was enough of a Harvard man to use fantastic properly. "Values have sunk to fantastic levels." That doesn't mean, oh, wow, fantastic, man. No, it meant you could not have ever believed in the summer of 1929 how far stocks had fallen.

"Our banks are shut down all through this country." Indeed, there were almost no functioning banks anywhere in the 48 states when he was inaugurated. "The goods of the farmer lie rotting in the field while people in the city do not have food to feed their children. Foreclosures of homes and farms throughout this country destroy families and their hope of the future. Millions of Americans have seen their savings of a lifetime disappear. Millions of Americans are without work and millions of others toil without adequate recompense. Why? We have not been struck by a plague of locusts. This is not a natural disaster. This is still a land of plenty, a land of tremendous natural resources and wealth. But the wealth lies expiring at our doorstep. No, this depression is the result of the failure of the leaders of the exchanges of the goods of mankind. It is the result of the failure of our business and financial leaders. They have admitted their failure. They have abandoned their trust. Oh, they've offered some solutions always in the old worn out mode. We've lost all of your money so loan us more, bail us out, that is what they say. Well, they knew these business and financial leaders, only the values of a generation of self-seekers. They had no vision and when there is no vision, the people perish. We will drive the moneychangers from the high temple of our civilization and we will rebuild it on enduring moral values. We will put an end to people speculating with other people's money.

My dear friends, this trying time will be worth all the misery it has caused us if from it we learn once again that it is our mission in life not to just take care of ourselves, but to take care of others. If we learn that work in and of itself is a joy, that high positions in business and in government are not simply a matter of enriching yourself or of pride—they are a public trust, they are an obligation, they are responsibility—and each and every one of us should not look first to what our salaries are, how much money are we making, but rather to the joy of work, to do a good day's job because someone has entrusted you to do that job. But, our recovery from this depression is not just a matter of ethics, it is a matter of action and action now.

And that is what the American people want, is action now. So I will put in place immediately a series of proposals to Congress to put people back to work. Now let me tell you, this is a global situation, it is a global economy, but we're going to look to America. We cannot fix the world. This is an American problem and we will fix it as Americans. We will be good neighbors to anyone who wants to be our neighbor, but we are going to look to America." He did not go globetrotting around the world trying to solve the problems of the world.

"We can put people to work by drafting them in the same way we did during the Great War. We will setup a corps of men giving them work, using the resources of our nation to build bridges, parks, to build sidewalks and streets, monuments that will endure, monuments that will give work to millions, good solid hard work. And we will mobilize immediately the systems of communication, the railroads, everywhere the government can act properly. We will organize; reevaluate the cost of government and the charities that government can provide. We will take action and the action we will take can be done under our traditional form of government." Here he speaks of democracy.

"The constitution given to us by our founders is such a flexible instrument, the best ever devised, that we can solve this with our traditional balance between the executive and the legislative branch. But let me tell you this, I will send my proposals to Congress. I will expect Congress to send me proposals. But if Congress does not act upon my proposals, and if Congress does not send me suitable proposals immediately, then I am prepared, under the Constitution, to ask for executive powers as broad and sweeping as if we were invaded by a foreign foe for we are at war with this depression.

So Americans, we march forward in the warm glow of national unity. We march forward in the clear consciousness that we are restoring old and sacred values. We march forward in the clean satisfaction of every American doing his duty. Democracy has not failed. The American people have not failed. They have gone to the polls and they have registered mandate for change, and I am the present instrument of their will. On this day of national consecration, each and every one of us must ask the blessing of God upon our nation. May he protect each and every one of you and may God guide my steps in the days to come."

The Atomic Bomb Is Dropped (1945)
Lecture 32

It is an absolutely crazy idea that there is something called Jewish physics, but it fit in with the whole Nazi ideology. There was Jewish art, as there was Aryan art; there was Jewish philosophy, as there was Aryan philosophy. There was also a Jewish way of looking at the natural world and an Aryan way. Since so much of nuclear physics had been developed by men like Albert Einstein, it was suspect in German universities.

The atomic age began on August 6, 1945, with the bombing of the Japanese city of Hiroshima by the United States. By 1949, the Soviet Union had developed its own atomic weapons, and from that point to the present, the world has stood permanently on the brink of nuclear disaster.

Only two months separated the assumption of leadership in their respective countries by Adolf Hitler and Franklin Roosevelt. Hitler believed that parliamentary democracy had failed and his nation required the leadership of a Führer, while Roosevelt affirmed his commitment to democracy. By the spring of 1933, Hitler had passed laws barring Jewish professors from teaching. Leading nuclear physicists, including **Albert Einstein**, left the country, crippling Germany's ability to develop an atomic bomb.

Six years later, in 1939, Einstein wrote a letter to Roosevelt, outlining the dangers of an atomic weapon in the hands of Germany and suggesting that the United States speed up research to develop its own nuclear bomb. This first letter never seems to have reached Roosevelt. By the summer of 1940, the president knew that the United States was headed for war, but isolationist sentiments were still strong in Congress. Roosevelt decided to give the British all the help he could, short of involving his country in war.

At the same time, the Nobel Prize–winning physicist **Werner Heisenberg** had been given considerable resources in Germany to develop an atomic bomb. Still, the most promising research along these lines was taking place in Britain and America, conducted primarily by scientists who had been driven out of Germany by Nazi hatred. Two physicists working in Britain calculated that only a small amount of uranium-235 would be required to produce an explosion equivalent to 20,000 tons of TNT. They also determined that plutonium could be used to produce a bomb. Their work reached the attention of Winston Churchill, who shared the information with contacts in the United States. With further prompting from the British, the **Manhattan Project** was finally launched.

In September 1942, Leslie Groves, a high-ranking officer in the Corps of Engineers, was appointed as the military leader of the Manhattan Project. J. Robert Oppenheimer, a professor at Berkeley, would be the civilian director. The work began at Los Alamos, New Mexico, in 1943. Huge plants were built in Oak Ridge, Tennessee, and Hanford, Washington, to provide materials for the project. Hundreds of mathematicians were brought in to work on selected portions of the calculations needed by the scientists. Step by step, the work progressed.

By the spring of 1945, Groves could confidently report to Henry Stimson, Secretary of War, that the bomb was ready to be tested. By now, Germany had fallen, but the war with Japan continued. President Truman was convinced that an invasion of Japan could result in up to a half million American casualties. In July 1945, the bomb was successfully tested, and Truman decided to use it against Japan, convinced that doing so would save American lives. The Japanese were warned that their country would be destroyed if they did not surrender, but they refused. On August 6, the bomb was dropped on the city of Hiroshima, exploding with a blast that shook the world, both literally and historically. As Roosevelt had warned when the Japanese attacked Pearl Harbor, America had won an "absolute victory." ■

Names to Know

Einstein, Albert (1879–1955): German-born Nobel Prize–winning physicist, whose theoretical research laid one of the foundations for the atomic bomb.

Heisenberg, Werner (1901–1976): German Nobel Prize–winning physicist. Heisenberg headed the effort by German scientists to develop an atomic bomb during World War II.

Manhattan Project: Code name for the U.S. program to build an atomic bomb, initiated in late 1941.

Suggested Reading

Ferrell, *Harry S. Truman.*

Rhodes, *The Making of the Atomic Bomb.*

Rose, *Heisenberg.*

Questions to Consider

1. Should the Americans have dropped the atomic bomb on Japan?

2. Was it ever feasible to think that the spread of nuclear weapons could be contained?

The Atomic Bomb Is Dropped (1945)
Lecture 32—Transcript

Our theme in this lecture is the development and use of the atomic bomb, the atomic bomb that was first dropped on August 6th, 1945 on the Japanese city of Hiroshima. It was an event that changed history forever. It changed it immediately in the most terrifying form. Perhaps as many as 200,000 citizens there in Hiroshima were killed or died later from the effects of this terrifying new weapon. President Truman announced it to the American people with the ominous warning that we would continue to drop such death from the skies until Japan either surrendered or was totally obliterated.

It began, the atomic age, and there were newspapers in this country that carried huge headlines—"Atomic Age Begins." One of the most primary duties for President Truman immediately became how to organize international control of these atomic weapons. It became of the most pressing duties of the Soviet Union, under Joseph Stalin, to break America's monopoly. By 1949, the Soviets had their own atomic weapon.

The atomic bomb and developments like the hydrogen bomb meant that from that moment on, in 1949, until right now—as we lecture and you listen and watch—the world stands permanently on the brink of nuclear disaster. It was not possible to constrain the growth of nuclear weapons. By 1964, China, under the leadership of Mao Zedong, had developed its own nuclear force. Nuclear proliferation continues to be, I believe, the most dangerous single movement in history and the greatest problem facing us at this moment.

How did this all begin? To understand what happened on August 6th, and then what happened three days later on August 9th at Nagasaki, we go back to 1933, to the two leaders we've been discussing—Adolf Hitler and Franklin Roosevelt, who took leadership of their countries in the very depths of the Depression—Adolf Hitler in January and Franklin Roosevelt in March. Only two months separated them, and in fact, only a few days would separate their deaths in the year 1945. But, Franklin Roosevelt would die, mourned by an entire nation, his body being carried all the way from Warm Springs back to Washington. Thousands, all along the way, lined up to bid farewell to this most beloved leader of the free world. Adolf Hitler would blow his brains out in a dank bunker in the middle of Berlin with his whole country in ruins.

They took two different paths. Hitler believed that parliamentary democracy had failed and only the leadership of a Führer could bring Germany back while Franklin Roosevelt said no, democracy has not failed. Hitler had written his book *Mein Kampf* and Roosevelt was one of the very few politicians who actually read it. When people said, in 1933, some of Roosevelt's advisers, "Hitler's not that bad," Roosevelt said, "Have you read this book? Read it in German. Don't read it in the authorized translation, this man is evil." Sure enough, already in the spring of 1933, Adolf Hitler had passed the laws barring Jewish professors from teaching in the university.

So it would be that Hans Bethe, one of the greatest nuclear physicists of his day, would go into his lecture room in the spring of 1933 and his students would fail to rap on the desk—the traditional symbol of respect for the professor. Instead, they began to boo him and say we're not going to learn any more Jewish physics. Bethe in fact was not even Jewish. His wife was Jewish, his mother had been Jewish, but both had converted and were Christians. But, that didn't matter. It was race, not religion, and you had to prove that you were racially—whatever that meant—Aryan—whatever that meant—going back generations. Bethe was terminated from his position at the University of Tübingen. He had tenure; he had a contract. He was a civil servant.

It also happened in Italy. Enrico Fermi, one of the most brilliant of nuclear scientists, left that country as Mussolini began to use his power to carry out an anti-Semitic program as well. Albert Einstein saw what was coming and already in 1932, he had planned a set of lectures in the United States. He planned on taking up residence in Princeton, New Jersey, and never going back. Other leading physicists began to be driven out of German universities or were wise enough to leave and find, in Britain and in this country, universities that would allow them to continue their work in the fundamental understanding of the atom. In other words, it was the leadership of Adolf Hitler which crippled, at the very beginning, the attempt of Germany to develop an atomic bomb and ensure that we would develop this bomb that would end the war that Hitler started.

It is an absolutely crazy idea that there is something called Jewish physics, but it fit in with the whole Nazi ideology. There was Jewish art as there was Aryan art; there was Jewish philosophy as there was Aryan philosophy. There was also a Jewish way of looking at the natural world, and an Aryan way. Since so much of nuclear physics had been developed by men like Albert Einstein, it was suspect in German universities.

The next step in this intriguing and illuminating story would come in the year 1939, six years after Hitler was in power. Albert Einstein, at his summer home on Long Island, would be approached by several leading physicists like Leo Szilard who had also been driven out of Nazi-occupied Europe. It was still August of 1939, but war was on the horizon. These physicists came to Albert Einstein and said, "You know what is going to happen. You know what has been clear since 1938. Germany will develop an atomic bomb and they will use it to destroy everything that civilization holds dear. The only nation in the world with the power and the scientific knowledge to preempt them is the United States where we have been given refuge. The war is going to come and America will be forced into that war. If the Americans do not have the atomic bomb first, the United States will be destroyed."

Einstein said, "What can I do? I am not involved in politics." "You are the most famous single scientist in the world. We have written a draft letter, go over it, sign it, and send it. The address is here—F.D. Roosevelt, President, White House." "You want me to write President Roosevelt directly?" "Yes! Tell him that a bomb is possible, the technology is possible, the Germans are going to develop it, and the Germans are already hard at work developing an atomic bomb. They are trying to put a monopoly on crucial elements like uranium. Tell Roosevelt all of that and send it."

Einstein did. It came into the White House mailroom, went through several different secretaries, and was just put off in a "never look at again" file. Two months later, at a meeting of a Jewish Federation, Einstein was talking with Alexander Sachs, one of the most trusted advisers of President Roosevelt.

Einstein said, "You know, I never even got the courtesy of a response from President Roosevelt when I sent him a letter two months ago." "What did you write him about?" "I wrote him about the possible development of a bomb of enormous power." "Well, I'm going to see Roosevelt later in the week, I shall talk to him."

Alexander Sachs sat down with the president. "Mr. President, did you get a letter from Albert Einstein?" "No, why would Albert Einstein write me anything?" "Well, he has written you about some terrible bomb." "A bomb?" "Yes, he sent it in August, but you know, since then, Germany has invaded Poland and the war is on." "Yes, yes, yes I know. Here, I'll put somebody on it." Nobody was really put on it and the letter just continued to sit there. The war got gloomier and gloomier and gloomier. By the summer of 1940, France had fallen. Franklin Roosevelt knew that our country would be dragged into this war. He knew that Britain was fighting for what was good and he knew that the Nazis were evil, but had to walk a very careful line. He had such strong isolationist feeling in Congress. He would give Winston Churchill all the help he could, short of involving this country actually in war.

This close, personal relationship between Churchill and Roosevelt also had close, personal relationships between nuclear scientists working in both countries—in America with men like Arthur Compton, with men like the president of Harvard University, James Conant, and in Britain, with large numbers of scientists, particularly the very well connected Dr. Mark Oliphant. All of these were pondering how soon Germany would produce this bomb. After all, it had been Germany that was the very center of the growth in the understanding of the atom and its power. France had made their contribution with Madam Curie and her husband developing and understanding what radiation is all about. England had made its contribution. In fact, it had been Ernest Rutherford who had been one of the first in the early part of the 20th century to understand that the atom was not just a solid substance like a billiard ball, but had various elements moving around inside of it. He also understood that it could be split.

Albert Einstein had already provided the means of understanding how powerful such a splitting of the atom would be with his equation of $E =$

mc^2. By the 1920s, leading German physicists were probing ever deeper into how fission could occur and how much energy would be unleashed. The most brilliant of all of these was Werner Heisenberg. He was a student of Niels Bohr, the Danish physicist who had contributed so much to the understanding of the atom. Heisenberg won the Nobel Prize at a very early stage. But, his academic career in Germany after he won the Nobel Prize was somewhat hindered by the fact that he taught Jewish physics. He lost one prime academic post. The Americans believed that not even the Germans could be stupid enough, once they were in this war, not to make use of talent like Werner Heisenberg to develop an atomic bomb given their scientific knowledge and their industrial capacity. Sure enough, by 1940, the Nazis had understood enough to realize that Werner Heisenberg was enormously valuable and gave him considerable resources to build a scientific team to work on the development of an atomic bomb.

The best of all the research was going on in Britain and America through the scientists who had been driven out by Nazi hatred. Two of these scientists working there in Britain—Frisch and Peierls, both Jewish and born in Germany and who had come to Britain—began to ponder how much actual uranium would be necessary to create a bomb. They were working extensively with one of the isotopes of uranium, uranium 235. It was understood that that could produce such a nuclear result. It was very hard to get more than the tiniest proportion. The scientists were working along the assumption that it would take pounds and pounds, maybe hundreds of pounds, of uranium 235 to make a bomb. Working out on their calculations, these two came instead to the idea that maybe no more than one pound would be necessary. Also, maybe a good bomb could be made with plutonium. That one pound of this uranium 235 could produce 20,000 tons of TNT in an explosion. That calculation of one pound was only a tiny bit off, just a little bit too low. The calculation of the amount of energy unleashed was very close to what would happen on the August 6th, 1945.

They met with Mark Oliphant who had been following their work very carefully, himself a nuclear physicist. They said, "We believe a bomb can be made and we need to do it right now." This is now about 1940. "Britain's going to lose this war and America's not even involved." Oliphant said,

"I absolutely agree. I'm going to meet with Winston Churchill's scientific advisers." Churchill, by this time, had become extremely interested in the bomb. It would later be said by Leslie Groves, the general who oversaw the Manhattan Project where our atomic was developed, that Churchill was the best friend the atom bomb ever had. Churchill said, "Put together a committee that actually does something, tell us what the next steps need to be, and then send a secret memo to the Americans to President Roosevelt and tell him we will cooperate fully."

The committee worked fast and sent it off. President Roosevelt, in the meantime, had become more interested in the atomic bomb. He had put in place Mr. Briggs; he was the head of the Bureau of Standards. Mr. Briggs understood absolutely nothing about atomic bombs and he had filed this all way. Then this letter came from the British committee, the MAUD Committee as it was called—simply a made-up name to fool any German espionage agents about what they were up to. Then came the letter from the MAUD Committee and that had been filed away too.

Mark Oliphant, distinguished physicist, got into an airplane, unheeded, scrunched [ph] up, and flew across the Atlantic. He went directly to his old friend Arthur Compton at the University of California at Berkeley laboratories and said, "How come nothing's been done with all the information that you have been sent in order to build an atomic bomb? You know one can be built." Compton said, "Yes, yes, I know it can be built, but I haven't heard anything about it. Let's go to Washington." They do and sure enough, they found it lying there in the files. This time action was taken or as Churchill would say, "Action and action now."

The committee began to develop into a concrete project—The Manhattan Project it was called as a code name, but also because its original office was located in Manhattan. Again, nothing concrete happened until the right man was put in place. Roosevelt again turned his attention to this and he talked to the Secretary of War, Henry Stinson. He said, "That bomb, how is it going along?" Stimson said, "We're not really getting a lot of action." "Get somebody and put them in charge who would make it work."

He turned to Leslie Groves, high ranking officer in the core of engineers, who had built the Pentagon in record speed. Groves then took over in September of 1942. He began to interview all the best scientists. Time and again, the answer came back that what you need is a think-tank with the best scientists assembled there. You need that directed by the best organizing mind who truly understands the nature of nuclear fission. You need other plants that have enormous amounts of hydroelectric power to produce all of the uranium that we need, of 235, and to produce all the plutonium that we need. You need a place to assemble all of this. This has got to be done fast. This is because American scientists remained convinced that, with the brilliance of Werner Heisenberg and other indications that were coming, Germans were building factories that could be related to the production of a super bomb—and that Germany would get this bomb sooner than America and use it on us and the entire world.

Who's the best man to organize all of this? J. Robert Oppenheimer, professor at Berkeley. "Oh, I've looked into that guy, he's a pinko. He would be a terrible security risk." "You don't know anything about Oppenheimer. He's a brilliant teacher, a superb physicist. He is, yes, liberal in his political leanings. He may have joined various organizations in the 1930s that today are suspect, but he's the man and he's the man we'll work under." You got to have somebody that can get all of these prima donnas, these physicists, to cooperate.

Oppenheimer was offered the job. He came from a wealthy family. He had traveled extensively, he had studied in Germany. He knew how evil the Nazis were, and he was ambitious. He wanted to build the first atomic bomb. The work began at Los Alamos in 1943. A huge plant was built at Oak Ridge, Tennessee. Another huge plant for plutonium was built in Washington State, Hanford. The plant at Oak Ridge—this huge, vast facility employing thousands—was kept so secret that the governor of Tennessee didn't even know that it existed.

There was a senator from Missouri, Harry Truman, who in 1943 was making a name for himself by investigating boondoggles. Here was something called the Manhattan Project that was ultimately costing $2 billion. Truman tried to find out what was going on and he ran up against a complete stone wall. The secrecy was extraordinary. There, in two years, what private industry, free science, and the government working together can achieve was shown. Step by step, enough of the material, U-235, was produced at Oak Ridge and enough of the plutonium was produced at Hanford. The ideas were tested again and again and again.

Even before he began directing the scientists, Oppenheimer had, in his mind, traced out what a bomb might actually look like and how it would work. To get all of the theoretical material, all of the calculations, done in a time when there was nothing like a computer, hundreds of young, bright mathematicians were brought in to work on selected parts of the calculations. Then, the technology and then an aircraft to drop such a bomb were needed. But, step by step, it was done.

By the spring of 1945, Oppenheimer was working very well with Leslie Groves. They were totally different men, the general and Oppenheimer. Groves was a big, fat man always smoking a cigar. Oppenheimer was a very intellectual, thin figure puffing away on his pipe. One of them was quoting Sanskrit literature and Groves was swearing all the time. In fact, one of the people who knew Groves said, "He was the most evenly tempered man I ever knew." He was always in a rage, pushing and pushing and pushing these scientists. But, he also had this practical engineering sense and he could understand what they were talking about. He gave them free reign.

By the spring of 1945, Groves could confidently report to Henry Stimson, Secretary of War, that the bomb was about to be tested. By now, Germany had fallen. It had collapsed. Werner Heisenberg was found in May of 1945 in a little summer cottage in the Black Forest. He was arrested and, along with a number of other leading German physicists, was sent to Britain where they were interred in very comfortable circumstances. They were very carefully examined over what they knew about the atomic bomb. It was clear that they knew very little about it. Germany had made almost no progress whatsoever.

The war with Japan continued. The estimate given to President Truman, now that he had assumed power, was that it would cost up to one-half million American casualties to invade Japan. The day he became president, Mrs. Truman came into the White House and said, "I hate this place, Harry." Then, Mrs. Roosevelt came in and Truman said, "Is there anything we can do for you?" Mrs. Roosevelt said, "Harry, you're the one who needs help now." Then, there was Secretary of War Stimson saying, "Mr. President I must inform you that we are about to develop the most powerful weapon ever imagined. It will destroy an entire city with one bomb." "Why wasn't I told about this sooner?" "I don't know, President Roosevelt didn't want it shared." "Wait a minute, that's not—what is that called?" "Manhattan Project." "That's that screwball thing I was investigating! That really produced a bomb?" "Yes." "How much did we spend?" "Two billion." "Is it ready yet?" "No, but it ought to be tested by this summer." "Well, let's hope the war with Japan is over and they will negotiate a peace based on unconditional surrender." It didn't happen. In July of 1945, meeting with Comrade Stalin and now the new Prime Minister of Britain, Clement Attlee, in Potsdam amidst the ruins of Germany, President Truman got his message that the bomb had worked.

He talked about it to Stalin. Stalin seemed unimpressed, just said, "Well, I'm glad you got a new weapon." This is because Stalin had been carefully informed all along about what America was doing. Russia, in fact, had its own nuclear project. There were spies like Klaus Fuchs working intently there at Los Alamos to be sure that information reached Stalin. But, now the question was to use it or not to use it.

Truman made his decision very confidently, absolutely convinced that it was the best thing to save American lives. The Japanese were warned that either they would surrender or Japan would be destroyed. The Japanese would not surrender. Time and time again, the question came up of what will happen to the emperor. Time and time again, those militarists who had brought Japan into this terrible war and fought it with no mercy whatsoever, squashed any attempt at peace. The great bomb was transported. The aircraft was available. The trained crews under Paul Tibbets, superb pilot, were all ready for this date with destiny.

On August 6th, the crew got into its aircraft, named Enola Gay after Tibbets' mother—isn't that sweet? He named it after his mother. It took off with the first of these bombs. They named it Little Boy. Robert Oppenheimer had planned very carefully. He had been one of the most decisive voices in what city was to be picked, Hiroshima. It was a city of military value. It was also a city that had been very little bombed so it would be an ideal experiment for the destructive power of the bomb. Oppenheimer and his colleagues traced exactly at what height the bomb should explode. A camera was loaded to record it. Early that morning the plane flew. It was a very small number of planes flying and the Japanese didn't even send up any fighters to try to shoot it down. They didn't even have enough fuel. Even the air raid siren was turned off because it seemed to be maybe no more than one plane.

It fell down upon the city of Hiroshima, exploding with a blast that could be seen for miles and that shook the world both literally and historically. The Japanese had brought this upon themselves. As Roosevelt had warned, when they attacked Pearl Harbor on December 7th, 1941, America would win through to the inevitable victory, so help us God. Hitler's insane racist policies had prevented the Nazis and the Germans from developing the bomb. Our land, as a beacon of freedom, brought the intellectual power and the moral authority to bring World War II to a close. The atomic bomb—history has never been the same.

Mao Zedong Begins His Long March (1934)
Lecture 33

> Freedom is not a universal value. Democracy is not a universal value.
> There have been many people in many places in many times who have
> chosen the perceived advantages of absolute rule over the awesome
> responsibility of self-government. So it was at the beginning of history
> in the Middle East and so it has been throughout Chinese history.

The proclamation of the People's Republic of China as the government of the Chinese mainland and Mao Zedong as absolute ruler on October 1, 1949, didn't immediately seem of significant consequence. It seemed that it would be only a matter of months before the nationalist government that had been supported by the Americans under Chiang Kai-shek would return. Instead, communist China grew stronger and is now one of the great forces of our time.

In the year 1900, China was a dying dragon, carved into various trading concessions by the Western powers and led by an incompetent and corrupt dynasty. Over the course of the first two decades of the 20th century, two leaders, Sun Yat-sen and Chiang Kai-shek, sought to modernize China and institute socialism. At the same time, the ideals of communism took hold among Chinese intellectuals. In 1921, the Communist Party in China was formed, with Mao Zedong as one of its earliest members.

Mao Zedong (1893–1976), one of the founders of China's Communist Party and advocate of the "peasant strategy."

Mao began spreading the ideas of communism among the peasants of China. Chiang Kai-shek set out to exterminate communism in China, using weapons provided to him by the United States and other nations. In 1934, the Long March, a retreat of some 8,000 kilometers, saved the Chinese communists from defeat at the hands of the national army. Mao, personally assuming a crucial role in the Long March, became the acknowledged leader of the communist party and the communist movement in China.

Americans watched the situation in China carefully, concerned lest the communists win out over the nationalists. After the surrender of Japan in 1945, Truman had to decide whether or not the United States should intervene in China. But the power of the Chinese communists had been underestimated. When General George Marshall was sent to research and report on the situation, he said, "China is lost."

On October 1, 1949, the People's Republic was proclaimed, and the nationalists fled to Taiwan. The communists had won because their all-encompassing worldview presented to ordinary Chinese people a means of elevating themselves and their country. Mao undertook to fully communize China by inculcating this worldview in young people.

In 1949, when the Soviet Union announced that it had exploded its first atomic bomb, the hope that America could maintain a monopoly on nuclear weapons faded away. At the same time, the Soviet Union had amassed a huge empire. By the fall of 1949, the American people lived in a world in which more than half the population was communist—and armed with the atomic bomb.

Then, in 1950, North Korean troops invaded in an effort to bring communism to South Korea. The United Nations declared war, and American troops were sent in to bear the weight of the conflict. Toward the end of the year, Chinese "volunteers" poured into the Korean War, sent there to fight by proxy for the Soviets. Over the course of three long years, more than 55,000 American troops died in this war to "stop the spread of communism."

As Mao Zedong grew older, he became more concerned with the dwindling of enthusiasm that had marked the early days of communism. In 1966, he unleashed, through the hordes of young people who looked upon him as a divine figure, the Cultural Revolution. When he passed away, Chinese communism was adapted, slowly and carefully, to use aspects of the free-market economy in retaining authoritarian rule. ∎

Suggested Reading

Chang, *Mao*.

Wright, *The History of China*.

Questions to Consider

1. What might prevent China from becoming the dominant superpower of the 21st century?

2. Is China, like Russia, another nation that proves freedom is not a universal value?

Mao Zedong Begins His Long March (1934)
Lecture 33—Transcript

Our theme in this lecture is Communist China and the rise of China in the 20th century to becoming one of two superpowers of the 21st century—indeed a century that many are calling, the 21st, the Chinese century. We take as our epic-making date, October 1st, 1949, with the proclamation of the People's Republic of China as the government of the whole of the Chinese mainland, and Mao Zedong as absolute ruler. He was chairman of the Communist Party, and one of the most powerful figures in Chinese history since the first emperor of China. Mao Zedong and Communist China—it perhaps immediately didn't seem to be epic making.

The nationalist government that had been supported by the Americans under Generalissimo Chiang Kai-shek had gone to Taiwan. It seemed as though it be only a matter of months before they came back armed by the Americans, but it didn't turn out that way. China grew ever strong and ever stronger, adapted its communist system, developed an atomic bomb, and now is one of the great forces of our time.

You would not have predicted that in the year 1900. You would not have predicted that 100 years later, China would be a superpower. In fact, China was a dying dragon in 1900. It seemed as though the humiliation of China at the hands of the western powers was reaching an apex. The Chinese were humiliated, carved into various trading concessions. China was described as one big cow or that the powers of the day Britain, France, the United States, Italy, Japan, Germany, were all carving up. The other phrase was, "Let's carve up the Chinese melon." The old dynasty of the Manchu's was incapable, incompetent, and corrupt. In 1900, the Chinese became so frustrated that various organizations calling themselves the Righteous and Harmonious Fifths, or the Boxers as they were called by Europeans, rose up in revolt and began killing symbols of western oppression such as missionaries or Chinese who had studied in missionary schools. The Chinese government was either unwilling or unable to put down this revolt of the Boxers.

The great powers sent troops. Russia, France, Germany, Italy, the United States, and Japan sent troops into China to quell the rebellion and show the Chinese absolutely they were not masters in their own home. The Boxer Rebellion of 1900 was a prelude to the collapse of the old monarchy for there were forces bubbling up in China that were determined to take China out of the past and into the present.

The leader of this was Sun Yat-sen. He had been educated very well in the Confucian classics. But, he believed that Confucius belonged to an outdated and outmoded way of thinking. He and his followers proclaimed, get rid of the old curiosity shop of Confucius. He has kept us backward here in China. Many of them studied at universities in America, some of them studying at Columbia with John Dewey. They brought back to China a belief in positivism and science. Many of them had begun studying in missionary schools in China and then had gone to study in the United States. Then, they came back to reform their country on the basis of science and democracy— out with Confucius, up with Mr. Democracy and Mr. Science.

In this heyday, the Chinese Republic was proclaimed in 1911. It was based upon Sun Yat-sen's great ideas of socialism, democracy, and nationalism. Yes, democracy, yes, the people should rule, but it should be the form of democracy in which the individual is less important than society as a whole—traditional Chinese idea of the importance of the collectivity. It was a socialistic style of democracy and nationalism—China for the Chinese. China would develop an army. China would develop a financial system. While China would be as good a neighbor as they could to the other great powers, China would take its own course. But, China was not prepared for democracy. It is a question that we can discuss throughout this course. We talked about in the Wisdom of History course.

Freedom is not a universal value. Democracy is not a universal value. There have been many people in many places in many times who have chosen the perceived advantages of absolute rule over the awesome responsibility of self government. So it was at the beginning of history in the Middle East and so it has been throughout Chinese history. As the Russian Revolution did not produce a democracy, the Chinese Revolution of the early part of the

20th century did not produce a democracy. In fact, it made China even more desperate. Grasping warlords carved up huge provinces of China, poverty stalked the land, there were epidemics of cholera, and a total failure of any notion of democracy to take root.

Out of this chaos, one of the followers of Sun Yat-sen, was Chiang Kai-shek. He had studied in Russia. He was a trained soldier. He had come away from his studies in Russia with a deep obsessive hatred of communism. He would become the leader of the Nationalist Forces, a party that pretended to and some ways actually did, continue the policies of Sun Yat-sen. They led China on a path to democracy, nationalism, and socialism, but under one strong figurehead, Chiang Kai-shek, the generalissimo. But, in the midst of this intellectual turmoil, communism had begun to take hold among some Chinese intellectuals.

In 1921, the Chinese party in China was first formed. One of its earliest members was a man with some education who had grown up in the rural countryside of China. He was an assistant librarian at the University of Peking. The University of Peking was, in the first part of the 20th century, a hotbed of radical ideas. It was formed on the basis of American universities. It didn't teach the Confucian classics; it taught real science, real history, and philosophy. One of the philosophies taught was Marxism. One of the professors at the University of Peking became a leading Marxist expert. The librarian, the boss of Mao Zedong, this young man, was also a committed communist.

Mao Zedong continued his study of Marxism. Yes, he believed absolutely in the evil of capitalism. He believed that all that was oppressive to the world would be swept away with the abolition of private property. He believed that this western concept was what would lead China into the future—not the old notions of Confucius, but the western concept of the historical inevitability of the triumph of communism. He admired what was happening in Russia in the 1920s. It was proof that communism could work. But, the more he pondered the lessons of the Russian Revolution, he began to believe that Lenin and then later Stalin had made one crucial error. They had not understood the role of the peasant.

Russia had a limited number of workers. It was a peasant country when the revolution broke out. Had the Soviets been more successful in organizing the peasants, the road of revolution in Russia would have been smoother. Mao began careful work in spreading the idea of communism in the countryside of China. Chiang Kai-shek decided communism was becoming a great danger and he set about to exterminate every communist he could find in China, making use of weapons given to him by the United States and others in the 1930s. In 1934, he had the communist army that had been built up by Mao Zedong, Jun Li [ph], and other communist leaders, all but surrounded. But, they made their way out, the communists did. Their march—according to tradition—of some 8,000 kilometers and 370 days of marching, the long march to safety became part of a heroic legend of communism in China and the Red Chinese army. Mao, personally assuming a crucial role in this long march, became the acknowledged leader of the communist party and the communist movement in China. There was a full blown civil war throughout much of the '30s between the Chinese communists and the Nationalist Army under Chiang Kai-shek.

Then came the war with Japan. Both sides spent almost as much time fighting each other even during the war with Japan as they did fighting the Japanese. The Americans were watching carefully. China was crucial to American foreign policy. Of course, Americans had already been involved in China's struggled against Japan before Pearl Harbor. The heroic story of the Flying Tigers that went to the aid of Chiang Kai-shek was familiar to every American in the late '30s and early '40s. America was deeply interested in China and deeply concerned lest the communists win. Japanese were going to be beaten—that was clear—sooner or later.

What would emerge in China? Would it be Chiang Kai-shek leading China towards democracy? Would it Chiang Kai-shek following in his old path of corruption, or would it be the communists? It wasn't totally out of the realm of possibility. The communists had won in Russia. The more seriously Chinese experts studied the situation in China, along with the more the reports of generals like Joseph Stillwell—who knew Chiang Kai-shek very well and despised him—they became convinced that, without massive American involvement, the communists would win. This is because the communists were winning the hearts of the countryside, the hearts of the peasants. The communists were not just fighting the nationalists. They were bringing better hygiene, better schools, better medical care, and better means of planting crops. They were getting rid of corruption at all levels of society, and they were winning the heart of China.

The war with Japan came to its end in 1945. It is a most remarkable four years of history—from 1945 until 1949—when the atomic bomb was dropped upon Japan and surrender was then signed by the Japanese. The United States was the only atomic power. The United States, in that late summer of 1945, possessed a large, extremely well equipped army—probably the greatest military machine that had ever been mustered. It had vast numbers of aircraft, the best equipment in tanks, and it had a monopoly on the atomic bomb. It had the moral authority to see to it that the world never again was plunged into war.

I know that President Truman had very difficult decisions to make. I know that he is a man who grew to his job. When he first came to the Senate, he was known as the Senator from Pendergast—that was his political boss Tom Pendergast who ran the Kansas City politics. He followed his boss's advice. He kept his nose clean, answered his mail, and kept his mouth shut. He was a good pick for Roosevelt who was looking for a non-controversial vice presidential candidate for the election of 1944. I know some of you think that Roosevelt should not have run for that third and fourth term, but I'll explain it to you the way Truman saw it.

By the time the third term rolled around in 1940, Europe was on the verge of war. Britain was on the verge of falling into the grasp of the Nazis. Europe was at war. Roosevelt had the deep ties to Churchill and a deep understanding of the situation in Europe that would enable us to guide us. He might very well have wanted to step back, but he stood for the third term. Then, by 1944, he knew he was sick. But, he believed he could live on long enough to fulfill the dream of Woodrow Wilson, to have a new United Nations, a better form of the League of Nations.

However, his vice presidential candidate was a great liability—Henry Wallace, who was very far to the left. Therefore, Truman, who had the reputation of being a moderate, of coming from a border state, and of having been tough on government spending, was chosen as the vice president. Roosevelt won. It had very little to do with Truman. Suddenly, in April, all of this felt upon the shoulders of Harry Truman.

In his memoirs, he explains what guided him. One, he was determined never again to have a major war, never a World War III. Two, he wanted to control the growth of this atomic power. Third, within that framework, he wanted to continue the New Deal, to bring the American soldiers home as quickly as he could, and put the world back to a normal state of peace. That was his goal. He and his advisers terribly misunderstood and underestimated the power of the communist in China by 1945 and the corruption of Chiang Kai-shek's government. Expert after expert was sent in that critical period, from 1945 until 1949, including the man that Truman trusted most, George Marshall.

When Marshall had stepped down from all the duties of being in charge of the army during the war, all of the duties he had had in the later years, he was looking forward to retirement with his wife. They had built a beautiful home out in the Virginia countryside. They were just moving in. On the day they were moving in, the phone rang. Marshall picked it up and said, after listening for a few minutes, "Yes" and hung up. The next day, he went to the White House. He went in and Truman said, "General, why in the hell did you hang up on me yesterday?" "Because, Mr. President, I have promised my wife I would never take another job that you gave me. And I agreed. I said yes, I'll go to China and evaluate the situation for you. But, I wanted to try to get to my wife and tell her before your White House leaked the news." "Did you do it, General?" "No, by the time I could get from where the phone was to where my wife was, the news radio already had it." "Uh, what happened, General?" "Well, there was hell to pay, Mr. President. But, at any rate, I'll go to China for you."

He went to China. He read carefully all the reports that generals like Joseph Stilwell had sent back, reports that had been neglected because they did not present the view that the administration wanted—that Chiang Kai-shek could win with enough material aid from America. After studying the situation, meeting time and time again with Chiang Kai-shek, getting to know more and more about the communists, trying to get negotiations between the communists and the nationalists, weighing the military abilities of some of the communist leaders like Mao Zedong and Jun Li, Marshall came back and said, China is lost. On October 1st, 1949, Chinese People's Republic was proclaimed. The nationalists fled to Taiwan. The American press asked over and over again, how did we lose China?

We lost it because one, it never was ours; it was the Chinese's. Secondly, it is because communism presented to the ordinary Chinese a means of elevating himself, his family, and, above all, his country. It is difficult perhaps in these days which we live now to understand the power that communism had in the 20th century. Communism, as much as Christianity, is a religion. Communism has its prophet—Karl Marx, Friedrich Engels, Vladimir Lenin, and Mao Zedong. It has its holy scriptures—the writings of Marx, Engels, Lenin, and Mao Zedong. It provides an all-inclusive world view; the economic determinism of Marxism explains how history has taken its course and how it will go in the future. It provides a means of understanding law. All law that existed before was but a statement and embodiment of the values of the exploiting class—slaveholders, feudal landlords, and bourgeois.

Communism will erect upon this ruin, laws that reflect the communist society. You have one evil for the world, private property, and you get rid of it. It provides an all-encompassing world view. It has its sacred scriptures. It even promises paradise—not in heaven, but paradise on earth. It can be inculcated. Whether in Russia, China, or North Korea, the first thing that is done—just as was done in Nazi Germany—is to take over the schools and teach communism. The young people had—from the very beginning of communism in China, back when Mao Zedong was a young assistant librarian—always been the bearers of communism. Mao Zedong undertook fully to communize China and assumed absolute rule.

Another very bad year for the Americans was 1949. This is because, in that same year, the Soviet Union announced that it had exploded its first atomic bomb. America was an absolute sieve in leaking strategic information about the nuclear weapon to the Soviet Union. The Rosenbergs were executed for their role in leaking this information to the Soviet Union. Stalin would later offer a toast to the Rosenbergs for all the help they had given. The Russians had also captured a large number of German scientists. They exploded that bomb. The hope that America could keep a monopoly of nuclear weapons faded away. That same period, from 1945-1949, under Stalin, the Soviet Union had gained an empire that would have astounded even a czar. Poland, Czechoslovakia, Hungary, Bulgaria, Romania, Yugoslavia, Eastern Germany, Estonia, Latvia, Lithuania—all of these were part of the Soviet empire. Poland—which had suffered the agonies of the German invasion and for which Britain had declared war—was allowed by the Americans, while they still possessed the power undisputed of the nuclear bomb, to go under Russian control.

It was an empire in Eastern Europe. Now, it was the Russians who were seen as the ultimate winners in the victory of communism in China. By fall of 1949, Harry Truman and the American people looked at a world in which more than half of it and its population was communist—and armed with the atomic bomb. There were communist governments in Germany and even in North Korea. This is because there's another aspect of ending the war as quickly as possible. In 1945, the Americans allowed the Soviet troops to go into the northern part of the Korean Peninsula which they immediately sealed off and turned into a communist government.

Then, in 1950, the hopes of avoiding another war were dashed when, in the far-off peninsula of which Americans knew absolutely nothing, North Korean troops invaded in an effort to bring communism to South Korea. The United Nations declared war. The Soviet Union had stormed out of the meeting of the Security Council so that the vote could be carried. The American troops bore the weight of that great war. The American public asked itself, why are we now involved in another war and what are we doing in Korea? They had even bigger questions to ask by Thanksgiving time when, in 1950, the Chinese poured into the Korean War. "Volunteers" they were called. They were sent there to fight a proxy war for the Soviets. Mao Zedong took that trained veteran army that had beaten the Chinese Nationalists and hurled them at the Americans. For three long years, more than 55,000 American troops died in a war that nobody even understood. It was never fully explained to the American people except in terms of stopping the spread of communism. Many, of course, asked, why that had not been done much sooner? Was it even feasible or did it even make sense? Maybe these people in China, the Soviet Union, and North Korea wanted communism.

The war ground to its halt. It had achieved its purpose. It had shown the might of communist China. It had shown that the Soviet Union would stop the expansion of American democracy. Stalin himself had died, but Mao Zedong remained. He had sharp differences with the Soviet Union. They began to split apart over idealogical, but even also over territorial issues. Mao Zedong, as he grew older and older, became more and more concerned about what seemed to him to be the dwindling of the enthusiasm that had marked the early days of communism, the long march, and intellectuals like himself as they came to grips with how to spread communism. He believed that revolution comes from the barrel of a gun, it's never made by debating societies. He believed that revolution should be eternal, enduring, and ever renewing itself.

In 1966, he unleashed, through the hordes of the young people that looked upon him as a divine figure, a cultural revolution to wipe out all of those who were deviationist. Millions of young Chinese travelled all over the country waving and reciting the quotations of Chairman Mao. "Down with authority," locking their teachers up in closets and them letting them out only to beat them; forcing all sorts of intellectuals to go out into the land to go back to the peasant way of life. Then, as quickly as it had started, he could turn it off.

Some doubted how physically able he was, so pictures and newsreels were shown of him swimming across the river. He was a great, huge man and probably could swim by kind of floating on his bloated stomach. He grew more into himself; spoke only some obscure rural dialect. He enjoyed most basic peasant food like winter melon and hog jowl, but remained alert enough to receive a visit from Richard Nixon. The great opening of China to the west would begin. When Chairman Mao passed away, communism could be adapted, carefully and slowly, so that all the authoritarian rule remains in

China today. There is an absolute lack of any freedom of thought, but aspects of the free market economy prove useful to maintain that absolute control that Mao had established.

John F. Kennedy Is Assassinated (1963)
Lecture 34

[In the 1950s and 1960s,] "communism" was synonymous with evil. … There were wonderful movies made, like *The Invasion of the Body Snatchers*. … Every one of us, immediately, in watching the movie, said, "That is how the communists are going to come. They're going to take over our bodies and we'll look just the same, but we will be doing evil communist things."

John Kennedy was a flash of brilliance amidst the rather dreary America of the 1950s. As we all know, he was born to wealth and privilege. His father, Joseph Kennedy, was an astute businessman and diplomat, well-connected in both the United States and Europe. Kennedy himself served in World War II and returned to America a hero. He was elected to the Senate and took a moderate approach on such issues as civil rights but was strong on national defense. In 1960, he was elected president on a ticket with **Lyndon Johnson**. His inaugural address was the most inspiring speech to the Americans since the first inaugural address of Franklin Roosevelt.

Once in office, Kenney took a bold stand on civil rights. Because he was a product of the Cold War, he also held to a firm foreign policy. Soviet leader Nikita Khrushchev met with Kennedy and concluded that both the president and America itself were weak. Perhaps the greatest sign of American weakness for Khrushchev was its response to the situation in Cuba: The plot to land U.S.-backed

John F. Kennedy's presidency was a spiritual end to the dreary 1950s.

199

Cuban exiles at the Bay of Pigs and overthrow Fidel Castro had ended in disaster. But Kennedy proved himself a strong and pragmatic politician in his solution to the Cuban Missile Crisis of 1962. He did not negotiate out of fear, but he did not fear to negotiate.

Kennedy and his wife, Jacqueline, traveled to Europe, where he won over crowds in West Berlin by declaring "*Ich bin ein Berliner*." America would not allow the takeover of Berlin by the Russians. Despite his popularity in Europe, Kenney was not loved by all Americans. Some in the African American community doubted his deep commitment to civil rights, while southerners thought he was far too strong on the issue. Others throughout the country believed that he was weak on communism or a communist himself. Many in the Democratic Party hated Kennedy.

The question of whether Kennedy would win reelection was raised already in the fall of 1963. Kennedy was confident because he believed that most Americans supported a moderate approach to civil rights, the containment of communism, and other issues. There was, however, a minority that found its embodiment in Barry Goldwater, who believed in absolute resistance to communism and a return to the economic and social system of the time of Herbert Hoover. In fact, the Republicans nominated Goldwater as their candidate for the 1964 election.

Kennedy debated whether or not he should retain Lyndon Johnson as his running mate. Johnson had not proved to be as effective at manipulating the Senate as Kennedy had hoped. Moreover, Johnson didn't seem to be able to control the Democratic Party in Texas, which was badly split into liberal and conservative factions. Kennedy agreed to a goodwill trip to Texas to try to reunite the party.

As we know, Kennedy flew into Fort Worth on the morning of November 22, 1963. After speaking to the Chamber of Commerce there, he flew to Dallas and began the procession through the streets, past the Texas School Book Depository. Lee Harvey Oswald shot the president at 12:30 p.m. central time, and Kennedy was pronounced dead a little more than 30 minutes later. Had he lived, the history of the United States from the time of Vietnam to the present would likely have been very different. ■

Johnson, Lyndon Baines (1908–1973): President of the United States (1963–1969). As a senator, Johnson proved to be a highly successful politician. As John Kennedy's vice president, he became president when Kennedy was assassinated.

Suggested Reading

Kennedy, "Inaugural Address," in Safire, *Lend Me Your Ears*.

Manchester, *Death of a President*.

Questions to Consider

1. Discuss the idea that the Kennedy family is one of the most fateful legacies in American history.

2. Why was John Kennedy so successful while Lyndon Johnson proved such a failure with the press?

John F. Kennedy Is Assassinated (1963)
Lecture 34—Transcript

Our theme in this lecture is November 22nd, 1963, the assassination of President John Kennedy. Someone asked me, how can you say that the assassination of John Kennedy changed history? Why is it worthy to rank alongside the Law Code of Hammurabi? In the first place, anyone who was of reasoning years—10 or above in 1963—knows forever that the assassination of this president changed his or her life and will believe to the end of their days that it changed the history of our country. You have to remember that I am an unabashed patriot. I believe that America is the greatest force for good that the world has ever known. The assassination of President Kennedy changed America and its reverberations are with us still today. It was, and this is a very meaningful expression in these terms, a loss of innocence for our country. It was a loss of a sense that the whole of our future would be ever upward.

Kennedy was a flash of brilliance amidst the rather dreary America of the 1950s. That was the age when the Cold War seemed at its height. But, I must also tell you that I don't think the Cold War has ever ended. The Cold War seemed at height in the 1950s. We had a very well-meaning President Eisenhower. He was very popular. He was deeply patriotic. He believed in his duty to uphold the law. He believed in his duty to contain communism, but he just wasn't very striking or inspiring. Our foreign policy seemed to be one group of setbacks after another. China lost in 1949. There were reports coming out of China of famines in which millions died. The Soviet Union was boasting that it would bury America and capitalism, and then even sending a satellite into space faster than we did. Our whole educational system began to question itself because communism seemed to be working better in education even. It was a gloomy time for Americans and suddenly there was John Kennedy. The world became brighter for us.

He was born, like Roosevelt—whom he admired enormously—to wealth and privilege. In fact, his father Joseph had been ambassador to Great Britain in the very time that Britain seemed most likely to collapse before the Germans. In fact, in the spring of 1940, Joseph Kennedy had sent telegram after telegram to President Roosevelt saying the British won't fight, they're going to collapse, and don't send them any aid. Of course, Roosevelt listened to the speech of Churchill—"We shall never surrender"—and gave the British all the aid he possibly could. Joseph Kennedy was a very astute businessman and a serious diplomat connected as high as possible throughout America and widely connected in Europe.

While he was an ambassador there in London, his son, John, was there studying at the London School of Economics. He was finishing up his Harvard honors thesis which was *Why England Slept*. Winston Churchill had written a very powerful treatise called *While England Slept* which described why the Nazis were able to build such a war machine. But Kennedy went into the politics of why the English had at first followed a policy of appeasement and negotiation, gaining time for themselves to become a match for the military power of Germany. One of his professors at Harvard gave it a magna cum laude. The other just gave it a cum laude, but it is a very fine book. Of all our presidents, Theodore Roosevelt and, I believe, John Kennedy, are the best authors. Thomas Jefferson was a genius, but he didn't write all that much into what we call a book.

Kennedy wrote this book on England and the interwar years. He came back to this country, and was a war hero. His older brother was killed in action and Kennedy was almost killed in action. PT-109—the name will live forever for Americans of the 1950s and '60s. PT-109 sunk and Kennedy, exhibiting great valor and winning medals, saved his crew. As always, he had a little witty thing to say about it. "How did you win those medals?" "Oh, I got my boat sunk." He was a war hero. He now became his father's objective for political power. He ran for Congress as soon as he got back and then was elected to the Senate. He was a dutiful senator. He married very well. He took a moderate approach to things like civil rights, but was very strong on national defense.

When he ran in 1960, it looked as though it was going to be a very close election. Eisenhower, of course, could not run and it was going to be his Vice President Richard Nixon, a very capable and experienced man, but who would be his opponent? There was Linden Johnson, absolute master of the Senate. He was a capable, shrewd, craft politician. It looked as though he would sweep to an easy victory. But, Americans didn't want a politician of that old stripe and Kennedy grabbed their attention. In hard-fought campaigns, spending a great deal of money, Kennedy won the nomination. Then, he took Linden Johnson on as his vice president—balancing his Massachusetts' geography with Linden Johnson's Texas and balancing his aristocratic background with Johnsons' homespun humor. They won.

But, like everything that John Kennedy did, it didn't come easily. There were enormous discussions over vote fraud. But, he was inaugurated as president. There, on that brilliant, cold January day, snow lying all around, John Kennedy was inaugurated. He gave the most inspiring speech since Franklin Roosevelt had given his first inaugural address. It was a speech that would highlight the values of America at mid-century, the highlight of the "American century" as it would already be called. His beautiful wife there— charming, speaking perfect French, and another breath of fresh air sweeping across the country. Mrs. Eisenhower had been such a nice lady, but she was your grandmother. Jackie Kennedy, dressed beautifully, had an elegant air about everything that she did.

He spoke. He told the world that a new generation was in America now. It was a generation that had fought the war and had been hardened by a Cold War. It was a generation that was taking up the torch of freedom. Throughout that inaugural address, he calls Americans to their role in bearing freedom to the world. Just as certainly as President Bush would in his second inaugural, Kennedy insisted that freedom is a universal value, that all people in all places and in all times want freedom. It is our duty to bring it to them. He demands that we dedicate ourself to our country and to our country's great mission. He wants us to ask not what our country can do for us, but what we can do for our country. He demands that we reach out to the world. "Let us never negotiate," he says, "out of fear, but let us never fear to negotiate." Those words still, when you read them in scribe there at Arlington Cemetery, move you to tears. It was a call to young Americans. He immediately gave them a task as important as Roosevelt had with his civilian conservation core. This was the Peace Corps. Thousands of young people would feel a new sense of doing something for their country—learning a foreign language, going off to help bring hygiene to places in Africa and Asia, going to Persia, and going to teach English in schools. They were caught up in this fervor that now America was once again on the move and things could change.

He took a bold stand on civil rights. When the University of Mississippi students rioted because an African-American student had enrolled, he sent the troops in. He wasn't afraid of controversy. People said, you can't make your brother Attorney General. "Why?" said Kennedy. "He needs the experience. He needs the experience of being a lawyer." He had this magnificent way of dealing with the press. No president, except Franklin Roosevelt, has been anywhere near his equal as a speaker to a large crowd, as a holder of press conferences, and as a debater on television. Again, see the old footage—there is Vice President Nixon looking much more experienced, knowing a great deal more than Kennedy, but looking shifty eyed and nervous under the cameras and even a little sweat coming out on his lips. Kennedy never showed he was worried at all. From that first debate on TV, he was going to win. He carried that majesty all through his term as president.

He had a strong stand on civil rights. He called the youth of America to a new task. He had a firm foreign policy because Kennedy was the product of the Cold War. The Cold War led to the communist takeover of China and the Soviet atomic bomb. All through the 1950s, it had everybody in America terrified that one day might be their last day because of atomic explosion. Kids were taught to dive under their desk in case there was an atomic explosion—though it was never explained to me in those days how that would help me. Kids were even issued dog tags so that they could be identified once this nuclear holocaust had come.

But, from the beginning, Kennedy was determined to negotiate—negotiate not out of fear, but not fearing to negotiate. He met with the then Soviet leader Nikita Khrushchev. You could not imagine two more different people meeting there in Vienna—the handsome, debonair, well-dressed Kennedy born in wealth and privilege, and Khrushchev who had grown up a peasant. Khrushchev was a great fat man, bald headed, snaggled tooth, a brute, and a hooligan. He had been in charge in the 1930s of Stalin's systematic starvation of millions of Ukrainians. He had risen to power after Stalin's death by treachery and brutality.

He met with the young president, and the first test of Kennedy didn't go so well. Khrushchev decided he was weak, young and inexperienced. Khrushchev decided—and the Soviet politburo went along with him—that America itself was weak and would not stand up. After all, it had been only seven years since the Korean War had come to an end. There, from Khrushchev's point of view, in that war, the Americans had not been willing to fight to the end. They weren't willing to use the atomic bomb. They wouldn't take that final step. Perhaps the greatest sign of weakness of all was Cuba.

Going all the way back to President James Monroe, we had said, European powers have no business in America. All through the 1920s, we had patrolled places like Haiti, a clear sign of our ability to enforce our will in the western hemisphere and no one else dare interfere. But, Fidel Castro had overthrown the corrupt dictator Batista. Once again, the American State Department in the late '50s looked totally uninformed just the way it had been in China. They looked upon or claimed Castro to be sort of an agrarian reformer. He was a communist and he set in place one of the most ruthless communist dictatorships in the world—every bit as ruthless as Mao Zedong's China. Suddenly, there was a communist foothold in the western hemisphere.

Again, unless you lived during the '50s and '60s, the word communist doesn't invoke the kind of fear it did to people then. Communism was synonymous with evil. Children grew up believing that once the communists took over America, they would confiscate your Bible. There were wonderful movies made like *The Invasion of the Body Snatchers,* the original version, in which these pods come to earth. Every one of us, immediately in watching the movie said, that is how the communists are going to come. They're going to take over our bodies and we'll look just the same, but we will be doing evil communist things. Here was a communist foothold in the western hemisphere. President Eisenhower had done nothing about it. Kennedy, at the very start, tried to do something about it and failed.

There was a plot already under foot when he became president to land Cuban exiles at place called the Bay of Pigs there in Cuba and overthrow Fidel Castro and the communists. This was rather like when we went into Iraq some years ago and everybody was convinced at the high government levels that these Cuban exiles would be recognized as liberators. They weren't. The Cuban army was extremely well trained, armed with Chinese and Soviet guns. It was a fiasco. Kennedy, early on in his administration, looked totally incompetent in foreign affairs. You could literally, one of his friends said, see him began to sink into his chair. One said to another, Jack Kennedy's never lost anything. The Bay of Pigs was a fiasco. Khrushchev picked up on it. That was another sign that America would not go the whole length.

America was possessed of nuclear missile sites that surrounded Russia, for example, there in Turkey. Therefore, Khrushchev decided that missiles bearing nuclear warheads could be put into Cuba and the Americans would do nothing about it. Fidel Castro wanted the weapons there; they would be his security. Then, the Cuban Missile Crisis of 1962 came about. Almost the way they had done at Roosevelt's first inaugural, Americans crowded around their televisions and radios that evening as Kennedy lay out exactly what was going to happen. These missiles were there in Cuba, they were in violation of our Monroe Policy, and if we allow them to stay there, no friend or foe would ever take our word seriously. Of course, he had many in the government who wanted him drop the big ones, start it, let's get this nuclear war over. But, no, he was a pragmatic politician. John Kennedy was a patriot, he was an idealist, and he was pragmatic. He and his advisers, his brother playing a key role, Robert Kennedy, they found a way out that allowed the Soviets to save some face. We took away obsolete missiles from Turkey, Russians took out their missiles, no armed engagement took place, and the world breathed easier.

He had not negotiated out of fear, but he had not feared to negotiate. That dreaded nuclear holocaust was postponed. He went to Europe. He didn't globetrot a great deal. He went to Europe, taking his beautiful wife with him, speaking her French, and introducing himself as, "I'm Jacqueline Kennedy's husband." Again, crowd's in his hands. Going to Berlin to make a statement—in those years, Berlin was divided by a great wall. One side was

East Germany—a constant statement of the failure of communism to work, down at the heels, grey, drab, many destructions from the war, and many buildings that were ruined were never even repaired. On the other side of the wall was West Berlin—a little island of freedom amidst the communist world with bustling, well-fed, well-clad people who were saying what they wanted and writing what they wanted. Kennedy went there and proclaimed our utter devotion to the freedom of Germany and Berlin.

Once again, Khrushchev and the Russians believed that America would back down and they might be able to take over all of Berlin. It didn't happen. "*Ich bin ein Berliner*," he said. The translator said, "*Ich bin ein Berliner*." Kennedy stopped and said, "I want to thank the translator for translating my German." Again, the crowd was his. No nation mourned more deeply when Kennedy was killed than did the Germans.

He had a strong and vigorous foreign policy, but he was not loved by every American. Even news media like *Time Magazine* were frequently critical of him. There were elements in the African American community who weren't sure how deep his commitment to civil rights actually was. He was hated as weak on communism by very influential, well-funded groups throughout America who looked upon him as a communist. Of course, some of these were the same people who had called Dwight Eisenhower a conscious tool of the international communist conspiracy, but, nonetheless, Kennedy was hated by them. In the south, he was looked upon as far too strong on his civil rights policy. There were many in the Democratic Party who hated him.

The question of whether he would actually win reelection became a real one, already, in the fall of 1963. Would he win reelection? He was confident he would because, on the one hand, was John Kennedy and most Americans who believed in a moderate approach to containing communism. In other words, this meant not blowing ourselves up. They believed in a moderate approach to civil rights, that African Americans had the right to vote, to go to any school they wanted, and to have all the freedoms of every American. They also believed that an educated public devoted to its country was willing to consider many different forms of ideas, that even fundamental tenants of Marxism were worth debating openly.

On the other hand was a minority that found its embodiment in Barry Goldwater. Goldwater was a very patriotic man. He was an intelligent man. He became the embodiment of these ideas that communism must be absolutely resisted, that it was better to be dead than red, and that America must pursue a return to a social and economic system back into the time of Herbert Hoover. Kennedy accepted the New Deal, he wanted to make it work ever better, and he wanted to expand healthcare. We were past Herbert Hoover's days. He believed in a liberal approach to the economy. Kennedy believed that government had an important role in the economy. One of his most trusted advisers and one of his speechwriters was John Kenneth Galbraith who was responsible for some of the very witty phrases that Kennedy used. He believed in a liberal view of the economy with government having a role in it. Barry Goldwater said, government has no role whatsoever. Kennedy was quite convinced that the Republican Party was so self-destructive that they would nominate Barry Goldwater—which is what they actually did in 196—so, he thought he would win.

The question, as far as he was concerned, pragmatically, was who was going to be his vice presidential candidate? Linden Johnson just had not worked out. Linden Johnson was very loyal to Kennedy. Kennedy was very good with Johnson, keeping him informed as much as possible about everything that was developing and including Johnson in every important meeting, but Johnson just had not proven to be what Kennedy thought he would be. John Kennedy believed that Johnson, having been the master of the Senate when he was a senator, could continue successfully to twist arms in the Senate and get senators to vote the way he wanted them to. Johnson was just a man now without a power base in the Senate. Senators just didn't listen to him. He was Vice President. As more than one vice president has said, it's a job, being vice president, that's not worth a pitcher of warm spit. Johnson just wasn't able to have the political clout Kennedy had hoped for. Moreover, Johnson didn't seem to be able even to control the Democratic Party in Texas. It was badly split between a liberal side that admired Kennedy and a very conservative Democratic faction that was opposed to civil rights, wanted a doctrinaire approach to communism, and wanted government totally out of business. They had fallen out. Senator Yarborough and the Governor of Texas John Connally were not even speaking.

If Johnson couldn't even control the Democratic Party in Texas, how much help would he be? Kennedy decided to give Johnson another chance and agreed to go on a goodwill trip to Texas, to try to get the feuding parts of the Democratic Party together again and give some exposure to his ideas. He was warned against it. Adlai Stevenson, one of the real pet hatreds of this conservative wing of America, had been to Dallas. He had been beaten on the head with posters held up by protestors. He begged Kennedy not to go to Dallas, it's dangerous. There were even some in Texas who said, you know, you are really hated here, don't come.

But, Kennedy was never a man to be afraid. He and Mrs. Kennedy flew into Fort Worth. He was going to speak to the Chamber of Commerce that morning of the 22nd. She was late and he said, "Mrs. Kennedy is late, but when she gets here, she looks a whole lot better than the rest of us." Then they flew on from Forth Worth to Dallas. It wasn't necessary, but the press secretaries believed presidential landings, getting off of a plane, always looked good. They landed and they began that drive, that procession, coming before the Texas Book Depository. There, as we are told, was this lone assassin, Lee Harvey Oswald, a failure in everything he had done. He had spent a good deal of time in Russia. His background was never fully understood and his reasons for what he did were never clear. But, if what we are told is true, he fired that rifle with extraordinary marksmanship—and he had been a marksman in the marines—and John Kennedy was dead. It was 12:30 Central Time, November 22nd, 1963 when he was shot, and he was pronounced dead a little more than 30 minutes later.

Had Kennedy lived—it's one of those fascinating questions of history. Would the world have been different? I believe yes. We were already involved in Vietnam. We had already sent military advisors there, but Kennedy was reevaluating the situation. I believe he had the political wisdom, political stature, and political courage, to have understood by 1965 not to increase our effort in Vietnam, but to withdraw. That one issue, Vietnam, tore our country apart under President Johnson. It broke the spirit of that brave and capable man, Linden Johnson. It led our country to a divisiveness that we have never overcome. It also led us to a distrust for our government, a distrust for what we are told by a president, by Congress, that continues to cast a shadow over

America today. In the immediate aftermath of Vietnam, one more country had fallen to communism. John Kennedy's assassination changed history and changed it for the worse.

Dr. King Leads a March (1963)
Lecture 35

> Martin Luther King drew upon Gandhi and his own deep belief in God, the God of the Old and the New Testament, the God who had proclaimed on Earth: "Do unto others as you would have them do unto you."

Along with Abraham Lincoln's Gettysburg Address, Franklin Roosevelt's first inaugural speech, and John Kennedy's inaugural address, the speech given by Martin Luther King on August 28, 1963, represents a high point in American history. It embodied the hopes of millions of Americans and the promise for the future.

As we all know, the Civil War abolished slavery and promised to all citizens of the United States—without regard to race—the protection of the federal government in life, liberty, and property. But of course, even after the Civil War, African Americans were oppressed, and a system of segregation emerged in the South that lasted well into the 20th century.

Martin Luther King was born as Michael King Jr. in 1929 in Atlanta, Georgia. King's father later changed his own name and that of his son to honor the German leader of the Reformation, Martin Luther. As a young man, King studied to become a minister, attending Crozer Seminary in Pennsylvania and receiving his doctorate in philosophy from Boston University. In the course of his studies, he was touched by the lessons of Gandhi, who had brought the British Empire to its knees and liberated an entire nation through nonviolence.

King took a position as a minister in Montgomery, Alabama. When a confrontation over segregation on buses emerged, he urged people to resist nonviolently by boycotting the bus system. He gradually became one of the most important voices speaking out for an end to segregation—but through nonviolent means. During this time, King wrote his "Letter from a Birmingham Jail," highlighting injustices taking place across the South and calling for equality for African Americans under the law. Having witnessed the violence in Birmingham and Selma, Alabama, the conscience of the nation began to turn against segregation. On August 28, 1963, King gave his "I Have a Dream" speech in Washington DC, closing with the words from a spiritual: "Free at last, free at last."

When President Kennedy was assassinated, Lyndon Johnson took up the cause of civil rights, but he was also focused on Vietnam. He was determined that America would not suffer defeat in Southeast Asia. Johnson expected that King would lend his voice to the war effort, but King, winner of the Nobel Peace Prize in 1964, refused to acknowledge that the conflict in Vietnam was a just war. Johnson viewed King as a traitor; thereafter, the FBI stepped up its surveillance of King.

As a young man, King studied to become a minister, attending Crozer Seminary in Pennsylvania and receiving his doctorate in philosophy from Boston University.

The more he studied the question of African Americans in this country, the more King realized that just being allowed to exercise the right to vote did not solve the entire issue. Democracy must encompass economic viability. Thus, he began to mobilize protests against poverty. This work took him to Memphis in the spring of 1968. On the evening of April 3, 1968, he delivered his "I've Been to the Mountaintop" speech before a group at the Mason Temple in Memphis. He promised that America would reach the Promised Land that he had proclaimed so many times—the Promised Land he had spoken of earlier in Washington DC, where people would not be judged "by the color of their skin but by the content of their character."

The following evening, King was shot at the Lorraine Motel in Memphis. Forty years later, in 2008, President Barack Obama fulfilled Dr. King's dream that America would reach the Promised Land of equality. ■

Suggested Reading

King, speeches in Safire, *Lend Me Your Ears*.

Oates, *Let the Trumpet Sound*.

1. Can you think of other examples of the success of passive resistance?

2. Apart from the role of Dr. King, what other elements foreshadowed the end of segregation in America of the early 1960s?

Dr. King Leads a March (1963)
Lecture 35—Transcript

Our theme in this lecture is Martin Luther King Jr., August 28th, 1963, and a speech that promised Americans that we would as a nation, all of us, overcome finally the legacy of slavery and realize the true meaning of the Declaration of Independence. Along with Abraham Lincoln's Gettysburg Address, Franklin Roosevelt's first inaugural, and John Kennedy's inaugural address, the speech of Martin Luther King represents a high point in American history. It was a speech that was meant to be given at just that moment to embody the hopes of millions of Americans and the promise for the future.

Jamestown was settled in 1607 and shortly thereafter, the first African American slaves arrived in what was to be a land of freedom. The American Civil War took the lives of 623,026 Americans, and at the end of it, slavery was abolished. The 13th, 14th, and 15th Amendments came out of this patriotic struggle by the north, ending slavery with no compensation. Not even slave owners who had been loyal to the Union in states like Delaware received any compensation. It was one of the greatest social revolutions in history, and African American males could vote. All citizens of the United States, without regard to race, had the promise of the protection of the federal government in life, in liberty, and their property.

Already in 1776, we had proclaimed to the world our founding principle that all men are created equal and endowed by their creator with the unalienable right of liberty. But, even after the end of the Civil War, while African Americans were no longer held in legal slavery, they were kept oppressed. All though the latter part of the 19th century, a system grew up in the south and in many parts of the north as well, that was as evil as apartheid in South Africa. It was a result of politics. Southern votes were needed. This was a way of bringing the south back into the Union by playing upon all the prejudices that had brought the Civil War into being. Some of our most progressive presidents, in the terms of those days, were among the most radical segregationists.

Woodrow Wilson was a graduate of Johns Hopkins with a Ph.D. He was a highly popular professor at Princeton and he wrote very influential books on political science and history. He was president of Princeton University and governor of New Jersey; he set out to clean up the politics of New Jersey. He became president of the United States on a progressive platform to clean up government and to spread democracy throughout our country. He led our country into the war, a war to make the world safe for democracy. He was a radical racist. He put in place segregation regulations in the civil service. At the first stages of our entry into World War I, some of the first American troops were African Americans. They fought in French uniforms and when Wilson learned that they were receiving decorations for their bravery in battle—the Germans were terrified of these African American troops and their gallant fighting—Woodrow Wilson told the French you must not give them the Croix de Guerre. France, to its great credit, said, we give military decorations without regard to race or color. Wilson's favorite movie was that horrifying racist picture *Birth of a Nation.* Part of this progressive movement were also immigration quotas.

The most progressive ideas in America still found their root in racism. Just as in 19th century Europe, in the early 20th century of the United States this racism was thought to be based on science and Darwinism—perverted, but that's what was thought. In fact, there's an anecdote about a governor of Georgia going through a hospital and being led through the blood bank. He said, "Well, I hope we also have just as good a facility for the blood bank for our African Americans." And they said, "What do you mean? It's all the same blood." He said, "Oh no," and immediately the two blood banks had to be separated. That was the level of ignorance.

Atlanta, Georgia was one of the more progressive parts of the south. Racism existed there; Atlanta had had a terrible race riot. Right around the turn of the 20th century, the great cotton state's exposition was held in Atlanta. Atlanta business leaders began to believe that, if they became a kind of model of a moderate city in which African Americans and white Americans worked together and there wasn't a lot of blatant racial violence, that Atlanta could outstrip other cities in the south. There was already a strong African American community. Atlanta became a center for African American education—fine schools like Spelman College for women, Morehouse College for men, and an umbrella institution, the Atlanta University, which educated large numbers of African American intellectuals and professional people.

It was into this Atlanta, in 1929, that Martin Luther King was born as Michael King. His father was also Michael King, so this was Michael King Jr. Atlanta was still segregated. At the state capital itself, there were drinking fountains for whites and drinking fountains for African Americans. There were restrooms for African Americans and restrooms for white Americans. There was complete segregation in restaurants and movie theaters. Of course, basic institutions of American life, like the United States Army, were still segregated.

Early on, King's father took a trip to Germany. He came back with so much admiration for Martin Luther, who had made his stand for the truth, that he changed his name and that of his son to Martin Luther—Martin Luther King the pastor and his son, Martin Luther King Jr. King the younger was a very good student. He went to Morehouse College at a young age and was determined to become a minister. He went off to a seminary, Crozer Seminary in Pennsylvania, where he could be free to study as he wanted to do. He then went on to Boston University and received his doctorate in theology. In the course of these studies, he became profoundly touched by the lessons of the great Gandhi, Mohandas Gandhi, who had brought the British Empire to its knees and had liberated an entire nation and people by nonviolence—not using the sword to overthrow evil, but to use the truth. In the words of Gandhi, followed by Martin Luther King Jr., "You must be strong in the truth, and the truth will set you free."

He read over and over again and would practice Gandhi's morning prayer: "Let me stand up for the truth, I will do injustice to no one today, but I will not stand by idly while injustice is done to anyone." Martin Luther King drew upon Gandhi and his own deep belief in God, the God of the Old and the New Testament, the God who had proclaimed on Earth, "Do unto others as you would have them do unto you."

He was a brilliant scholar at Boston University and there were not a large number of African American professors in those days. He could have had a very comfortable, safe life teaching at a northern university with his books, just following the life of ideas. But, King believed it was the same kind of choice that Jesus had to make—Jesus who was tempted in the wilderness. King, just like Jesus, decided he had to go out into the world. He applied for positions as a minister in the south. His father told him, you should at least be a minister here in Atlanta. No, he wanted to go into cities like Birmingham and be a minister. His father said, you can't imagine what racism is like until you go to some of those cities. But, he got an offer and a very good salary and so, he began his mission. When African Americans in Birmingham and in Montgomery began to feel that they should not sit at the back of a bus— they paid the same fare, they paid the same taxes, and they began to resist. It was King who took the fundamental role in saying make this resistance without violence—no violence whatsoever.

Instead, economic force was used. Hit this evil of segregation right in the pocketbook, and the busses were boycotted. African Americans walked to work. Some even rode in a mule cart. King was there to lead them. He gradually became one of the most important voices speaking out for the end to segregation, but on a nonviolent path. He would be thrown into jail and his letter written from a Birmingham jail is a classic. It takes its place right alongside Boethius and his *Consolation of Philosophy*, and the dialogues that Plato wrote about Socrates in jail. King knew these all. His understanding of nonviolence, his understanding of the power of conscience and the freedom of conscience, was deeply rooted in his philosophical as well as his biblical background.

He found that the most difficult people to convince were those who were most well meaning, like the white ministers there in Birmingham. They had sent him a letter while he was in jail just for wanting to sit at the same lunch counter with other Americans. They sent him a letter and said, "Don't you understand that you are violating the teachings of our lord, that you are bringing trouble into the world, that you are making it so difficult for your people? Do not rush. Obey the law; what a terrible example you are setting for young people by disobeying the law. Segregation is the law of the State of Alabama and you are a troublemaker. Nobody even thinks you should be here."

And King wrote back, "I get lots of letters," he suggested lots of letters from cranks, "but I believe you white ministers actually think you're good and have our best interest at your heart. You are so wrong. Troublemaker? I will tell you who was a big troublemaker, that was Paul. He was thrown out of city after city for preaching the Gospel. You tell me I have no right to be down here in Birmingham, I have no right to be in jail in Birmingham? I was invited here under the auspices of a legal corporation and entity. But, I'll tell you something else, who actually invited Paul to go to Macedonia? The Macedonian called and Paul went. No, we have been waiting since 1776. We have been waiting since America began, and we will wait no more. But, let me tell you gentleman one more thing. What we are doing is based on natural law. If you are ministers of the Gospel, you understand that God created the law for all of us. There is neither Jew nor gentile, Greek or barbarian; we are all one in Christ Jesus. I see no segregation in the teachings of our lord or of Paul. And one more thing, if this movement does not achieve our goal which is simply our equal rights under the law, then there will be others who will come who will be far more violent than anything you have seen yet."

His letter from a Birmingham jail, his courage and that of thousands of African Americans and Americans of all ethnic backgrounds crossing the bridge that you can still see there in Selma, Alabama—being beaten bloodily, rebel yells resounding through the crowd as the state troopers beat them with clubs, unleashed dogs upon them—yes, it was bloody, yes, it was painful, but it also struck the heart of a nation. Americans north and south alike began to realize how long segregation was and the conscience of a nation turned. For a good nation like America, once that conscience is turned, then there is no holding it back.

That great day would happen on August 28th when King would proclaim with all the majesty of the old African American spirituals that we will be free at last, free at last. All of these coming together—Birmingham, Selma, the march upon Washington, step by step. When President Kennedy was assassinated, President Johnson took up the cause of civil rights. He would himself say before Congress, "We shall overcome." African Americans were registered to vote and began to transform the politics of the south and this country. America and its promise of freedom was on the march.

Johnson was a politician and he believed quite rightly that he had done very important things for the Civil Rights Movement. Having brought about the Civil Rights Act, he was focusing now upon Vietnam. It was a legacy he had gotten from John Kennedy. He was determined, in all the spirit of that Cold War, that we were not going to suffer a defeat in Southeast Asia. Johnson believed fully, as did most Americans, in 1965, that we were at war with communism. Khrushchev had said, we will bury you. Communism had to be contained and it had to be contained there in Vietnam.

We could not allow the government of South Vietnam, however corrupt it might be—it was still a democracy as we called it—to fall to the communists. We had stopped them in Korea and if we allowed Vietnam to fall, then, like dominos, all the countries of southeast Asia would fall. Who knows, the communists might even reach Australia. Johnson was not going to be the first American president to lose a war. Fighting that war were Americans of all ethnic backgrounds, side by side. I've said some critical things about President Truman, but he integrated the army. In Korea, Americans of all ethnic backgrounds learned that it is not the color of your skin, but the courage in your heart that matters. There were large numbers of African American soldiers serving there in Vietnam.

As a politician, Johnson of course expected that Martin Luther King would lend his voice to this war effort. But, King believed his principle of nonviolence. How could we be a model to the world when we were carrying out a violent war against a country that just wanted to decide for itself? It wanted that same self determination that we had proclaimed in the Declaration of Independence. Why was communism any more of a threat than any other form of government? These were people's republics and we had enough issues here in our own country. No, he would not proclaim that this was a just war.

In fact, he pondered deeply, Martin Luther King Jr. did, about the meaning of a just war. To him, the most fundamental principles laid down by St. Augustine for what makes a just war were not in play there in Vietnam. We had not been attacked, he was not sure even an ally had been attacked. No, and so, he came out against the war. He had already, in 1964, won the Nobel Peace Prize—one of the youngest to ever receive it and one of the most deserving. He had won it because he had taken what was a very dangerous violent situation in this country with many African American leaders calling for riots. He had taken it and channeled it into a peaceful solution and now he lent that same voice to the idea, get out of Vietnam. It is not our war and we are not a model for democracies until every one of our issues here at home has been solved. President Johnson looked upon him as a traitor. He began to be followed and tapped by the FBI which indeed had been looking into his activities for years, but he believed and he followed it.

The more he studied the question of African Americans here in this country, he realized that just receiving the vote, being allowed to exercise their constitutional right—while important, while transforming over the years—nonetheless, did not solve the entire issue. There had to be an economic viability to democracy. America had yet to fulfill its promise to bring wealth and affluence to every member of American society, and to make every member of American society able to have equality of opportunity.

Just as he saw that the struggle for the African American in this country had its parallels with the struggle of the Vietnamese for their own self determination, he realized that poor people in this country, whether African American or of any other ethnic background, all shared in common. Thus, he turned his attention now to what President Johnson had proclaimed was a war on poverty. He wanted to see that realized in this country. The billions of dollars that were being poured into Vietnam, transferred back here to provide opportunities and jobs. He knew he was being followed by the FBI. He knew he was taking a very dangerous path, but just like Martin Luther, his namesake, King said, "Here I stand. I can do nothing else, God help me."

It began to play an important role in mobilizing protest against poverty. It took him to Memphis, Tennessee in the spring of 1968. There he took the side of and marched alongside African American garbage collectors. What a thing for a Nobel Peace Prize winner to march alongside ordinary Americans, those who picked up the garbage of other people. People at the time said, why do they deserve a living wage? A lot of them can't even write. Just because a person can't read or write doesn't mean it costs them any less to take care of their families. King took this path.

He knew, sooner or later, this man of destiny, that he would die, that he would be killed. The night before the assassination would occur, April of 1968, he was supposed to give a speech and he didn't want to give it that night. People don't understand that a great speaker like Martin Luther King—speaking from the heart without using notes, not reading from a teleprompter, speaking from the heart—they just can't be wound up and let go. He just did not feel the spirit of the lord moving in him. He one time said to his wife, "You know, what depresses me more than almost anything is not the hatred that I encounter—I expect that—it is the constant number of people expecting me to speak and thinking that I ought to just be able to give a speech right there off the cuff and never understanding the way Winston Churchill did that every quote extemporaneous speech requires hours of preparation." In fact, for King, it required a lifetime of preparation and thought.

But, he went ahead and did it. He had given his word, and the spirit did begin to move in him. He said, "I am like Moses, I will not get to the Promised Land. I may not get there with you, but, as a people, we will get there together." As a people, he meant the whole of our nation. We would all reach that Promised Land that he had proclaimed so many times—where the sons and daughters of former slaves would sit down at the table of friendship with the sons and daughters of slave owners, where we would judge not by the color of your skin, but the quality of your character, where a whole world would be founded in the ideal of "do unto others as you would have them do unto you." In fact, we would not even notice the color of the skin of our neighbor because we were all just one.

The next day was there at the Lorraine Motel in Memphis, Tennessee. You can still visit it. It is one of the best museums I have ever seen, a remarkable display conveying powerfully but factually the Civil Rights Movement in our country, the same way that the birthplace of Martin Luther King in Atlanta is a remarkable museum, a moving learning experience. At both of these museums, at Memphis where he died and in Atlanta where he was born, one of the most prominent figures is a statue of the great Gandhi.

King knew how Gandhi had died. Riots had broken out all over India with its partition. The hatreds that Gandhi had tried to channel into nonviolence led Muslims to kill Hindus, Hindus to kill Muslims. Gandhi, trying to make them live together in peace, was shot by an assassin, the last words on his lips being, "God," his soul thus going straight to heaven. Gandhi had died. Christ had known he was going to die. He had said, "Let that cup pass." These were not historical figures to Martin Luther King Jr. They were great examples that guided every one of his steps. Maybe this cup would pass from his lips this time, but sooner or later the fanaticism would kill him.

He was going to go off to a friend's house, have the kind of meal he liked, the kind of friendship and fellowship he liked. He walked out just for a breath of fresh air there at that motel which is preserved just the way it was then. The shot rang out. Like John F. Kennedy, like Kennedy's brother Robert—so devoted to the Civil Rights Movement—in that same year 1968, Martin Luther King was assassinated by, we are told, a lone assassin. But, his spirit still moves. His speech still moves us to tears when we see it in the old footage. But, more than that, he changed history. In the year 2008, President Obama would bring to fulfillment the promise and the dream of an entire nation that would get to that sacred and holy land. Martin Luther King, he was a key force in bringing America to the realization of its true mission in the world.

September 11, 2001
Lecture 36

Human nature never changes. We feel the same passions, love, hate, desire for domination, desire to wage war, and wishes to live in peace that the men and women of the age of Hammurabi felt.

Many believed that the advent of the new millennium brought with it an age of peace and prosperity. The Soviet Union had collapsed, and the emergence of democracies around the world seemed to prefigure the end of war. Economists predicted ever-growing affluence in the new global economy, and scientists foresaw the end of famines. Then, suddenly, this golden age was shattered by the terrorist attack on the United States on September 11, 2001.

The background of this event can be found in the Middle East. As we have said in the last few lectures, the axial age of our day was set in motion by the Cold War, and U.S. involvement in the Middle East is one more legacy of the Cold War. Both Britain and France received mandates to govern parts of the Middle East after World War I, and both failed utterly. The United States took up the challenge of the Middle East after World War II, largely to protect its interests in its oil.

In 1948, Palestine was in complete ferment. Britain had promised a homeland to the Jewish people in Palestine, and they were determined to proclaim their nationality in what is now Israel. President Truman recognized the new state of Israel, despite advice that doing so would poison relations with the Arab world for generations. From this, the hatred of America grew, reaching fruition on September 11, 2001.

The events of that day forever shattered the myth that America is all-powerful. Before September 11, Americans looked upon themselves as the new Roman Empire, establishing peace around the world. Americans are now faced by new potential superpowers in economics and military strength: China, India, and North Korea. The world is now a far more dangerous place than it has been at any time since 1962 and the Cuban Missile Crisis.

Our course has been based on the conviction that history is made by great individuals, great ideas, and great events. We began with the Middle East and we conclude with the Middle East and America's involvement in it today. Along the way, we looked at crucial ages in history, such as the period from 600 to 400 B.C., when the spiritual ideas that still guide much of the world today were born. We also looked at ideals of beauty, including Dante's *Divine Comedy* and Michelangelo's Sistine Chapel. At the same time, we explored great events in science, from the birth of scientific medicine in Athens in the 5th century B.C. to the transformation of medicine and our understanding of our own origins in the 19th and 20th centuries. We've also witnessed technological developments, including travel by air and the harnessing of atomic power. In our own age, the world had witnessed the discovery and understanding of DNA and the advent of cloning.

Despite the technological and scientific advances humans have made, we've also learned in this course that human nature remains the same.

Despite the technological and scientific advances humans have made, we've also learned in this course that human nature remains the same. That is why history is always our great light. As we've seen, it is not that history repeats itself but that humans repeat the mistakes of the past because they refuse to learn the lessons of history. In this age of science and technology, we must continue to be guided by the lessons of Confucius, Buddha, Jesus, and Socrates. If we can live by their truths starting right now, then truly, the world will never be the same. ∎

Suggested Reading

Ferguson, *Colossus*.

1. We draw lessons from history both as citizens of a democracy and as private individuals. How have imponderables shaped your life?

2. Could someone in 1900 imagine the world of today? Where do you think the world will be in 100 years?

September 11, 2001
Lecture 36—Transcript

With this, our final lecture on events that have changed history, I want you to go back with me to September 11th, 2001. You could be anywhere in this great nation of ours. If you're a late rising professor in the State of Oklahoma, maybe you're just having breakfast, getting ready to go to class. If you're in New York City, it's a beehive of activity, everyone working as hard as they can, and the great Twin Towers soaring into the heavens. Or maybe you're on an airplane, worried about being late to a business meeting that didn't even need to be held in the first place.

You're in the America of a new millennia. It is a new century and it is a new millennia. How foolish people have been to think that this would somehow be a catastrophe. These ideas of a changing millennium have tortured the human race since the year 1000 when prophets predicted the fall of the world. But, 2000 had come, Y2K, isn't that what it was called? Who today even remembers that? All the people storing food, how foolish they looked in retrospect—one of the few things I was actually right about.

The millennium has come, nothing bad has happened. It is a new dawn of peace and prosperity. In fact, books have come out entitled the *Triumph of Liberty.* Books have come out entitled the *End of History* because everywhere in the world, democracy and freedom are on the march. The Soviet Union has collapsed; countries have emerged from its rubble like Estonia, Latvia, Lithuania, and Poland, to begin their course towards democracy. It is an age of a global economy and the economists are predicting ever-greater prosperity. Science is predicting that there will never again be terrible famines. We can produce so much food through various hybrids that no one need to go hungry in this world. Democracies make for good neighbors our political figures tell us. There will be democracies all along the world and therefore, no more wars. We in America are safe. We won the Cold War and the terror of the old Soviet Union is gone. China is our friend now, our trading partner. It is a golden age of peace and prosperity.

Then, suddenly, watching the TV while you have breakfast, catching a glimpse of it from a corner of your eye as you walk the busy streets of New York, there is this terrifying scene that is burned forever into the memory of anyone who was there or saw it on television. Just as the Twin Towers collapsed, so our world around us seemed to collapse and nothing was what it had seemed to be. September 11th, 2001—it changed history immediately. The Twin Towers struck, the Pentagon, the very symbol of our nation's power, and one more plane just crashing down into a field. It had been aimed, we were told, at the White House itself. With all of our military might, we seem to be helpless before a few fanatical terrorists. Terrorists—we knew what the word meant, we knew what terror was. But, it took on a whole new meaning to us because it seemed that the whole of the world—and it still seems to us right now—the whole of the world was united into a global terror network determined to bring pain and suffering and death to our country, terrorism.

Then, following rapidly upon it were economic troubles, invasion of Afghanistan, invasion of Iraq, a bumpy economy right on down until our own day, and security precautions. Every aspect of our life—no doubt quite rightly—was subjected to ever greater scrutiny lest somehow a terrorist sneak through and carry out again one of these terrible devastating acts. How can we protect ourselves? Was this but the forerunner of an atomic attack? As we have discussed in this course, nuclear proliferation remains our greatest single danger. What if, the next time around, one of these terrorists unleashes a nuclear explosion in one our great American cities? Bacteria—what about unleashing some killer virus? From being confident, we became scared. We acted—and should act—as though terror is all around us.

What was the background for this world changing event of September 11th, 2001? Remember, I am convinced that America is the greatest force for good in the world and whatever changes America forever changes the world forever. The background lay in the Middle East. As we have said in our last several lectures, the axial age of our day was set in motion by the Cold War. Our involvement in the Middle East is one more legacy of the Cold War. Army after army has passed through the Middle East. Before us, the last great powers to try to solve the issues of the Middle East were Britain and France. Both received mandates in that area—the authority to govern parts of the Middle East after World War I. Britain and Iraq, France and Syria—both failed entirely. We took up that legacy after World War II. It was also a matter of national security. It was also a matter of bringing democracy to the Middle East which had never known it, perhaps never wanted it. It was a matter of oil.

You want at world changing event—it was the drilling of the first commercial oil well in Pennsylvania in 1859, a product of an energy crisis. Lamps had been lit with whale oil and we were exterminating the whales. Thus, petroleum—which had already been known, as far back as the time of Herodotus—now became a vital natural resource. Of course, it went right along with the development of the internal combustion engine. Winston Churchill had already foreseen how petroleum would transform the world. Quite rightly, Churchill is looked upon as one of the 100 most important oil people in the world's history. As First Lord of the Admiralty, in 1911, he began transforming the British Navy from coal burning to oil. Churchill struck the first big oil deal in Iran in order to get oil for the British Navy.

Oil has brought us into the Middle East. We were so confident in 1919 that, when it was suggested as part of the peace negotiations at Versailles that America might take a mandate in some part of the Middle East like Iraq one of the advisers to President Wilson said why do we need Iraq? We've got Texas. We still have Texas, but we need that oil. The oil brought us into the Middle East, but also the moral fiber and courage of President Harry Truman.

It's 1948. The State of Palestine, the area of Palestine, was in complete ferment. It was a British Mandate. Going back to the time of Winston Churchill and largely led by Winston Churchill at the time for the First World War, Britain had promised a homeland to the Jewish people there in Palestine. Churchill fought for that for the rest of his political career. In 1948, the horrors of the Holocaust had been unveiled to the entire world. Jewish people, knowing that the only safety they would ever truly have was in their own country, were determined to put in place a Jewish homeland.

Truman was faced with a decision. The Jewish people, in what was now Israel, said we're going to proclaim our nationality, our nation, and we want America to be the first to recognize us. The man that Truman admired most of all, George Marshall, came in and said, "I am Secretary of State, Mr. President, and I must tell you that the entire State Department is opposed to the recognition of Israel. It will poison our relations with the Arab world for generations to come." Truman pondered it and then he said, "I am going to recognize Israel." There were two reasons; one, the Jewish people have suffered beyond any possible human imagination, and two, it's in the Bible. God promised them a homeland and now all these centuries later, if I can do anything to help the Jewish people get back that homeland, I will do it. If it embitters our relations with the Middle East, so be it, because it is the right thing to do. The hatred of America, America as the great Satan, grew and grew and grew. It reached its fruition in this terrorist attack that changed history.

Will 100 years from now a potbellied professor tell you that September 11th, 2001 changed history? I believe that person will. I believe that it forever has taken away from us the veil that we are all-powerful. It has recreated a series of superpowers in the world. We looked upon ourselves, before September 11th , as the new Roman Empire, establishing a Pax Americana like the Pax Romaña of the 1st and 2nd century A.D. We are not that. We are now faced by superpowers. China has a larger army and a more vibrant economy. Russia is armed to the teeth with nuclear weapons. It has a history of being xenophobic and chauvinistic, feeling a deep humiliation at the loss of its empire and deep frustration at the failure of the Americans to step in after the collapse of communism and rebuild Russia on a viable economic basis for democracy the way we used the Marshall Plan to rebuild Germany and Japan after the war. Countries like India are developing rapidly economically, but are also armed with nuclear weapons.

There is one more legacy of the Cold War—North Korea. Who would have imagined that more than 50 years after the conclusion of the Korean War that that little tiny country stuff off on a peninsula of Asia would be a nuclear power to threaten us, making us ever more dependent upon China not just financially, but in terms of our foreign affairs and dealing with North Korea?

No, we are no longer the world's absolute superpower. The world is a far more dangerous place than it has been any time since 1962 and the Cuban Missile Crisis. It has changed forever our perception of ourselves and it has changed the course of history in the Middle East.

Event after event, great events that shape history—we have studied 36 of them in this course. We have begun our course in the firm conviction that history is made by great individuals, great ideas, and great events. This is our history of the world taught through the great events that have shaped it. We have looked at great ideas like the concept of law, tracing it back to the first Law Code of Hammurabi. We've looked at that great event which we call the birth of civilization, the invention of writing, of monumental architecture, of the use of metals, and of complex government structures in the Middle East. We have understood that the history of the Middle East defines it as the crucible of conflict and the graveyard of empires.

We began with the Middle East and we conclude with the Middle East and America's involvement in it today. Will we be only one of those who have passed through like the charioteers of Ramses II in the 13th century, like the Roman legions of Julius Cesar, like the crusaders of Richard the Lionheart, like the soldiers of Napoleon, like the camel core of Lawrence of Arabia— simply to pass through and be forgotten? Or will we, with our blood and treasure, change the Middle East forever?

Then, we have looked at those crucial ages in history like the period from 600 to 400 B.C. when the spiritual ideas that still guide much of the world today were born. The Buddha, Confucius, the Hebrew prophets—their ideals form the spiritual framework for all the centuries to come. We've looked at ideals of beauty—Dante and his magnificent *Paradise* celebrating the love of God, the supreme beauty of the Sistine Chapel and Michelangelo—great events that gave us enduring statements of what beauty is.

Science—science has propelled us to a whole new level of civilization. The birth of scientific medicine in Athens in the 5th century B.C. and with it, the idea we still grapple with today—can every citizen in a democracy have the best possible medical care made available to them just because they are a citizen? Is it part of their unalienable right of life, liberty, and the pursuit of happiness? But, it was the 19th and 20th century that, above all, created our age of science—the transformation of medicine, of travel by flight, and of our entire understanding of the nature of human beings. These are ideas that still reverberate with us right now—every time a school board debates whether or not evolution or intelligent design will be taught in its schools.

In fact, the 19th and 20th century, and going on into our 21st century, those have formed the axes upon which our world will spin off into the future because it has placed into our hands the knowledge first described in the book of Genesis. "Partake of the fruit of knowledge and you will become like gods, you will know good and evil." Right there, there's the lesson of history. We are become like gods; our knowledge of medicine enables a doctor today to bring you back from the dead. If I have a heart attack lecturing right here, they'll rush in and bring me back and I'll start right back up without losing a beat. We have come to understand the power of the atom itself. We are able to unleash it and harness it to bring electricity to the entire world. We have unlocked the secrets of life so that no child in the world needs to go hungry. With our communication, technology, and ability to move food everywhere in the world, there should not be a hungry child in Somalia or anywhere in the world.

We have become like gods, almost able like the Lord in the book of Exodus to spread out manna before the hungry. Then, we've gone even further. We have looked deeply into the very structure of human life. The discovery and understanding of what DNA is, is an event that has changed history forever. This is because, with that knowledge, we can now remove every evil disease from the world theoretically. We can clone an entire new generation that will never know some dreaded rare neurological disease, epilepsy, or cancer—who knows, that may never have to die. You see, our science, our human brain, it can create a new paradise. Our brain is no bigger, we're not even any more intelligent than those who raised the first pyramids. But, step by step, the world has evolved into this scientific and technological revolution of our day. It has put into our hands the ability to decide fate itself.

Our life lessons from the great books—we have looked at Greek tragedy. From the time of the Greeks going right back in fact to the time of ancient Babylonia and the great story of the Gilgamesh, humans have wondered, why do I have to die? They have wondered why, if God is good, does evil exist in the world? Why, if God is good, do terrible diseases exist? Why, if God is good, are there serial killers? Now, just like eating the fruit of knowledge, we have come to understand. We can link it all to chromosomes, to DNA. We have the power to alter these. DNA has become our modern answer to the Greek question of fate versus free will. In the play *Oedipus the King*, the playwright Sophocles already asked the question, are there families that are fated for disaster? In the *Oresteia* of Aeschylus, Cassandra says, "I see this family filled with all the blood of disaster." The Greeks already understood that somehow these were passed down to us, but now we understand it. Now, when I read *Oedipus the King,* I no longer tell my students that Oedipus had free will, that he could choose not to marry a woman old enough to be his mother after he had received an oracle that he would kill his father and marry his mother. No, he had no free will whatsoever and none of us do; it is all set up from the time we are conceived and we can do nothing about it.

Let's take a lighter note. Do you think I freely chose to be as bald as a cucumber? No. I want a head of golden curls right to the grave, but from the moment of my conception, it was determined that I would be bald. So it is with each of us. The Greeks also understood, the same way that the author of the Gilgamesh did—the Gilgamesh, already known and loved in the time of Hammurabi. Gilgamesh, like the Greek playwright, knew that the only free will you have is how you respond to the disasters or the good things that are built into your DNA. We have come to this wisdom. The question is how we are we going to use it. Yes, we live on an entirely different plane in terms of our technology and science—even the 19th century and even the generation that fought World War II. But, the trouble is science and technology advance.

All of that technology, all of that science with its power for ill as well as good, is put into the same human nature. That is one of our most fundamental lessons of history and one of the most fundamental truths revealed by or study of great events. Human nature never changes. We feel the same passions, love, hate, desire for domination, desire to wage war, and wishes to live in peace that the men and women of the age of Hammurabi felt. The 20th century, with all its knowledge, brought forth the two most destructive wars in history. The power of the atom unleashed, able to do enormous good, was first used to drop upon our fellow human beings—who had, in the minds of those who dropped it, my mind as well, fully brought it upon themselves by their desire to have war. Cloning—do you think that human cloning will not occur? It has not already occurred I'm quite sure. We will not stop striving until there is a class seated out in front of me—310 students, all listening intently, taking down notes, all with the same brilliant IQ.

All of this knowledge is poured into the same human nature. That is the one thing, despite our God-like intentions, that we cannot change—human nature. That is why history is always our great light. As the founders of our country saw, human nature never changes and therefore, the events of the past will be repeated again and again and again. It is not history that repeats itself, but as we have said, it is humans repeating the same mistakes of the past because they refuse to learn these lessons of history. It is with us right now—as President John Kennedy said, "With this generation to make one more step forward." One more step to see if we cannot break the cycle of war and starvation.

If we cannot, as a world entire, decide we will use our knowledge to feed the hungry, we will use our knowledge to spread the lesson of do unto others as you would have them do unto you. We will spread the lessons of love, peace, and charity throughout the world. We will get to the Promised Land where no one even says President Obama is the first African American president because we will simply take it for granted that we all have the same heart and moral values. The lessons of Confucius, Buddha, Jesus, and Socrates can guide us in the same age of science and technology; do unto others, search for wisdom, be just to your fellow human, be courageous in standing up for what is right, and be moderate. Be moderate. Judge what is right in each and every situation. If we did that starting right now, today, then truly, the world would never be the same.

Timeline

B.C.

3000.. Birth of civilization in Egypt
and Mesopotamia.

2500.. Pyramids; Indus Valley civilization.

2000.. Stonehenge.

1760.. Beginning of civilization in
China with the first historical
dynasty, the Shang, and the first
writing and bronze artworks.

1749.. Law code of Hammurabi issued.

1295–1225....................................... Ramses II, pharaoh of Egypt,
historical context of Exodus.

1250–1240....................................... Trojan War.

1027–256....................................... Zhou dynasty in China.

1000.. Beginning of Sanskrit literature in India.

594 .... Solon becomes governor of Athens.

563–483... Life of the Buddha.

551–479... Life of Confucius.

546–330... Persian Empire.

490.. Battle of Marathon.

480–404... Golden age of Athenian democracy.

430.. Hippocrates.

336–323... Alexander the Great.

259–209... Ch'in Shih Huang-ti, first true
emperor of all China.

218–146... Rise of Rome to the status of
superpower in the Mediterranean world.

48–31... Julius Caesar and Augustus establish
monarchy in the Roman Empire.

31 B.C.–180 A.D. .... Golden age of the Roman Empire.

A.D.

36... Trial of Jesus.

312... Conversion of Constantine.

476... Fall of the Roman Empire
in Western Europe.

622... The Hegira of Muhammad.

800... Charlemagne crowned Roman Emperor,
establishing what will become the Holy
Roman Empire of the German Nation.

988... Russia converts to
Orthodox Christianity.

1066... Norman conquest of England.

1088.. Founding of the University of Bologna.

1096–1272.. Crusades.

1155–1227.. Life of Genghis Khan.

1194–1500.. Gothic art and architecture
dominate Europe.

1215.. Magna Carta.

1254–1324.. Marco Polo.

1265–1321.. Dante.

1304–1564.. Renaissance.

1453–1521.. Golden age of the Aztec
Empire in Mexico.

1492.. Columbus's discovery
of the New World.

1517–1648.. Reformation.

1588.. Defeat of the Spanish Armada.

1648–1789.. Age of Enlightenment.

1688.. Siege of Vienna.

1769.. James Watt patents the steam engine.

1775–1789.. American Revolution and Constitution.

1789–1815 .... French Revolution.

1804.. Richard Trevithick and
the first locomotive.

1822–1895....................................... Louis Pasteur.

1823.. Samuel Brown begins production and
sale of internal combustion engines.

1861–1865....................................... American Civil War.

1903.. First heavier-than-air flight.

1909.. Henry Ford and the Model T.

1914–1918....................................... World War I.

1929–1939....................................... Great Depression.

1939–1945....................................... World War II.

1945–1989....................................... Cold War.

1989–?... United States as world's superpower.

Glossary

Akkadian: Language of ancient Babylonia. It was a Semitic language, related to Hebrew and Arabic, written in cuneiform, or wedge-shaped, script.

antibiotics: "Anti-life." Substances produced by microorganisms, such as fungi and bacteria, that have the ability to kill or inhabit the growth of other microorganisms.

Austro-Hungarian monarchy: The designation from 1867 to 1918 for the empire combining Austria and Hungary, as well as other political entities, under the rule of Franz Ferdinand as emperor of Austria and king of Hungary.

Balkans: Geographical and political designation for southeastern Europe from Slovenia to Greece.

birth of civilization: Convenient term to describe the invention of writing, monumental architecture, metallurgy, hydraulic engineering, and complex government structures that occurred at different times in the major centers of ancient civilization: the Middle East and Egypt, China, and India.

Bolshevik: From the Russian "majority party." Self-designation of Vladimir Lenin's faction of the Russian Communist Party in 1917.

capitalism: Economic system based on private ownership of the means of production, the setting of prices by the free market, and the accumulation of capital and wealth in the hands of private individuals.

democracy: Greek: *demos*, "people," and *kratia*, "power." As Lincoln said, democracy is defined as "government of the people, by the people, and for the people."

Holy Roman Empire of the German Nation: The political structure arising from Charlemagne's coronation in Rome in 800 as the new Roman emperor. The power and extent of this empire varied greatly over the more than 1,000 years of its existence. At its height, in the 15th and 16th centuries, the Holy Roman Empire encompassed more than 350 political entities, including free cities and entire countries, and stretched from the Czech Republic of today to Belgium. It was ended by Napoleon in 1806.

humanism: Intellectual current focusing on the use of the classical past to understand the present.

humors: The medical theory, going back to Hippocrates, that four "humors," or fluids, determined the medical condition of a human: phlegm, blood, yellow bile, and black bile.

liberal arts: A term first used in the Athenian democracy and defined by Aristotle as an education suited for a free citizen. In the medieval university, the liberal arts were the intermediary areas of study between the fundamental learning of reading and writing and more advanced professional study. The liberal arts included grammar, rhetoric, and logic, along with arithmetic, geometry, music, and astronomy.

Manhattan Project: Code name for the U.S. program to build an atomic bomb, initiated in late 1941.

Mesopotamia: Greek for the "land between the rivers." Classical term for the land and cultures of the area between the Tigris and Euphrates Rivers. Bounded on the north by the mountains of southern Turkey and on the south by the Persian Gulf. Mesopotamia is basically the same territory as modern Iraq.

microbes: Organisms so small they can be seen only with a microscope. In common use, synonymous with "germ."

Middle Ages: Historical term of convenience to define the period between antiquity and the modern age. A good basic definition of the Middle Ages is the period between the conversion of Constantine to Christianity in 312 A.D. and the fall of Constantinople in 1453.

Middle East: As used in this course, the geographical area from Pakistan to Morocco, including Turkey.

Mithras (Mithra): One of numerous gods of personal salvation in the Roman Empire. As Christianity came from Judaea, so Mithraism came from Persia. Like Jesus, Mithras was believed to be the son of god, who suffered for humanity. The cult of Mithraism was viewed as a hated competitor by contemporary Christians.

panic: As an economic term, it is the 19th-century word for what we today call a "market sell-off" or a recession or depression.

Protestantism: European religious current initiated by Martin Luther. The name derives from the adherents' "protesting" against corruption in the Roman Catholic Church and the authority of the pope.

Renaissance: Historical term of convenience but also used by contemporaries to describe the rebirth of Europe from "the ignorance and barbarity of the Middle Ages." A good working definition is the period in Italy from 1300 to 1600 and in northern Europe from 1453 to 1600.

Sanskrit: The language of ancient India; an Indo-European language and, thus, related to English, Latin, Greek, and many other European languages. The earliest literary texts in Sanskrit go back to 1000 B.C. Like Latin, it gave rise to numerous related languages, such as Hindi, spoken throughout modern India.

socialism: Economic and political concepts based on the ideal that the welfare of society as a whole is more important than the freedom of the individual members of society.

spontaneous generation: The theory that a living organism can arise from non-living matter.

Vedas: The "wisdom" literature of early India, written in Sanskrit and comprising hymns and other religious poetry. Composed by various authors from around 1000 to 600 B.C.

Biographical Notes

Diocletian (a.k.a. **Gaius Aurelius Valerius Diocletianus**, 245–313): As emperor from 284 to 305, Diocletian restored the Roman Empire, which had collapsed under political, economic, military, and social turmoil. The restored empire of Diocletian was highly structured and bureaucratic. Part of this structure was the insistence that all Romans worship the gods of Rome. The refusal of Christians to obey led to savage persecutions.

Einstein, Albert (1879–1955): German-born Nobel Prize–winning physicist, whose theoretical research laid one of the foundations for the atomic bomb. Einstein immigrated to the United States in 1933 and became a professor at the Institute for Advanced Study in Princeton. In 1939, Einstein wrote to President Roosevelt, stressing the danger of the development of an atomic bomb by Germany. This letter played a major role in Roosevelt's decision to initiate the development of an atomic bomb in the United States.

Galen (131–200): Greco-Roman doctor. Court physician to the emperor Marcus Aurelius, Galen played a fundamental role in the transmission of the medical knowledge of Hippocrates. Galen's own textbooks were determinative for European medicine until 1500.

Heisenberg, Werner (1901–1976): German Nobel Prize–winning physicist. Heisenberg headed the effort by German scientists to develop an atomic bomb in World War II. Heisenberg's role in the failure of this effort remains controversial.

Hoover, Herbert (1874–1964): President of the United States (1929–1933. Hoover, who was elected during a period of enormous prosperity, was one of the best educated and most successful men to become president. He was a superb businessman and administrator. His failure to deal with the Depression that began in 1929 and his role in causing it remain controversial.

Johnson, Lyndon Baines (1908–1973): President of the United States (1963–1969). As a senator, Johnson proved to be a highly successful politician. As

John Kennedy's vice president, he became president when Kennedy was assassinated. A great admirer of Franklin Roosevelt, Johnson put in place a broad social program known as the "Great Society." His influence was fundamental in bringing political success to the civil rights movement. His handling of the Vietnam War was highly controversial and divisive and led to his refusal to seek reelection.

Julius II (Giuliano della Rovere, 1443–1513): Pope from 1503 to 1513, Julius was a humanist, a lover of art, a diplomat, and a warrior. His goal was to unite all of Italy under the temporal power of the papacy. His love of art and his longing for immortality led to his granting of artistic commissions to Michelangelo and other great artists of the Renaissance.

Lee, Robert Edward (1807–1870): U.S. and Confederate soldier. As general of the Army of Northern Virginia, Lee's victories from 1862 to 1863 led him to be compared in the North and Europe to the greatest generals in history. His defeat at the Battle of Gettysburg (July1–3, 1863) turned the tide of the Civil War against the Confederacy. His noble behavior, his sense of honor, and his efforts after the war to reconcile North and South led Theodore Roosevelt to call Lee, along with George Washington, one of the "two greatest Americans."

Marco Polo (1254–1324): Venetian businessman, entrepreneur, traveler, and explorer. Marco Polo's lengthy travels throughout Asia and his published accounts of his adventures played a major role in encouraging the projects of Christopher Columbus and other explorers.

Pompey (a. k. a. **Gnaeus Pompeius**, 106–48 B.C.): Roman general and politician. Pompey was a brilliant general who conquered widely in the Middle East and solved Rome's problem with terrorists. At first an ally, he later became Caesar's most dangerous opponent. Pompey was supported by the legitimate government of Rome in the form of the Senate. He was defeated by Caesar in 48 B.C. at Pharsalus, and after fleeing to Egypt, he was murdered there on the order of the Egyptian king.

Ptolemy (a.k.a. **Claudius Ptolemaeus**, fl. 127–151): Greco-Roman mathematician, geographer, and astronomer. Working at the library of Alexandria, Ptolemy developed latitudes and longitudes and drew maps of the world that were determinative for European knowledge of geography until Christopher Columbus.

Ramses II (1292–1225 B.C.): Pharaoh of Egypt. Under Ramses the Egyptian Empire was at its height of military and political power. His monumental buildings and statues dedicated to himself remain among the most imposing monuments of ancient Egypt. Ramses is frequently thought to be the pharaoh of Exodus.

Raphael (Raffaello Santi, 1483–1520): The contemporary of Michelangelo who most rivaled him as a painter. Raphael's magnificent paintings in the Vatican, including The School of Athens, are masterpieces that are superior in style and color to the Sistine Chapel frescoes of Michelangelo. Raphael's work has a perfection that is lacking in Michelangelo but without the creative genius.

Bibliography

Note: In this bibliography, I have sought to recommend works that I thought best put our discussions into a broader context and works that I find clearest and most helpful. This means that I have frequently suggested older, more traditional works that are available. I have followed Lord Acton, the great British historian of liberty, and his dictum that it is the mark of an educated person to read books he or she disagrees with. Thus, I have frequently recommended books that disagree with me, because I find these most stimulating.

Alter, Jonathan. *The Defining Moment: FDR's Hundred Days and the Triumph of Hope*. New York: Simon and Schuster, 2006. A journalistic account but very solid in its knowledge of the history of the period.

Arberry, A. J. *The Koran Interpreted*. New York: Simon and Schuster, 1996. The best translation.

Aristotle. *The Athenian Constitution*. Translated by P. J. Rhodes. New York: Penguin, 1984. The most profound mind of Greece gives a history of the Athenian constitution, with a good discussion of Solon.

Bainton, Roland, *Here I Stand: A Life of Martin Luther*. Nashville, TN: Abingdon Press, 1990. The best biography of Martin Luther.

Barzun, Jacques. *Darwin, Marx, Wagner: Critique of a Heritage*. Boston: Little Brown, 1943. An intellectual history of the impact of these thinkers on the catastrophe of the 20th century.

Browning, W. R. F. *Oxford Dictionary of the Bible*. New York: Oxford University Press, 1996. A good orientation on the book of Exodus.

Bullock, Alan. *Hitler and Stalin: Parallel Lives*. New York: Knopf, 1991. Masterful parallel lives of these titans of evil.

Byrne, Patrick. *The Black Death*. Westport, CT: Greenwood, 2004. The best short introduction to the Black Death in medieval Europe.

Caesar, Julius. *The Civil War*. Translated by John Carter. Oxford: Oxford University Press, 1997. A convenient edition of Caesar's account of his decision to cross the Rubicon and its consequences.

Carrithers, M., M. Cook, H. Carpenter, and R. Dawson. *Founders of Faith: The Buddha, Confucius, Jesus, and Muhammad*. New York: Oxford University Press, 1990. Good, brief discussions of these four religious leaders.

Chung, Jung. *Mao: The Unknown Story*. New York: Knopf, 2005. A highly critical account of the life and crimes of Chairman Mao.

Confucius. *The Analects*. Translated by D. C. Lau. New York: Penguin, 1979. The best translation, with a valuable introduction.

Dante. *The Divine Comedy*. Translated by R. Sinclair. New York: Oxford University Press, 1991. Of the many English translations, I prefer Sinclair for the accuracy of his translation and the clarity of his notes.

———. *Vita Nuova*. Translated by D. Cervigni and E. Vasta. Notre Dame, IN: University of Notre Dame Press, 1995. An accurate translation with facing Italian text.

Darwin, Charles. *From So Simple a Beginning: The Four Great Books of Charles Darwin*. Edited by Edward O. Wilson. New York: Norton, 2006. A new edition of Darwin's major works.

Debre, Partrice. *Louis Pasteur*. Baltimore, MD: Johns Hopkins University Press, 1996. The best biography.

Donia, Robert. *Sarajevo: A Biography*. Ann Arbor: University of Michigan Press, 2006. A history of the city, with an excellent discussion of the assassination of Franz Ferdinand.

Dubos, Rene. *Pasteur and Modern Science*. Garden City, NY: Doubleday, 1960. An excellent brief treatment of Pasteur's achievement.

Ehrenberg, V. *From Solon to Socrates: Greek History and Civilization during the 5th and 6th Centuries B.C.* London: Methuen, 1968. Still the best and clearest introduction to this critical period in history.

Eusebius. *The Life of Constantine*. A. Cameron and S. Hall, trans. Oxford: Clarendon Press, 1999. The fundamental ancient source, very partisan, for the conversion of Constantine.

Evans, Harold, Gail Buckland, and David Lefer. *They Made America: From the Steam Engine to the Search Engine: Two Centuries of Innovators*. Boston: Little Brown, 2004. Outstanding biographies of America's most seminal entrepreneurs.

Ferguson, Niall. *Colossus: The Price of America's Empire*. New York: Penguin, 2004. A somewhat gloating prediction of the failure of the United States as a superpower.

Ferrell, Robert. *Harry S. Truman and the Cold War Revisionists*. Columbia: University of Missouri Press, 2006. An excellent introduction to the issues surrounding the origin of the Cold War by a distinguished specialist on Truman.

Foote, Shelby. *The Civil War: A Narrative*. New York: Random House, 1958. The most well written and informative history of the Civil War.

Freud, S. *Moses and Monotheism*. New York: Vintage, 1955. A work of genius and highly controversial.

Galbraith, John Kenneth. *The Great Crash*. Boston: Houghton Mifflin, 1988. A stylistic and historical gem by one of the most thoughtful economists of the 20th century. The obvious parallels between 1929 and 2008 are more chilling when you realize the book was originally written in 1955.

Goffen, R. *Renaissance Rivals: Michelangelo, Leonardo, Raphael, Titian*. New Haven: Yale University Press, 2002. A superb study of this constellation of genius.

Gokhale, B. *Asoka Maurya*. New York: Twayne, 1966. An excellent discussion of Buddhism and the political and intellectual context of its dissemination.

Goldhagen. Daniel. *Hitler's Willing Executioners: Ordinary Germans and the Holocaust*. New York: Knopf, 1996. A meticulous work of scholarship, documenting the terrifying degree to which everyday Germans lent themselves to the evils of the Nazi government.

Graham-Dixon, Andrew. *Michelangelo and the Sistine Chapel*. New York: Skyhorse, 2009. A good introduction.

Green, Peter. *The Greco-Persian Wars*. Berkeley: University of California Press, 1996. A detailed, scholarly account.

Hallo, William, and William Simpson. *The Ancient Near East*. New York: Harcourt Brace, 1998. A good, brief history.

Heilbroner, Robert. *The Worldly Philosophers: The Lives, Times and Ideas of the Great Economic Thinkers*. New York: Simon and Schuster, 1999. Now in its ninth edition, this is an instructive and highly readable account of the lives and ideas of Adam Smith, Karl Marx, and other influential economic thinkers.

Herodotus. *The Histories*. Translated by Aubrey de Selincourt. New York: Penguin, 1954. The most readable translation of our fundamental source for the Battle of Marathon.

Hippocrates. *Hippocratic Writings*. Edited by G. E. R. Lloyd. New York: Penguin, 1983. The most convenient selection, with good translation.

Hodge, M. J. S. *The Cambridge Companion to Darwin*. New York: Cambridge University Press, 2009. A standard work of reference.

Inalcik, H. *Social and Economic History of the Ottoman Empire*. New York: Cambridge, 1994. The standard treatment of the Ottoman Empire, detailed and scholarly.

Jones, A. H. M. *Constantine and the Conversion of Europe*. New York: Macmillan, 1949, numerous reprints. The best and clearest account of the issues surrounding the conversion of Constantine.

Kelly, John. *The Great Mortality: An Intimate History of the Black Death*. New York: HarperCollins, 2005. A popular book on the Black Death.

Lindberg, David. *The Beginnings of Western Science*. Chicago: University of Chicago Press, 2007. A definitive work, discussing the topic from prehistory to the Renaissance, including a good section on the intellectual context of Hippocrates.

Man, John. *Gutenberg: How One Man Remade the World with Words*. New York: Wiley, 2002. A popular story of the man and the invention that changed history.

Manchester, William. *The Death of a President*. New York: Harper and Row, 1967. Through this book, a generation unfamiliar with Kennedy can judge the impact of his assassination.

———. *The Glory and the Dream: A Narrative History of America from 1932–1972*. Boston: Little Brown, 1974. A beautifully written, evocative, and accurate account; good on both Roosevelt and Kennedy.

Marx, Karl. *Capital: A Critique of Political Economy*. New York: Vintage, 1981. An excellent English translation of Marx's definitive book.

Mattingly, Garrett. *The Defeat of the Spanish Armada*. Boston: Houghton Mifflin, 1984. A good account of the English victory.

McDermott, S. *England and the Spanish Armada: A Necessary Quarrel*. New Haven: Yale University Press, 2005. A broad study of the historical context and consequences of the Spanish Armada.

McLellan, David. *Karl Marx: A Biography*. New York: Macmillan, 2006. A solid and informative biography.

Morison, Samuel. *Admiral of the Ocean Sea: A Life of Christopher Columbus*. Boston: Little Brown, 1942. The best biography of Columbus ever written.

Newman, John Henry. *The Idea of a University*. New Haven: Yale University Press, 1996. A handsome new edition of the Victorian classic, defending the ideal of a liberal education after the fashion of Oxford and Cambridge.

Oates, Stephen. *Let the Trumpet Sound: The Life of Martin Luther King, Jr.* New York: Harper, 1982. A balanced biography.

Plutarch. *Lives of the Noble Greeks and Romans*. Translated by John Dryden. New York: Modern Library, 1992. The most convenient English translation, containing all the lives written by Plutarch.

Rashdall, Hastings. *The Universities of Europe in the Middle Ages: A New Edition*. Oxford: Oxford University Press, 1969. A revision of the most authoritative history of the medieval university.

Rhodes, Richard. *The Making of the Atomic Bomb*. New York: Simon and Schuster, 1988. A detailed account of the Manhattan Project.

Richardson, M. E. J. *Hammurabi's Law*. Sheffield: Sheffield Academic Press, 2000. A good recent translation and commentary.

Rose, Paul. *Heisenberg and the Nazi Atomic Bomb Project*. Berkeley: University of California Press, 1998. A detailed examination of the Nobel Prize–winning physicist's controversial and ambiguous role during World War II.

Safire, William. *Lend Me Your Ears: Great Speeches in History*. New York: Norton, 2004. A superb collection of speeches that have made history.

Scarborough, John. *Roman Medicine*. London: Thames and Hudson, 1969. The best introduction to Greco-Roman medicine, including Galen.

Shaara, Michael. *The Killer Angels*. New York: Random House, 1993. A gripping historical novel of the Battle of Gettysburg. It has been studied in war colleges because of its authenticity in re-creating the mental attitudes of soldiers in battle.

Sherwin-White, A. N. *Roman Society and Roman Law in the New Testament*. Oxford: Clarendon Press, 1963. The most knowledgeable discussion of the New Testament in the context of Roman history, by a distinguished historian of antiquity.

Smith, Adam. *The Wealth of Nations*. New York: Penguin, 1999. A convenient complete edition of the classic of free-market economics.

Smith, Preserved. *Erasmus*. New York: Harper, 1923. Still by far the best intellectual biography.

Spitz, Lewis. *The Protestant Reformation*. New York: Harper and Row, 1985. A solid historical survey of the critical historical period.

Stannard, David. *American Holocaust: The Conquest of the New World*. New York: Oxford, 1993. A chilling and well-documented study of the impact of European discovery and colonization on the original inhabitants of America.

Stoye, John. *The Siege of Vienna: The Last Great Trial between Cross and Crescent*. New York: Holt, 1965. The most detailed account of this epoch-making event.

Tobin, James. *To Conquer the Air: The Wright Brothers and the Race for Flight*. New York: Free Press, 2003. The competition to be the first to fly makes the achievement of the Wright brothers even more remarkable.

Tuchman, Barbara. *The Guns of August*. New York: Dell, 1963. A vivid re-creation of Europe's march to World War I.

————. *Stilwell and the America Experience in China*. New York: Macmillan, 1970. The best introduction to the failure of American policy to contain communism in China.

Wilson, Edmund. *To the Finland Station*. New York: Farrar, Strauss and Giroux, 1972. A brilliantly written account of the historical and intellectual context of the Russian Revolution by a notable American man of letters.

Wolfe, B. D. *Three Who Made a Revolution: A Biographical History of Lenin, Trotsky and Stalin*. New York: Dial, 1964. The story of the Russian Revolution told through biographies of Lenin, Trotsky, and Stalin.

Wright, David. *The History of China*. Westport, CT: Greenwood, 2001. An excellent, concise history of China, especially good on Mao.

Yao, X. *The Encyclopedia of Confucianism*. New York: Routledge/Curzon, 2003. Authoritative articles on all aspects of the teachings and influence of Confucius.

Notes

Notes

Notes

Notes

Notes

Notes